The Principles and Practice of Rational-Emotive Therapy

Ruth A. Wessler

Richard L. Wessler

Foreword by Albert Ellis

The Principles and Practice of Rational-Emotive Therapy

Jossey-Bass Publishers
San Francisco • Washington • London • 1983

THE PRINCIPLES AND PRACTICE OF RATIONAL-EMOTIVE THERAPY
by Ruth A. Wessler and Richard L. Wessler

Library of Congress Cataloging in Publication Data

Wessler, Ruth, 1938-
The principles and practice of rational-emotive therapy.

Bibliography: p. 261
Includes index.
1. Rational-emotive psychotherapy. I. Wessler, Richard L., joint author. II. Title.
RC489.R3W47 616.89'14 80-8319
ISBN 0-87589-473-9

Manufactured in the United States of America

JACKET DESIGN BY WILLI BAUM

FIRST EDITION
First printing: November 1980
Second printing: February 1983

Code 8041

The Jossey-Bass
Social and Behavioral Science Series

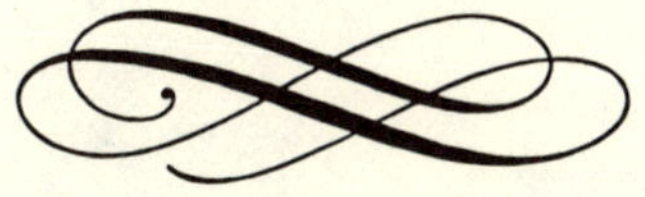

Foreword

I am naturally quite pleased by the publication of a number of recent books explaining the principles of rational-emotive therapy (RET) to professionals and to members of the public, but I am especially delighted with this one by Ruth and Richard Wessler. In many ways it is different, and, in several respects, it makes important and original contributions to the theory and practice of RET.

Since their graduation from the postdoctoral training program at the Institute for Rational-Emotive Therapy in New York, the authors have been among the most effective RET practitioners and supervisors in the world. Ruth Wessler now practices, teaches, and supervises in the Chicago area; and

Richard Wessler is the director of training of the Institute and chair of the International Training Standards Committee on RET. Between the two of them, they have probably helped more neophyte RET practitioners to an effective start than has any other supervising team (with the possible exception of myself and the associate director of the Institute, Janet L. Wolfe). From using RET with their own clients and from teaching professionals and students how to employ RET, the Wesslers know exactly what problems clients and therapists are most likely to bring up. In *The Principles and Practice of Rational-Emotive Therapy,* they give scores of down-to-earth, practical, discriminating examples of how to use and misuse RET.

This is one of the few books that not only accurately presents but also makes original, independent contributions to the theory and practice of RET. Like most of the graduate Fellows of the Institute, Ruth and Richard Wessler refrain from doing RET by rote; they think carefully about what they are doing therapeutically and why they are doing it. They often come up with novel concepts that adhere to the basic principles of this form of psychotherapy while also augmenting it. For example, in discussing the now well-known ABC's of RET, they show that although B stands for Beliefs and is largely concerned with evaluative assumptions and convictions about what is happening to the individual at A (Activating events), A also frequently includes perceptions and conceptions and therefore is not as crucially evaluative as is B but may easily involve some important misconceptions. The Wesslers' detailed definitions of what people usually include in their A's and B's when they have disturbed feelings and behaviors at C (Consequences) clarify and augment some of my own presentations and are sufficiently perceptive and original to give all cognitive behavior therapists, including myself, succulent food for thought.

Another aspect of the Wesslers' book that I particularly like is the consistent probing and exhuming to show the RET practitioner how to dispute the basic irrational Beliefs that almost invariably lie behind clients' disturbed and dysfunctional behavior. Several books that nicely and practically outline RET procedure somewhat neglect its fundamental philosophic aspects, but the Wesslers are virtually never lax in this respect. They fully realize, and in this book effectively show, that the main goal in RET is not (as it is in many kinds of behavior therapy) symptom removal. The main goal is to help clients make a profound philosophic change that not only will help them with their current presenting symptoms but will enable them to internalize the basic RET methodology and use it, often without supplementary therapy, on any new emotional disturbances that they may inflict on themselves in the future. The Wesslers demonstrate how this profound philosophic change can be produced. In espousing what I call the most "elegant" RET-type solution to neurotic problems, they also show the therapists to whom this book is mainly addressed how to help clients achieve a pronounced form of rational-emotive thinking and behaving that will very likely prevent them from creating future forms of self-disturbance.

The Wesslers demonstrate to RET practitioners how they can help ensure that their clients are not merely giving lip service to rationality or simply parroting the constructive beliefs that they learn in the course of their RET sessions. They specifically indicate how therapists can question their clients' rational or coping statements to see whether they truly understand them and are likely to act on them in their present and future lives. At the same time, the Wesslers emphasize that RET therapists had better think and act for themselves and not just follow some supposedly general rational-emotive rules that allegedly apply to all therapeutic interactions at all times.

Several aspects of RET that are often neglected in other rational-emotive writings are stressed here. In Chapter Eight, the authors assess progress as therapy proceeds; they deal not only with client variables when progress is minimal but with the personal and professional problems of the therapist that may interfere with the client's advancement. They also consider the self-actualizing, as well as the curative, aspects of RET and show how the former do not necessarily accompany the latter unless specific therapeutic efforts are made to encourage self-actualization.

Other unique elements in this book include the verbatim

transcript of an entire RET session with the Wesslers' critical comments on this session. Their comments are right to the point and emphasize RET methodologies that I sometimes neglect in my book of verbatim transcripts, *Growth Through Reason* (1974a). The long excerpts from a group therapy protocol in Chapter Ten also add significantly to the RET-oriented group literature. Finally, the self-supervision inventory that the Wesslers have adapted and devised as an appendix to their book is an original contribution to RET that will almost certainly help its growth and development.

The Wesslers have stated, in clear and precise form and with remarkable succinctness, most of the important clinical theories and findings of RET, and they have done so in a manner that is likely to benefit virtually every beginning and a great many advanced practitioners of this form of therapy. Although RET teaches its therapists and clients not to be absolutely certain about anything, I am *reasonably sure* that this will be a standard RET book for many years to come.

August 1980

Albert Ellis
Executive Director
Institute for
Rational-Emotive Therapy
New York, New York

Preface

Rational-emotive therapy (RET) is largely the creation of one person, Albert Ellis, whose writings dominate the literature of RET. Although prolific and precise in his delineation of RET theory and concepts, Ellis has written little about how to practice RET; and, unfortunately, those who have written about its practice have focused primarily on disputing irrational ideas. Admittedly, the notion that irrational thinking leads to disruptive emotions forms the foundation of RET and distinguishes it from other approaches to therapy. However, this narrow focus on disputing has contributed to RET being misunderstood and misrepresented as simply "arguing" with clients (Meichenbaum, 1977) and labeled as "shaming argumentative therapy" (Simkin,

1979). As we will show in this book, arguing with clients does not do justice to the basic cognitive approach of RET, and, more importantly, the therapy that is actually practiced by Albert Ellis and other RET therapists involves much more than merely the disputing of irrational ideas.

This book, then, emphasizes all aspects of the practice of RET. It grew out of our experience in teaching this practice to beginning and advanced psychotherapists. We intend its audience to be those who are interested in understanding and applying the principles of RET: experienced therapists and counselors, as well as graduate students and others training to be psychotherapists and counselors. No previous background in rational-emotive theory is necessary to understand the principles we describe. To practice RET, however, the reader should have at least a minimal background in interviewing and therapeutic skills; although we cover a variety of interviewing techniques, we only touch on such basic skills as how to clarify, how to ask clear questions, and how to obtain feedback from the client.

In Chapter One we describe Ellis's cognitive theory of emotions (the *ABC* theory) and our own expanded model, the emotional episode. We also briefly discuss aspects of RET practice: the process, the techniques, and the structure of sessions. Chapter Two explains and illustrates the sentence "The term *irrational belief* has a very specific meaning in RET" and describes the three components of irrational beliefs: awfulizing, demandingness, and evaluation of self and others. Chapter Three, as its title indicates, presents the goals and values of RET. The middle chapters (Four through Seven) deal with the practice of RET. They are followed by a presentation of an actual, annotated, therapy session (Chapter Eight) and a discussion of RET in groups (Chapter Nine), including an illustrative group therapy session.

Our intent is to show how RET is practiced over the course of therapy, from beginning to end. In the beginning, goals are set, problems are assessed, and a working relationship is established. As therapy progresses, more time is spent on helping the client find ways to change in light of the established goals. As the client reports or exhibits change, progressively more time is spent assessing and reinforcing the changes that are made until therapy comes to a natural end. People are subject not only to irrational thinking but also to misperceptions, misconceptions, and illogical thinking. These, too, are grist for the mill in RET and often become the content of therapy. But if they are the exclusive content, then it is not RET that is being practiced. In Chapter Ten we show how RET is similar to, yet distinct from, other approaches to psychotherapy. Following Chapter Ten is a checklist for RET practitioners to use in self-supervision of their work with clients. In addition, it serves as a summary of the competencies, skills, and techniques important for the practice of RET.

We wish to acknowledge René Diekstra, whose ideas strongly influenced our thinking in developing the emotional episode. Our sincere thanks are due to Dorothy Conway, our copy editor, whose imprint is found on every page. Finally, this book would not have been written without the inspiration and sense of dedication acquired from our mentor, Albert Ellis. Working with him has been a joyous experience, for he practices what he preaches.

September 1980

Ruth A. Wessler
Downers Grove, Illinois

Richard L. Wessler
Pleasantville, New York

Contents

The Authors

Ruth A. Wessler is professor of psychology and director of the Social Science Division at George Williams College in Downers Grove, Illinois. She received a Bachelor of Arts degree in psychology from Grinnell College in 1960 and a Master of Arts degree (1962) and a Doctor of Philosophy degree (1965) in clinical psychology from Washington University in St. Louis. At Washington University she became a research associate for a test development project resulting in *Measuring Ego Development* (with J. Loevinger and C. Redmore, 1970). She subsequently became a member of the counseling center and associate professor of psychology at Parsons College in Fairfield, Iowa. Before coming to George Williams College, she served two years as a postdoctoral fellow at the Institute for Rational-Emotive Therapy in New York City.

Richard L. Wessler chairs the Department of Psychology at the Westchester campus of Pace University in Pleasantville, New York, where he is also professor of psychology. After a year at Missouri University, he completed his formal education at Washington University, where he received a Bachelor of Arts degree in psychology in 1958 and a Doctor of Philosophy degree in clinical psychology in 1966. After teaching at St. Louis University for several years, he became the director of institutional research and later presidential assistant at Parsons College. He also completed the postdoctoral fellowship program at the Institute for Rational-Emotive Therapy.

Both authors remain active in the practice of rational-emotive therapy, each maintaining a private practice and active involvement in the training and supervision of persons learning to practice RET. Richard Wessler is the present director of training for the Institute for Rational-Emotive Therapy, where Ruth Wessler serves as a member of the training faculty. Both have served as editor of *Rational Living,* the journal of the Institute for Rational Living.

The Principles and Practice of Rational-Emotive Therapy

1

Overview of RET Theory and Practice

As its name suggests, rational-emotive therapy (RET) places great emphasis on *rational thinking* and has as its primary goal *emotional change.* RET shares this goal with other therapies, but, unlike many approaches, attempts to effect the change differently, employing a variety of techniques to alter cognitions that produce emotions.

Early roots of RET can be traced to Alfred Adler and his concern for treating "discouraged" (not "sick") people by helping them change their outlook on themselves and life. Ellis (1974b) points out the one major difference between RET and Adler's individual psychology. Specifically, Adler stresses social interest as a route to adjustment, whereas RET emphasizes enlightened self-interest.

Karen Horney also exerted a strong influence on Ellis's thinking. Her list of the ten "neurotic needs" acquired by the insecure child to gain security (Horney, 1942)—for instance, the neurotic needs for affection and approval and for perfection and unassailability—has its counterpart in Ellis's enumeration of irrational ideas (Ellis, 1977d). In Horney's view, however, neurotic needs grow out of insecurity and are attempts to gain security and reduce basic anxiety, whereas Ellis views neurotic needs (irrational ideas) as beliefs that create rather than reduce anxiety. In the 1950s, Ellis, previously trained as an analyst of the Horneyan school, began to experiment with a more active and directive approach to therapy and to consolidate his theory of emotional disturbance and change (Ellis, 1957), culminating in the publication of *Reason and Emotion in Psychotherapy* in 1962 (see Ellis, 1977d). Although some of Ellis's thinking has changed since the publication of this book, it remains a classic introduction to RET.

In the 1950s and early 1960s, RET was something of a maverick, outside the first force in psychology (psychoanalysis) and the third force (the so-called humanistic approaches, represented at that time primarily by client-centered therapy). Interestingly, there was no second force in the field of psychotherapy at the time. Like RET, behavior therapy was just beginning (Wolpe published *Psychotherapy by Reciprocal Inhibition* in 1958). There was little in common between early behavior therapy approaches and RET, except that Ellis, since his departure from psychoanalysis, made heavy use of behavioral, primarily operant, techniques as a part of his eclectic repertoire. But Ellis wanted to change more than his clients' behavior. He wanted to change the ideas mediating the emotions of the client—ideas that were, in turn, leading to approach or avoidance behaviors. Ultimately, behavior therapy began to broaden, so that it included cognitions as legitimate and important human behaviors that can be learned and modified in the same way as any motoric or autonomic response. Rimm and Masters (1979), for instance, include RET—with a bit of apology for its being a "depth" approach—in their book on behavior therapy: "It should be pointed out that, in sharp contrast to the traditional depth approaches, the kinds of cognitive activity so essential to Ellis's theoretical position can be specified in a relatively concrete and unambiguous manner" (p. 5).

As the RET approach gained acceptance by some behavior therapists, other behavior therapists began to develop their own views of the cognitive components of people's problems and to develop approaches and techniques to modify cognitions. We speculate that much of behavior therapy today is no longer of the strict S-R variety but, rather, cognitive-behavior therapy. During the 1970s, Lazarus (1971, 1976) developed a multimodal approach, which includes cognition as one of the modalities; Beck (1976) recognized the role of cognitions in depression and in the treatment of emotional problems in general; Meichenbaum (1977), in his work on stress inoculation, emphasized the cognitive aspects of behavior modification; and Selye (1976), the man who invented the word *stress* as applied to humans and other animals, included a role for cognitions as mediators between the stressor and stress. As we enter the 1980s, cognitive-behavior therapy has arrived; and, thanks somewhat to its own influence, RET is no longer a maverick.

What makes RET different from other cognitive-behavior therapies is the careful and systematic exposition of what kinds of cognitions (irrational beliefs) lead to emotional upset. While most forms of cognitive-behavior therapy include the proposition that thoughts and emotions are intricately related, Ellis goes much further by categorizing beliefs according to a philosophy or conception of rationality. It is this systematic conception of rationality that makes RET unique among cognitive therapies.

The roots of RET reside in philosophy as much as in psychology. Although the ancient Stoic Epictetus, who contended that it is not events but our opinions of events that disturb us, is often cited in RET writings (Warren and Hymen, 1980), RET owes more to Bertrand Russell (1930). In fact, the core of RET might be characterized as the applied philosophy of Russell. The earliest applications can be found in Ellis's writings on sex (Ellis, 1960a, 1960b, 1969b), in which he advocates a sane and rational approach to a then strongly taboo topic.

Ellis's definition of *rational* is based on humanistic philosophy. Personal ethics, including sexual ethics, can be derived from a few principles. Basically, situationally relative rights and wrongs can be derived by humans based upon whether their conclusions result in pleasure or pain and whether they are in both one's long- and short-term interests. Relations with other people are a matter of enlightened self-interest. Thus, RET espouses most rules of social ethics as being in a person's best interest, but, eschewing dogmatic thinking and all absolutes and imperatives, RET holds that people do not *have* to abide by these rules.

The Emotional Episode

Ellis calls his cognitive theory of emotions the *ABC* theory. *A* stands for the *A*ctivating or antecedent event; *B*, the *B*elief about *A*; and *C*, the emotional *C*onsequence. The idea that emotions have cognitive components has many influential adherents. Ellis's theory was influenced by and is similar to that of Arnold (1960). Others who later developed cognitive theories of emotion include Lazarus (1966) and Schachter (1964).

The *ABC* model is useful for giving clients a simple and nonmysterious account of the emotional experience and for showing clients that they have some control over these experiences. Because of its simplicity and because it corresponds to Ellis's writings, we shall use the *ABC* model throughout most of this book. However, the model is sometimes confusing, in part because it does not specify several important steps in the emotional process and in part because the distinction between *A* and *B* is difficult to grasp. The difficulty occurs because *A* can involve cognitive content and can be subdivided into four steps. We call our expanded model of the *ABC*s the emotional episode (see Table 1).

Step 1 is the stimulus that begins the episode. The stimulus can be overt or covert. An overt stimulus might be other people's actions, a "phobic" object, or the loss of something tangible. Covert stimuli—for example, bodily sensations (such as nausea) and thoughts (especially memories and anticipations)—

Table 1. Model of an Emotional Episode.

	Step	*Event*
A	1. Reality	Stimulus (S)
	2. Input and selection	S competes with other stimuli; awareness of S
	3. Definition and description	What S is, S = S′; covert or overt verbal description of S′
	4. Interpretation	Nonobservable aspects of S′ or of observer
B	5. Appraisal	Positive, negative, or neutral
C	6. Affect	Arousal if positive or negative
	7. Action tendency	Approach if positive; elimination of stimulus if negative: (a) avoidance, (b) destruction
	8. Feedback	Reinforcing consequences of responses (Steps 6 and 7)

Note: A, B, and *C* are Ellis's notation.

play an especially important role in what we later discuss as secondary symptoms or problems.

Step 2 is input and selection. Here we refer to the action of the sensory neurons. We also refer to physiological processes that give us information about present motive states, such as hunger or thirst. Finally, we refer to the assumed physiological processes that serve the *function* of sensory neurons to give us input from our own cognitive processes, leading to self-awareness and self-consciousness. So, at any given moment, we may become aware of and attend to a noise, our physiological arousal, or our own thoughts.

Step 3 consists of perceptions and symbolic representations of perceptions. It is convenient to treat them together because in therapy we deal with clients' statements about their perceptions rather than the perceptions themselves, which are silent. This step, which is distinctly cognitive, includes definition and description. Definition can easily be conceived of as a perceptual process. In psychology, perception is almost universally treated as the first, though nonconscious, step in information processing, provided there is some input. Perception is a process whereby incoming information is organized and categorized—that is, defined. Description involves verbal statements of the experienced stimulus. The statements may be said aloud or simply thought: "I see a dog; I hear music; I hear and feel my stomach growling; I am thinking about going on a vacation." It is to Step 3, especially, that Michael Mahoney (1977) refers when he writes that it is not environments that impinge upon us, but representations of environments. However, this is not an essential step in the emotional episode because one may have a visual image of a dog, for example, and immediately process that information at the step of appraisal (Step 5): Dogs are dangerous (and therefore bad). Or a person might perceive a dog and immediately experience arousal (Step 6), following a classical conditioning model. When Step 3 is omitted, however, we believe that the person is most likely to process the information at Step 4.

Step 4, interpretation, refers to the making of inferences about nonobservable aspects of the perceived stimulus (S′) or about oneself. Here are some examples: S′ = a piece of wood; interpretation = the wood is hard (however, it might be soft balsa wood). S′ = man walking toward post office with letter in hand; interpretation = he intends to mail the letter (however, he might be taking the letter home from the office). S′ = a person does not speak to me; interpretation = he is not friendly. S′ = a person does not speak to me; interpretation = I am not likable. Interpretations can be either relatively enduring (All people are not trustworthy) or relatively specific (This person is not trustworthy). The specific interpretation may simply be a special case of the more generalized and enduring one (All people are not trustworthy; therefore, this person is not trustworthy). Although interpretation is not an essential step, humans usually do make interpretations—a fact that is the basis of attribution theory in social psychology (Wegner and Vallacher, 1977).

Steps 1, 2, 3, and 4 comprise the activating or antecedent events in the *ABC* model. In some accounts of rational therapy (Maultsby, 1975; Zastrow, 1979), however, only Steps 1 and 2 comprise *A*; Steps 3 and 4 are treated as part of *B*. Diekstra and

Dassen (1979) prefer to gather all symbolic behavior under *B*. We shall follow Ellis's practice of restricting *B* to appraisals or evaluations, although Ellis himself has not always done so consistently.

Step 5, appraisal, is the step that Arnold (1960) emphasizes in her theory of emotion. Appraisal is a crucial step in the emotional episode; for, as both Arnold and Ellis note, if the appraisal is neutral (or indecisive or ambiguous), no affective response follows. Lazarus's (1966) conception is similar, except that he includes reappraisal, a step that follows appraisal. We do not include reappraisal in the emotional episode, but reappraisal is the goal of the "disputing" questions frequently used in RET. For example: "Was it really so awful that you did not get the job you wanted?"

Step 6, affect, refers to the arousal of the autonomic nervous system following nonneutral appraisal. The greater the deviation from neutral, the greater will be the arousal. In the *ABC* model, this step is called the emotional consequence (*C*).

Step 7, action tendency, is the tendency to behave in certain ways toward a perceived stimulus: to approach, to move toward, and to try to obtain that which we evaluate positively; to eliminate that which we evaluate negatively. One way to eliminate a negatively evaluated stimulus is to avoid or escape it. Another way is to destroy the stimulus. The destruction can be literal, but it can also be figurative; that is, one might change the stimulus in such a way that it is no longer evaluated negatively—for example, by slapping a screaming child, who is now quiet and apologetic. When there is a strong negative appraisal, the action components of the "fight-or-flight" response occur. The action tendency is referred to in the *ABC* model as the behavioral consequence (*C*).

Step 8, functional feedback or reinforcing consequences of action, is not strictly part of the emotional episode but a result of it. We include it to underscore its effect on subsequent emotional experiences and behavior and because it often is the focus of treatment in other therapeutic modalities. "Reinforcing consequences" simply means that rewards or penalties occur as a result of behavior and thereby affect future behavior.

Humans, operating on hedonistic principles, tend to repeat those actions that bring satisfactions. Behaviorists call these satisfactions *reinforcing consequences*; psychoanalysts call them *secondary gains* (for the ego's satisfaction); and Greenwald (1973) calls them *payoffs*. Step 8 does not have a corresponding letter in the *ABC* model but, because it is a significant factor in the complete emotional episode, is an important addition to the theory.

RET as it is actually practiced is very eclectic. An experienced RET practitioner might intervene at any of the eight steps of the emotional episode, although his or her focus would usually be on evaluative beliefs or appraisal. The emotional episode is, of course, a somewhat arbitrary division of a continuous stream of experience and behavior. In real life, as opposed to an abstract model, the steps may overlap and seem to occur nearly instantaneously and simultaneously. The cognitive mediators at Steps 2 through 5 may vary depending on many factors, thus explaining why a person may give different responses to the same stimulus on different occasions. For instance, if a person is already in an angry mood, a stimulus that he usually ignores, such as the noise of children playing in the street, may become paramount in his awareness. Similarly, a person who is fatigued may evaluate as extremely obnoxious something that she would normally evaluate as only slightly unpleasant.

Table 2 illustrates Schachter's (1964) theory of emotion. Arousal and action tendency become potential stimuli, which, if perceived, lead to an interpretation, such as "I am feeling angry." This interpretation derives from two sources. First, the person recognizes that he feels aroused; second, he searches the environment for cues to explain the arousal. Table 2 also illustrates that *C*s can be, and usually are, *A*s, which can lead to a second *C*. That is, when people become aware of their emotional state, this awareness is a stimulus to further cognitive processing, which, if the stimulus is appraised positively or negatively, leads to an emotion about an emotion, such as feeling guilty about feeling angry.

Let us take a specific example: a person who might say, "I was snubbed by a friend and felt ashamed" (Table 3, Steps

Table 2. Schachter's (1964) Theory of Emotion.

	Step	Event
C	6. Affect	Arousal if positive or negative
	7. Action tendency	Approach if positive; elimination of stimulus if negative: (a) avoidance, (b) destruction
A	1. Reality	The arousal and action tendency = Stimulus (S)
	2. Input and selection	S competes with other stimuli; awareness of S
	3. Definition and description	What S is, S = S′; covert or overt verbal description of S′
	4. Interpretation	Nonobservable aspects of S′ or of observer

Note: C and *A* are Ellis's notation.

1a through 4b). We carry the episode further, so that the person becomes more aroused and has a tendency to eliminate the shame (Steps 5b through 7b). Our person might say, "I was snubbed by a friend and felt ashamed and very anxious." How can these emotions be reduced? There are at least fourteen solutions, one for each step. Here briefly are the solutions; the explanations follow. The numbers given these solutions correspond to the steps in Table 3.

(1a and b) Avoid the initiating stimulus—stay home. (2a and b) Distraction—watch TV, get absorbed in a novel, meditate on one syllable. (3a and b) Change the definition and description—decide it was not a friend but someone else. (4a) Change the interpretation—"It happened, *but* my friend did not see me." (4b) Change the interpretation—"I am not feeling ashamed; I simply drank too much coffee this morning." (5a and b) Change the appraisal—"It's really not so awful." (6a and b) Reduce the arousal through the use of tranquilizers or some other biochemical means. (7a and b) Fight the avoidance—approach the friend first, so that the probability of the negatively appraised event is greatly diminished.

Solution 1, avoiding the initiating stimulus (for instance, by staying home), may not be practical and may, in any case,

Table 3. Example of an Emotional Episode.

	Step	Event
A	1a. Reality	Friend does not speak to observer (O) when passing on the street = S.
	2a. Input and selection	S competes with O's thoughts of vacation, attractive stranger getting out of cab; S becomes figure.
	3a. Definition and description	Awareness that S is friend passing and not speaking; thinking the same.
	4a. Interpretation	My friend is angry with me.
B	5a. Appraisal	That is awful.
C	6a. Affect	High arousal.
	7a. Action tendency	Elimination of the stimulus.
A	1b. Reality	The arousal and action tendency = S.
	2b. Input and selection	S competes with street noises, attractive stranger closing door; S becomes figure.
	3b. Definition and description	Awareness of S; thinking "I feel funny, I want to get away from here."
	4b. Interpretation	I feel ashamed.
B	5b. Appraisal	It's awful to feel this way.
C	6b. Affect	More arousal.
	7b. Action tendency	Elimination of the stimulus.

Note: A, B, and *C* are Ellis's notation.

give rise to other problems. Many depressed clients are people who have carried this strategy to such an extreme that they are receiving few rewards in life. Another major problem with this strategy is that the initiating stimulus does not have to be an external event. The initiating stimulus could be feelings (for instance, annoyance or anger—with a *B* of "It's awful to feel this way") or thoughts (for instance, of deserting one's family—with a *B* of "It's awful to think that").

Solution 2, distraction, is a commonly used strategy to avoid unpleasant feelings. A person may engage in distracting activities, such as watching television, going to a party, doing crossword puzzles *in order to* avoid becoming aware of stimuli that could lead to anxiety, guilt, or other disturbing emotions. Particularly when the initiating stimuli are thoughts, this strategy is effective only as long as the disturbing ideas are not recognized; so it is a short-term solution. If the initiating stimulus is anxiety, distraction will keep one from seeking more permanent solutions to reduce the anxiety. In contrast, the goal of RET is to help people *change* their basic philosophies leading to the negative appraisal that underlies the extreme negative emotions.

Solution 3, change the definition and description, refers first to a change in perception. Changing the definition means changing the S′ to some other S′, which may lead to the completion of a different emotional episode. For instance, our person could perceive that his friend had, in fact, talked to him or perhaps that it was a stranger, not a friend, who did not speak. He might feel happy in the first instance, indifferent in the second. Definition is a process that occurs automatically and nonconsciously. It is one of the processes often referred to as "reality testing," particularly when it appears to be faulty, such as in illusions and particularly hallucinations. (Delusions occur at Step 4 in our model.) We will say no more about perceptual definition in this book. We include it in the emotional episode because, in our thinking, it is an event that occurs between awareness and verbal description, an event that we usually take for granted but that, like the other steps, is subject to change.

Changing the description is much more under our conscious control. In fact, such a solution is the goal of several approaches to psychotherapy. For example, both general semantics and gestalt therapy encourage people to make more accurate descriptive statements that include the observer—"I statements." Rather than "My friend did not speak to me," the more accurate statement would be something like "I am aware that my friend did not speak to me," for it is my perceptual experience that I know. The formulation of more accurate descriptions can help persons not leap to conclusions—to Step 4 interpretations such as "He is angry" or "I am unlikable," what Beck (1963) calls "arbitrary inferences." But accurate description alone will not be effective in the long run because (1) many inferences are probably adaptive, giving meaning to the present and aiding the prediction of the future, and (2) it is not the inferences as such but, rather, the evaluation or appraisal of those inferences that leads to the affective response.

Solution 4a, changing the interpretation, is often advisable and is the object of many cognitive-behavioral interventions—particularly when the person interprets the situation erroneously (as when a friend does not speak because he is preoccupied, not because he intends to reject you). Reconstruing the event more realistically, perhaps at the descriptive level, will probably modify the emotional reaction. Likewise, reconstruing the event less realistically will also modify the response. For instance, a person with the belief that to fail would be awful could reconstrue failure on an exam not to mean that at all: "I didn't really fail; the test was unfair!" Such rationalization can, of course, reduce or eliminate feelings such as shame or guilt; but a goal of RET is to help people stop rationalizing, realistically perceive situations, and take responsibility for their behavior.

Solution 4b is similar to 4a, except that one's own affect is reinterpreted. This approach is sometimes used in behavior therapy and is called "reattribution therapy" (see, for instance, Försterling, 1980). For example, the person may reattribute the reason for his arousal to too much caffeine rather than to the fear of rejection. Thus, the person is no longer "anxious." This solution lasts as long as the person can maintain the reattribution—usually, but not necessarily, when the reattribution is valid. Even when not valid, the reattribution still has the effect of reducing further arousal and may lead to beneficial behavioral changes and outcomes. For instance, one may now study for a test and do well, instead of avoiding the studying because "I am anxious." However, a person who attributes her arousal to caffeine rather than to anxiety probably will not be motivated to reduce the anxiety by becoming aware of and changing her appraisals of failure, for the good reason that she is not "anxious."

Solution 5, changing the appraisal, is a basic solution in RET. We will return to it after discussing the remaining solutions.

Solution 6, taking tranquilizers or other medication, may also be effective in reducing the experience of disruptive emotions. However, there might be unwanted side effects to the medication; moreover, unless the person resorts to another solution, he may still be subject to anxiety or depression without the drug. Although this is a palliative solution, RET therapists are not averse to recommending that their clients—particularly those with extreme anxiety or depression—take appropriate medication under the care of a physician. However, the main goal of therapy remains the changing of cognitions that lead to the extreme upsetting emotion.

Solution 7, overpreparing, can be adaptive—studying twenty hours for a test rather than ten, spending several hours dressing, even rehearsing for a date. However, the possibility of failure or rejection always exists, even if it is only one chance in a million. Often that remote chance is sufficient to create anxiety (see Chapter Eight), with the possible consequences of poor concentration, avoidance behavior, ulcers, and the like, if the person believes that the undesired event, no matter how improbable, would be catastrophic. Also, people who view an event as catastrophic are likely to magnify the chances of its happening. A further side effect of overpreparing is that there is less time for other potentially satisfying activities. For instance, a person who spends eighteen hours a day studying has almost no time for making new friends, reading a novel, or building a model airplane.

We return to solution 5, changing the appraisal and associated irrational beliefs that underlie anxiety, guilt, and other extreme negative emotions. This is the ultimate goal of RET, for if a person's basic philosophy at *B* is changed so that *A* (particularly descriptions and interpretations) no longer triggers a particular upsetting belief, none of the other solutions will be necessary.

Some ways of changing *B* are ineffective because they are unrealistic. For instance, instead of believing that a particular event, such as failure, is awful, we can believe that it is good. Although there may be some truth to the idea that failure can be beneficial, as when something is learned from the experience, most failures usually have mixed outcomes. Thus, the assertion that failures are good is too simplistic and is difficult to maintain in the face of potential negative consequences of failing. Another usually unrealistic solution would be changing the appraisal from strongly negative to neutral—for instance, changing "I *must* succeed, and it would be awful if I failed" to "I don't care if I succeed." In some instances, a person may find that he really does not care about failure. However, practically all humans do care about some things in life and usually want to obtain what is important to them. Thus, in many cases the belief "I don't care" either cannot be maintained or is maintained to cover up the more painful "I do care and, in fact, absolutely must have success." These two examples point up some of the fine distinctions made in RET theory and practice: between bad and awful, between want and need. These and other distinctions will be discussed in greater detail in subsequent chapters. For the present, suffice it to say that the kinds of cognitive changes encouraged by RET practitioners are quite specific and that a good deal of time can be, and often is, profitably spent on issues of accurate semantic labels.

One of the first tasks in learning RET is to become immersed in RET theory. With this knowledge, the therapist becomes attuned to client statements that indicate irrational thinking and, even more important, can help the client see the errors of his or her thinking. If the RET therapist shares the client's belief that, for example, an event would be awful, the therapist cannot do much to help the client change that philosophy.

RET as Dissuasive Therapy

The main task in counseling and therapy is to dissuade people from their maladaptive ideas and unrealistic perceptions —in other words, to change attitudes. The three components of attitudes coincide with the *ABC*s: knowledge (*A*), affect (*B*) ("affect" in attitude theory refers to evaluations), and behavioral tendency (*C*).

The RET view of evaluative beliefs (the distinguishing feature of an attitude) is that they act as mediators of experiences and lead to behaviors. In RET we do not change the target behaviors themselves; instead, we try to help revise the belief system, so that the target behaviors will *then* change. Paradoxically, one of the better ways to change attitudes is to change behaviors. Rather than engage in a chicken-and-egg debate of whether cognitive-behavior therapy uses cognitions to change behaviors or behaviors to change cognitions (Wilson, 1978), let us acknowledge that the components of attitudes are interdependent. There are many ways to change them.

One way is through persuasion or, similarly, dissuasion. We lament the fact that we received no training in dissuasion as a part of our graduate education, nor are we aware that this topic is offered in contemporary graduate programs. Ironically, a classic book on psychotherapy has as the first word in the title "persuasion"; we refer to *Persuasion and Healing* by Jerome Frank (1961). Indeed, much graduate education socializes us to become "objective" scientists; and, although we keenly debate with each other over the merits of our version of reality and of psychology, we learn little about how to persuade nonpsychologists to believe this rather than that. Some people have reacted very negatively to our suggestion that counseling and therapy persuade people of the wrongness of their views (wrong, that is, if they wish to reach their human goals of survival and happiness). Labels such as "manipulative" and "forcing your values on the client" are but a few that we have heard. But what is wrong with trying to persuade people that what they believe to be dangerous is in reality not, or that what they believe to be awful is not so when viewed objectively? In our view, we err if we do *not* try to dissuade them.

But how do we do so? Here are some principles of therapeutic dissuasion that begin to give answers. They are derived from several accounts of the nature of attitudes, especially McGuire (1969) and Karlins and Abelson (1970). First, certain characteristics of the therapist or counselor are important to effective dissuasion.

1. There will be more attitude change in the desired direction if the therapist has high credibility rather than low credibility. Credibility, then, is an important characteristic of the

therapist or counselor who uses RET. How can it be acquired? Like other abstract concepts, it exists in the mind of the client. We can promote an image of credibility if we can show our expertise and our trustworthiness. Expertise can be communicated by credentials or reputation. A prime example of this form of credibility occurred when one of us was having a last session with a client who, after eight weeks of therapy, was no longer experiencing the severe anxiety attacks that had plagued him for seven years. The attacks had virtually disappeared after two or three weeks of therapy, but the client had remained in therapy to "practice" his new way of thinking—that is, he no longer demanded that his anxiety disappear but simply accepted it as an annoyance (discovering in the process that he was seldom initially anxious). He pointed out how illogical this new way of thinking seemed to him and said, "If anyone else had told me that simply accepting anxiety would reduce anxiety, I'd have said they were nuts. But [pointing to degrees and certificates on the wall] I figured you knew what you were talking about."

A confident manner and our own belief in what we are saying (see for instance, Frank, 1961) also tend to communicate expertise. The comment that we have successfully worked with such problems before not only reassures a client but also enhances the likelihood that the client will see us as credible. When we mention his irrational beliefs before he does, by making inferences from RET principles, we not only show empathy for the client but also enhance our image as experts in human affairs.

Trustworthiness occurs when clients see us as genuinely interested in helping them and not working with them for our own benefits. We begin to acquire trustworthiness when we show a genuine concern for helping clients—or at least no intention to work against the client's interests. We might even say to the client something like "I won't gain personally if you improve or if you continue to make yourself miserable. I'd like to see you improve, but it's your choice."

2. Therapist characteristics that are irrelevant to the client's belief system can influence acceptance of rational thinking. That is, even though their view of the therapist has little to

do with the merit of what he is communicating, clients may reject his therapeutic message because they do not like him. We, as therapists, do not care per se what our clients think of us. However, there is an interplay between how we are perceived and acceptance of our message. Thus, our ability to influence, and hence to help, *is* related to what clients think of us. This principle tells us that our "bedside manner" is important and that we had better try to present our message in a style that is acceptable to our clients.

3. The therapist's effectiveness is increased if he or she initially expresses some views that are held by the client. This principle seems to us to justify self-disclosure, especially the disclosing of *rational* beliefs shared by client and therapist. We can also express provisional agreement with the client's version of *A*: "OK, let's assume your mother didn't like you when you were a child." In our practice we find many things about which to agree with clients during each session. In more traditional terms, we can communicate empathic understanding of our clients and thereby show them that we are on their side.

4. The credibility of the therapist is less a factor later on than it is initially. This is known as the "sleeper effect." Change may occur later without the person's even recalling where or from whom he or she heard the ideas. For therapists, this principle suggests that we vigorously work to present rational thinking and a philosophy of tolerance, for even if the client does not agree during therapy sessions, the seeds of constructive change may have been planted.

5. The more extreme the change that the therapist asks for, the more actual change is likely to result. RET practitioners, following the example of Albert Ellis, often ask for a great deal of *attitude* change. We ask that clients accept themselves fully and without conditions when all their lives they have been doing just the opposite. We urge them to tolerate the foibles of the imperfect people who inhabit this planet. We take positions that are quite unlike those of conventional wisdom—for example, holding that the only needs we have are those necessary for survival and that most of people's so-called "needs" are irrational demands that they escalate from their

own desires. This principle concerns *attitude* change, not *behavior* change. To ask a client who has never approached members of the opposite sex to suddenly approach dozens of them daily is an extreme change, probably so extreme as to result in noncompliance. To ask this client to change an attitude from negative to neutral is consistent with this principle.

Now let us consider some other principles of attitude change.

1. Successful dissuasion takes into account the reasons underlying attitudes as well as the attitudes themselves. Effective therapists tailor their approaches to the client. One of the most interesting unanswered questions is "Why does my client believe something to be true?" Although we do not have the answer for people in general, we urge you to ask your clients how they know that something is true or how they know that it is awful or whatever. Ideally, RET is done with people who value evidence and logic but who have not applied them to their personal problems. It becomes rather simple to point out their misconceptions and fallacious reasoning. Because they prefer to see themselves as consistently reasonable people, they are likely to adopt the classical RET approach of questioning for the evidence of their beliefs and the accuracy of their reports of activating events.

Clients who are not committed to evidence and logic may believe what they do on the basis of faith, authority, or superstition rather than information. Some people believe that material reality is not the only reality; they may uphold, instead, anything from religious revelation to intuition to ESP. We had best work within the client's basis for belief, realizing that most people, including therapists, know relatively few facts about which they have first-hand information. For instance, we accept as factual the existence of Paris, atoms, and cancer. But how many of us have empirical evidence for these? Beginning RET therapists and counselors frequently are so intent on winning the argument that they risk losing the client. Even attempting to win with evidence and logic misses the point of therapy—which is simply to help the client. Why spend valuable minutes or hours trying to convince the client verbally of the wrongness of his or her view and the rightness of yours when demonstrations—appropriate homework assignments, carefully rehearsed new behaviors, and effective rational coping statements—are more effective? All clients, like other customers, want results. They like what works, and consequences are convincing.

2. People are more susceptible to influence when their self-esteem is low. Perhaps that is why neurotics are more successfully treated by verbal psychotherapy than any other diagnostic group. However, persons who are highly persuadable and who easily change can be equally influenced by counterarguments. The implication here is that therapists had better not feel too complacent about a quick cure. If there is reason to suspect that the client will return to an environment that fosters irrational thinking, the therapist would do well to try to insulate the client's beliefs from the influence of those others. The therapist can warn the client about the influence of other people and suggest rational coping statements, such as "When they encourage absolutistic thinking, remind yourself that there are no absolute rules in the world."

3. Active involvement is more effective than passive listening. Therapists who are inappropriately active, who lecture the client or fail to involve the client in a dialogue, do not follow this principle. Passive listening by the therapist also violates this principle. In Chapter Six we describe a number of ways to involve the client actively. The client who imagines that he is reacting with concern rather than anxiety over some obnoxious event, for example, and then reports the new beliefs that enabled the change to occur is actively involved in therapy. The client is demonstrating to himself the contingency between cognitions and emotions and the difference between rational and irrational thought content. Reversing roles, so that the therapist becomes the "client," puts clients into the position of committing themselves to the RET philosophy of tolerance for self, others, and reality by actively arguing against the intolerant position taken by the therapist.

This discussion has drawn heavily on social psychological principles, particularly those of attitude change or persuasion. The extensive literature on attitudes and attitude change

(McGuire, 1969) suggests additional factors central to therapeutic influence. From an understanding of these theoretical principles and empirical findings, creative, innovative interventions can be developed.

Process and Techniques

The process of RET follows certain stages, which we have called initiating RET, defining problems, and changing irrational beliefs. Much of the therapy is directed to the last stage. Initiating RET and defining problems may be accomplished rather rapidly. However, for the therapist inexperienced in RET, defining problems ties in most directly with the theory of RET and may be somewhat difficult at first. As we discuss the process of RET later in this book, we will suggest and describe a variety of techniques that can be used at each stage. Here we discuss several caveats regarding techniques.

First and most important, there is no one way to practice RET. For example, the present authors differ from each other in their styles, and we both differ in style from Albert Ellis. RET therapists' styles range from a gentle, evocative approach to a directly confronting approach (Eschenroder, 1979). More often than not, a therapist may use different styles, depending on the client and what is happening during a particular session. Thus, RET is not synonymous with a particular style. Nor is it synonymous with particular techniques. RET therapists differ in techniques used, amount of activity, and degree of directiveness, although we are all to some degree active and directive. Directiveness, naturally, implies a direction, which is why the theory is so important. A therapist conceivably could use the same techniques as a particular RET therapist but not be practicing RET. Practicing RET means engaging in psychotherapy according to RET principles. RET is not a set of techniques; it is a *theory* of neurotic disturbance and a way of understanding people that may be applied to helping them change. Although we will suggest and describe specific techniques, RET cannot be simplified into a series of questions to be asked or lessons to teach a client. Indeed, if therapy and counseling were so simple, we could hardly justify devoting professional time and effort to it.

Clients are complex human beings. The *ABC* model of disturbance and our model of the emotional episode are *simplifications* for the sake of convenience. But clients are more than just a series of problems to be solved through the persistent application of the *ABC* model plus intellectual disputing. If RET were only reeducation or relearning, our work would be much easier. The fact is, though, that in most instances clients do not learn from us as readily as we wish they would; and, as a result, some clients present problems for which the RET practitioner had best be ready with some novel tactics. We hope that everyone who practices RET will do so inventively rather than mechanically.

Finally, any form of psychotherapy is more than application of techniques. We partly agree with Rogers (1961) that certain important conditions—namely, unconditional positive regard, empathy, and genuineness of the therapist—facilitate change. Instead of "regard," Ellis speaks of "undamning acceptance." As is well known among counselors, using Rogerian techniques alone does not make a Rogerian. We also believe that these conditions for change are important, but they can be conveyed in a directive as well as a nondirective situation. If they are not conveyed, however, all the techniques in the world will be unlikely to lead to a successful outcome.

Structure of the Sessions

RET is an active and directive form of therapy because the therapist provides the structure for each session; the client provides the content. What is done in therapy differs as client and therapist progress from initial goal setting and problem identification, through actively working on change, to preparation for leaving therapy. To discuss these differences in structure, we have chosen arbitrarily the typical initial, middle, and last sessions. While we do not advocate following a rigid structure, or slavishly following any structure, we recommend that the sessions generally follow the steps we describe.

In the initial session, the first task is to establish a relationship between therapist and client. This does not mean that a great deal of time is devoted to developing a particular kind of relationship. Rather, the therapist strives to get the client to have confidence in the therapy and to talk freely about himself. In our experience, most clients will do this rather quickly. Reluctant clients, especially those who have been forced into therapy, are exceptions. With adolescents and some persons who are not sophisticated about therapy, the rapport-building period may extend over several sessions (Young, 1977). We prefer to get some basic information about the client's age, marital status, and so forth, not because these facts are so important to therapy but because they are social icebreakers. They lead to the opening of a dialogue. After some initial rapport is established, we begin the next phase, problem identification.

We can inaugurate this phase by asking, "What problem do you want help with?" or "What can I do for you?" These questions are open ended but problem centered. This second phase can be entered immediately if the client is eager to talk about a problem. The client may easily describe problems or may have difficulty and require the therapist's skilled questioning. Clients frequently theorize about their problems, although they may be unaware that they do so. Humans seem to want to explain their behavior and so will offer explanations or causes of their problems. In response to the question "What is your problem?" one woman replied, "My husband." Another might say, "I've been depressed for a long time." In other words, clients usually define their problems in terms of the *A* or *C* of the *ABC* model, and the therapist's task is to probe for *B*s. However, this probing will come later.

The third phase of the initial session is goal setting. It is usually safe to assume that a client wants help with a present problem or complaint. However, it does not take much time to check, and the therapist may discover additional goals, perhaps even conflicting ones. Further, both client and therapist would do well to express some positive goals—feelings and actions the client desires—rather than merely citing the ones he or she wishes to reduce or eliminate. Then, too, some goals are unrealistic, such as wanting one's spouse to change or wanting to achieve in fields where the client has no training or talent. A goal-setting question is "What would you like to see changed as a result of therapy?" The legitimate goal in RET is changes in *C*—emotional and behavioral consequences. So, regardless of the client's initial statement of goals, the final version would be an answer to the question "How would you like to feel and act differently than you feel and act now?" Goals are tentative, for they are always subject to review and renegotiation.

Closely related to goal setting is the task of helping to clarify the client's expectations about therapy. We want clients to know that their tasks are to present specific problems each session and to work at homework assignments between sessions. They can expect to receive help with the psychological aspects of their problems and, to a lesser degree, the practical aspects as well. It is also helpful to orient the client to cognitive-behavioral notions about disturbance and treatment. We do not advocate a long theoretical discourse but, rather, a brief orientation period. We stress to clients that RET is not a mysterious process, that the therapist will not hoard insights but will reveal them to the client, and that the client's questions will be answered. We also inform the client about the role of thoughts, images, evaluative beliefs, and inferences in people's emotions and actions and then let the client know that we will collaborate with him in trying to uncover and reevaluate the important cognitions.

When time permits, the first session can cover some problem solving. The therapist can question the client about his or her belief system and do some preliminary challenging of irrational beliefs (*iB*s). Toward the end of the session, the client and therapist can discuss and agree on a homework assignment. Here is a summary of the outline we have just presented:

1. Introduction, rapport building, initial collaboration.
2. Ask for problems; get *A*s and *C*s from client.
3. Goal setting, both positive and negative, in terms of emotional and behavioral consequences.
4. Orient the client to RET and the cognitive hypothesis of disturbance; show influence of *iB*s on *C*.

5. Begin to work on specific problem, probing for *B*s, clarifying and correcting *iB*s, and agreeing on homework.

Early in therapy, the structure of sessions is similar to that of an initial session. As therapy progresses, rapport building and orientation are given much less emphasis, because the collaboration or therapeutic alliance has been established. A good way to start a session is to check on homework assigned during the previous session. Questions such as "What happened this week?" or "How did you feel this week?" do not set a problem-solving tone for the session. If the session does not start with homework, we might ask a problem-oriented question, such as "What problem do you want to work on today?"

The second phase is to set goals, and the third phase is to uncover beliefs. These are important aspects of assessment. Assessment includes the understanding of the client in relation to his cognitive dynamics. During this inquiry, secondary problems might emerge, such as anxiety about anxiety or other emotional difficulties about one's thoughts, feelings, and actions.

Before moving to the disputing of irrational beliefs, the therapist will want to get the client's agreement to work on a problem. An error made by some therapists in training is to challenge an irrational belief—for example, one associated with anger—when the clients have clearly indicated that they did not consider anger a problem. To challenge beliefs without an explicit or implicit commitment from the client is to challenge them absolutistically. Beliefs are defined as irrational if they have dysfunctional consequences for the individual, not because they contain certain words, such as *must.* Also, even if the consequences are dysfunctional, but occur infrequently, the client is probably correct in perceiving that they are not a problem. It is *not absolutely wrong* to believe "I must not do X."

During the course of therapy, the intellectual disputing of ideas often is insufficient to induce change. There is a trend in RET to deemphasize intellectual or cognitive disputing and to emphasize many other forms of attitude and behavior change. Later chapters deal with this point in some detail; we mention it here because it affects the structure of a typical session.

A frequently made error in subsequent sessions occurs when the therapist repeatedly disputes the *iB*s that the client already knows are incorrect. When clients understand their *iB*s, their role in dysfunctional emoting and action, and how to dispute the *iB*s, the task of the therapist changes. When the client understands, the therapist's task is to encourage the client to act on his or her insight or to investigate why the client is clinging to old misconceptions instead of giving them up. Why, in other words, does the client not try to convince himself to act differently based on his intellectual insight? Rather than repeatedly teaching the client how to work on problems, the therapist may now focus on the client's low frustration tolerance about working on problems.

The resolution of the session is in the form of a behavioral-experiential homework assignment. In homework the client performs positive actions inducing attitude and emotional change. Therefore, the homework assignments are ideally not simply tossed off at the end of the session. Instead, sufficient time will be set aside for discussing and perhaps rehearsing the assignment in some detail. To summarize, here is the outline of a typical middle session:

1. Check on homework; ask for problem.
2. Set goals, both positive and negative, in terms of emotional and behavioral consequences.
3. After hearing *A* and *C,* probe for *B*s.
4. Get commitment to work on problems, goals.
5. Dispute *iB*s, using cognitive and other dissuasion methods.
6. Assign and rehearse homework.

Ideally, the last session of therapy is devoted to helping the client review progress made to date and to identifying continuing or potential problems. The developing of plans to work on future problems is the primary focus. The therapist may share his or her view of the client's remaining current problems and identify what may be remaining difficulties for the client. It is usually advisable to speak against perfectionism once more; some clients think that the end of therapy means that they will live happily ever after.

Since the emphasis is on consolidation and anticipation of future difficulties, the outline for the final session is quite simple:

1. Review.
2. Plan.

Include in the plans the option of the client's returning at some future time. We do not have "last" sessions ordinarily; we simply agree to postpone the next one until the client calls.

Narrowly conceived, RET consists of identifying irrational beliefs and correcting them. This approach to RET focuses on Step 5 of the emotional episode and is usually given high priority by teachers of RET because this emphasis gives RET its uniqueness in the broad field of cognitive-behavior therapy. However, not all clients respond well to this approach. Experienced, creative RET practitioners are able to work at any step of the emotional episode, even though these others are given lower priorities.

Many client problems do not involve irrational evaluative thinking, or they involve it only minimally. In these cases, working with a client's problems in a comprehensive manner is strongly indicated. For example, men with secondary impotence can benefit from learning to focus their thinking on more erotic, arousing thoughts. In addition, the therapist can dispute the belief that the impotence is "awful," or the client may figure it out for himself once he knows that he can do something about the condition. A client who contemplates changing jobs may benefit from practical suggestions. Clients may want to discuss other plans, such as marriage, perhaps even seeking the therapist's impression of a potential mate. A client whose spouse threatens physical violence can be advised to see an attorney and then leave home or, in the most extreme instance, to leave town and change her name.

While some information giving may be factual, some is based on broad psychological principles. For example, in relationship counseling we find it helpful to furnish information about social exchange principles and to translate this information into terms usable by clients. There are many similar opportunities in psychotherapy and counseling to "give psychology away." In counseling couples, the therapist might try to improve communications rather than working on belief systems. (Of course, if irrational thinking were interfering with the relationship, it would be the focus of attention.) The partners may be taught to encode and decode messages more accurately, as well as to speak assertively and to share their feelings. There is no special RET way to deal with communications; the therapist or counselor can obtain information and techniques from other sources.

As we have done elsewhere in this book, we encourage therapists and counselors to be complete and well-rounded professionals. All the "non-RET" topics we mention here and later form a legitimate part of RET and are important aspects of what RET practitioners actually do.

2

Irrational Beliefs and Emotional Responses

RET shares with other cognitive explanations of emotions and behavior the assumption that the content of thoughts leads directly to emotional responses. In addition, RET makes another assumption: that rational beliefs typically lead to emotional responses appropriate to personal goals, whereas irrational beliefs lead to sustained, dysfunctional emotional responses. Consequently, one of the main goals of RET is to eliminate or greatly reduce irrational beliefs. For example, a person who is experiencing anxiety about an examination may hold one or more irrational ideas, such as "It would be truly disastrous for me to fail." If the person gives up this irrational belief, he might still appropriately believe that it would be disadvantageous to fail (a rational belief) and continue to experience concern and even some tension. Concern and tension might move the person to additional study and preparation (responses appropriate to his goals), whereas anxiety can be strongly inhibiting and tends to immobilize rather than to motivate.

Distinguishing *B* from *A*

The term *irrational belief* (*iB*) has a very specific meaning in RET. People may have any number of ill-founded, anti-empirical thoughts, such as "The world is flat," "The Martians are trying to capture me," "My husband hates me." If such thoughts enter into the *ABC* of an emotional episode, they are *A*s–not *B*s or even *iB*s. *A*s are cognitive events, as illustrated in the model of an emotional episode, and are often expressed as an opinion or an impression of an event. If a person tells us, "I failed my math exam and I feel anxious about it," we usually accept the claim "I failed my math exam" as a statement of fact. It might be true or it might not. The important thing is that the person believes it to be true. Now if the person said, "I *think* I failed my math exam," we could be tempted to wrongly classify that statement as a rational belief (*rB*) or an irrational belief (*iB*). Actually both statements, "I failed my math exam" and "I think I failed my math exam," are equivalent for RET purposes. Both are statements of what a person holds as true at that time. They are *not* rational or irrational beliefs in RET. They are simply descriptions of events by that person. The difference is that one is asserted while the other is stated tentatively. What varies is the degree of certainty. As we will discuss later, in RET we usually accept what a person says as true, even if our acceptance of the description of *A* is provisional; for example, "OK, let's say you did fail your exam. Now, what about that would make you anxious?" People do not become disturbed about things they know to be untrue or nonexistent.

In the *ABC*s of RET, *B* is a belief about *A*; it is an *evaluation* of something that a person believes to be true. *B* also includes the premises upon which the evaluation is made, which we describe later. In an article with the subtitle "Preferences

Need No Inferences," Zajonc (1980, p. 154) differentiates between "affective judgments and reactions, or hot cognitions, [and] their cold cognitive counterparts. . . . The first category is represented by the prototype 'I like Joe' and the second by 'Joe is a boy.' " In the model of the emotional episode, "Joe is a boy" is a description (Step 3), not an evaluation, while "I like Joe" is clearly an evaluation (Step 5). Confusion arises when a speaker says, "Joe is a likable boy," a semantic way of combining both statements but misattributing likeableness to Joe rather than to the speaker.

Almost everything we can think of or talk about contains some degree of appraisal or evaluation (Osgood, Suci, and Tannenbaum, 1957). To evaluate means simply to find something good or bad or somewhere in between; to appraise something as desirable or undesirable; to consider it as favorable or unfavorable. More directly and honestly, evaluation means that I like or dislike something and therefore label it as positive or negative. Thus, in *ABC* terms, *B* involves an evaluation of *A*. One of the first rules of RET is to listen for people's evaluations. Listen for them in these statements:

- I am a homosexual.
- My husband does not love me.
- I think my son is on drugs.
- I think I'm going to be fired.
- If I do well, I may get a promotion.

Unless we read into these statements our own evaluations, which is not a wise thing to do, they are simply statements of fact or presumed fact. If any or all of these presumed facts are upsetting to a person, we may be tempted to reassure that person that the fact is not true—for instance, by asking, "Where is the evidence that you are a homosexual?" and following with a lecture on bisexuality. This may or may not be advisable at the time, but it is an *error* when the therapist believes that he or she is disputing an irrational belief. The therapist is not. The therapist is disputing *A*. A great deal of cognitive therapy is devoted to helping clients test reality more accurately;

that is, to clear up misconceptions (Raimy, 1975). However, RET focuses primarily on evaluative beliefs and secondarily on the cognitions regarding the truth or falsity of activating events.

Distinguishing *rB* from *iB*

If the *B*s in the *ABC*s involve evaluations, how can we distinguish between rational evaluations and irrational evaluations? Several possibilities exist. All of them have to do with what is realistic and demonstrable versus unrealistic and magical.

Ellis and Harper (1975) have proposed a simple definition of *rational* and of *irrational. Rational* is anything that promotes individual survival and happiness. *Irrational* is anything that blocks, inhibits, or works against individual survival and happiness. This definition is helpful in understanding the overall theory and goals of RET, but it is difficult to use in practice. It is difficult to use because the therapist or counselor and the client are forced to wait for the outcome of a thought to occur, or at least to be able to forecast the consequences with a high degree of accuracy. Some thoughts—such as "I think I'll kill myself" or "I can drink a quart of gin a day without ill effects"—are obviously not helpful to individual survival, but many are more subtle. Further, when it comes to happiness, the picture is even less clear. How can one say that job X will bring more happiness than job Y? Or even if one knows that loafing all day is more enjoyable than working, loafing all day will probably not bring future happiness. Hence, whether we are talking of survival or of happiness, it would be better to compare the pleasures of the moment with the pleasures of the future and to seek compromise solutions. This philosophy is known as the hedonic calculus, an idea that plays a central role in RET.

Closely related to the happiness-survival definition of rationality are the five criteria proposed by Maultsby (1975):

> Criterion 1: Rational thinking is based on objective reality or the known facts of a life situation.

Criterion 2: Rational thinking enables people to protect their lives.

Criterion 3: Rational thinking enables people to achieve their goals more quickly.

Criterion 4: Rational thinking enables people to keep out of significant trouble with other people.

Criterion 5: Rational thinking enables people to prevent or quickly eliminate significant personal or emotional conflict.

Criterion 1 concerns itself with whether the activating event (*A*) is true or false and is not directed to an evaluation of *A*. Moreover, "objective reality" is a difficult notion; what is meant is better termed "verifiable reality" or "consensual reality." Criterion 2 is a difficult rule to apply except in very obvious situations. How do I know whether the birth control pill I take today will protect or endanger my life in the future? Regarding Criterion 3, it may be easy to determine a course of action that will *not* achieve my goals quickly; for example, loafing instead of studying when I want to earn a degree. But many choices are a good deal more subtle, and to apply this rule, in our view, requires knowledge of the future. Criteria 4 and 5 also require us to forecast the future, with respect to avoiding trouble; and this cannot be done consistently. Further, the word *significant* is defined as the amount of conflict or trouble that one does not want to have. This is hardly a helpful guide to therapists and counselors who are attempting to listen for and identify clients' irrational thinking. So, while the five criteria can be helpful in decision making, especially when there is plenty of information about the future, they do not involve *evaluations* of *A*. Except for Criterion 1, objective reality, which refers to checking the activating cognition against the activating stimulus, all these criteria are based on behavioral results of thinking.

Can we speak of the beliefs themselves, the evaluations at *B*, as being rational or irrational? Yes, given a particular frame of reference. That frame of reference in RET is reasoning from evidence, the basis of the scientific method and of jurisprudence, which posits that knowledge can be based only on what is observable. From this point of view, we find that by far the most useful definition of *rational* in counseling and clinical situations centers on empirical proofs about the basis of one's evaluations of *A*. If I say that something is good and mean that I like it, I can easily find evidence for this assertion, for my preference exists. If, however, I insist that it is inherently good, I venture into the realm of the unempirical and the unprovable, for another person may find it bad.

Irrational thinking consists of evaluations derived from nonempirical premises stated in absolutistic language. Rational thinking consists of evaluations that are relative to what can be proven empirically: one's preferences and desires. Irrational thinking ignores reality in favor of what the individual says should exist. Irrational ideas are often expressed in sentences containing such words as *should, must, ought, have to, got to, need*—words implying unconditional prescriptions or demands. In most instances, there is no empirical basis for using these words. How, for example, can I prove that things *ought* to be the way I *prefer* them to be? I can sensibly tell you that I wish it would not snow, but I cannot legitimately escalate this preference into the statement "Therefore, it should not snow." Or picture me shouting to the sky, "You must not snow! I don't like it!" The fact is that snow will fall when weather conditions determine it, not when I desire it, no matter how absolutistic or loud my demands.

But words themselves do not constitute irrational beliefs. RET is concerned with meanings. The experienced counselor or therapist listens for meanings, not for words. Ellis coined the term *musturbation* to refer to absolutistic prescriptions and other unconditional imperatives. Colorful words and phrases like *musturbation* may alert us to irrational meanings, but the word *must* does not in itself always signal an irrational belief. Inquiry is called for to check out our hypothesis that a key word, such as *should* or *ought* or *must,* signals irrational thinking, since the meaning (but not the language) may reflect rational, reality-oriented, nonabsolutistic thinking. To give a brief example of focusing on words and not on meaning, here is a paraphrase of a therapeutic interaction one of us once heard:

Therapist (T): Your fear of rejection seems to be keeping you from having the close relationships you want.
Client (C): Yes, but I don't know if I can overcome the fear. It will be hard for me.
T: But the effort will be worth it, won't it?
C: Yeah, I guess it will be. I guess I should try.
T: Why should you?

Words such as *must, should,* and *awful* serve as cues to irrational thinking, but they are only cues, not absolutes.

Feelings and thoughts also can serve as activating events and get evaluated at point *B*. A person might become angry, for example, and express this anger indiscriminately. He may then become guilty in response to his indiscriminate display of anger, in which case the angry behavior would be both an expression of *C*, the anger, and an *A* related to the guilt, another *C*. Some people feel guilty simply for *feeling* angry in a situation, even when they do not express their angry feelings. In this case, the *C*, feelings of anger, also serves as an *A*. So when clients tell us that they feel angry and guilty when their mother criticizes them, for example, they are probably holding two related sets of irrational beliefs. First:

A: Mother criticizes me.
(*rB:* I don't like that; I wish she wouldn't do it.)
iB: She must not criticize me. I can't stand her putting me down that way.
C: Anger.

and second:

A: Realization of feelings of anger.
(*rB:* I wish I wouldn't feel this way toward my mother.)
iB: It's horrible of me to feel that way about my own mother. I'm a rotten person for feeling that way.
C: Guilt.

Perhaps a more typical example is feeling anxious and then escalating the anxiety by feeling anxious about the anxiety. Let us say a person is afraid to give speeches and panics when called on to do so. First:

A: Anticipates the audience's disapproval.
(*rB:* I want to do a good job and have them appreciate it.)
iB: They must appreciate my talk. If they don't, that will prove how inadequate I am.
C: Anxiety.

and then:

A: Feelings of anxiety.
(*rB:* I'd prefer not to feel uncomfortable.)
iB: I must not feel discomfort. It is awful to feel anxious, and it proves how inadequate I am because I feel anxious.
C: More anxiety.

As these examples show, both rational and irrational beliefs can occur in response to *A*. Minimizing or eliminating an irrational belief does not lead to a vacuum between *A* and *C*, for the rational belief remains.

A goal of RET is to help people accept reality, including the reality of one's own thoughts and feelings, and to reject the baseless additional evaluations they attach to reality. It is not always pleasant to accept reality, particularly grim reality. However, we seem able to work best at changing reality when we first accept the present reality and refrain from demanding that it magically change because we do not like it. The old idea that we can work to change what can be changed and accept what cannot be changed seems appropriate here. It is *not* a goal of RET to eliminate all feelings, not even all negative feelings. Rather, the goal is to emote and behave in ways that are not dysfunctional in the long run and in ways that ultimately promote one's happiness and survival. By fully accepting reality and eliminating extreme, absolutistic evaluations of reality, we take major steps toward that goal.

Listen for the demands people make. Listen further for the meaning or evaluations they attach to not getting their demands fulfilled. You may wish to check at this point whether you can recognize an activating event (*A*), a rational belief (*rB*), an irrational belief (*iB*), and an emotional consequence (*C*). Try this quiz:

> A client tells you that he went for a job interview and now feels depressed. He says his thoughts were: "I don't think I got the job. It's horrible. I can't stand not getting the job, and I'll never get one."

The emotional consequence (*C*) is what he feels—depressed. The activating event (*A*) is his thinking he did not get the job. (As mentioned, *A* is a statement about reality as the client perceives it; a fact, not an evaluation.) No rational belief is stated here, although we can plausibly infer that the client would prefer to get the job. Several irrational beliefs (*iB*s) may be found: "It's horrible. I can't stand it. I'll never get one." "It's horrible" is clearly an evaluation, an exaggerated one at that. "I can't stand it" is both an evaluation of the horribleness of the event and a distortion of reality, for he is indeed standing it. "I'll never get one" is a depression-inducing exaggeration that might be true but is very unlikely. Further, there is an implied evaluation here (subject to checking with the client): "If I never get another job, that would be awful."

Given the definition of irrational beliefs as evaluations based on absolutistic, nonempirical assumptions, there are perhaps thousands of irrational self-statements. To the extent that each person is unique, each person has his or her own set of irrational thoughts. Each has favorite words to stand for personal meanings. The task of the counselor or therapist is to discover these meanings. For this reason, we do not favor memorizing lists of irrational beliefs. However, it can be instructive to study these lists and learn *why* each common idea is irrational and how each leads to disturbance. The reader is encouraged to consult Ellis (1977d) and Ellis and Harper (1975) for a detailed discussion of a number of common irrational ideas.

Here we will discuss in some detail one such idea. The idea we shall consider is that one must prove thoroughly competent, adequate, and achieving, or that one must have competence or talent in some important area (Ellis and Harper, 1975, p. 102). Note the demanding or absolutistic language. One does not merely *want* to be competent or talented; he *must* be competent or talented. There is some evidence that a desire for achievement leads to important human activity and can prove highly motivating (for example, Festinger, 1957; White, 1963); however, to *demand* what one wants is the essence of irrationality. Further, hardly anyone can prove competent and masterful in most respects, and probably no one can display perfect adequacy or achievement. Finally, accomplishment cannot be attained without discomfort or disadvantages. There is not enough time for outstanding achievement *and* many of life's other pleasures.

How does the failure to get what one *must* get, in this case achievement, lead to dysfunctional emoting? The answer lies in the *evaluation* of self, others, and the world in general. People often, perhaps usually, make absolutistic demands in order to prove their own worth as a human being or their own adequacy to cope with the world. Thus, the irrational belief that "I must prove thoroughly adequate and achieving" is simply the beginning of a longer thought, "I must prove thoroughly adequate and achieving; if I do not, it is awful and proves what an inadequate human being I am," which leads to anxiety when one contemplates failure. To this idea the person might add the thought "poor me" or other self-pitying statements associated with depression. Or the person might add, "It's unfair that I should have to strive so hard to achieve," a statement associated with anger.

Other Problems in Thinking

Evaluations and meanings that we impose on ourselves, other people, the world, life, and so forth, may become so habitual that we fail to take notice of them. Beck (1976) refers to such habitual thoughts as automatic thinking. We cannot easily identify some of our own automatic thoughts, although we can improve with practice. An experienced counselor or therapist (or other alert listener) can often point out assumptions that one would have to make in order to feel or act in a particular way. We usually assume a consistency among thoughts, feelings, and actions; therefore, from a client's statements about his feelings or from his behavior, or from both, a therapist can develop hypotheses or hunches about what the client might be thinking. By revealing these hunches to clients for their consideration, the therapist can help them become aware of their automatic or nonconscious thoughts. This process is probably accurately called interpretation, but since it is usually done in a tentative manner, it might be better called hypothesis testing.

To return to the example of the student who thinks she has failed an examination, we would expect that her thoughts or evaluations about the expected failure would be consistent with reported feelings and with anxiety-coping behaviors. Thus, the client may tell us only that she has failed an examination and feels anxious about it. Based on RET theory and our past experience, we quickly form hypotheses: the client (1) believes that failure is quite possible, (2) perceives failure as harmful or personally threatening, (3) evaluates failure as unpleasant, (4) further evaluates the failure as awful, and (5) believes that failing the exam would "prove" something about her worth or adequacy as a human being and that therefore she must do well on it. With these hypotheses as guides, the RET therapist can focus quickly on irrational beliefs that a client may be unaware of because they have become automatic.

To this point we have been discussing irrational beliefs as false premises. Take this syllogism as an example:

Major premise:	People must do well to be worthwhile.
Minor premise:	I did poorly.
Conclusion:	I am no good.

The conclusion follows logically from the major premise. (The minor premise, by the way, is *A*.) As we discover clients' conceptions of situations and their philosophical beliefs about them, it becomes apparent that many clients often engage in illogical operations as well. They may choose to believe what they want to believe and not what fits the evidence. Or they may evaluate activating events according to "psycho-logical" processes (Abelson and Rosenberg, 1958) instead of logical ones. They may attribute favorable evaluations to themselves or, more likely, unfavorable ones by overgeneralizing, over-including, and making other logical errors. Focusing on these logical mistakes as well as on invalid premises is a prime strategy in disputing and challenging irrational ideas, a process that constitutes the heart of RET and a topic we will come to in a later chapter.

There are also other errors of thinking that are not irrational beliefs. To return to *A*, the misconstruing of events is an example. The individual may interpret events in ways that are somewhat autistic or at least highly personalized, ways that are quite unlike what others may say about a situation. For example, a 55-year-old client complained that, despite her assertive requests, her 85-year-old father would telephone her and ask her what she was doing. She construed his inquiry as an intentional interference with her activities. The therapist offered the plausible alternative construction that he was simply lonely and eager for conversation and used a stereotyped query ("Hello, what's doing?") to initiate the conversation. She began to consider this alternative construction of the situation; and later, when she redefined the situation for herself, she found that she was less angry with the old man. Her solution was, strictly speaking, not elegant or ideal in RET practice, for the solution was a reconstruing of a specific *A*. The solution to psychological problems that RET attempts involves philosophical changes, not just redefinitions of stimuli. (In this case, however, the woman had not shown any inclination to a philosophical solution, and so this more empirical solution was attempted.)

Misconstructions or misinterpretations of situations do get dealt with in RET but usually after the person's belief system has been explored, irrationalities challenged, and ideas at *B* reconsidered. Hence, in this case we are using for illustration, the therapist began by stipulating, "Well, suppose your father does want to know about your personal affairs. What about that would anger you?" This resulted in uncovering the irrational belief that her father had no right to question her and that she strongly blamed him for it, righteous blaming so that she would not feel so guilty about thinking damning thoughts about her father. But she would not give up her irrational thoughts that he had no right to say things that displeased her and that wrongdoers, including her father, should be condemned. In short, when it became apparent that she would not easily change her evaluations of the situation, the therapist attempted to get her to rethink the intentions she had attributed to him.

Many approaches to cognitive therapy are based on correcting misconceptions. Raimy (1975) and Beck (1976) have written extensively about this approach. There is a great deal to recommend it to therapists and counselors. However, in RET, work directed toward correcting misconceptions at *A* is secondary to the attempt to change the highly evaluative, absolutistic philosophies at *B*. Changing one's philosophy is a deeper and more pervasive change, and, because they are not infallible, therapists or counselors cannot always determine what constitutes a true misconception (this client's father might, in fact, have intended to pry into her affairs).

Components of Irrational Beliefs

Irrational beliefs are composed of at least two of the following three components: awfulizing, demandingness, and evaluation of self and others. Awfulizing is the major evaluative component of irrational beliefs. Although we will begin by discussing this component, awfulizing does not stand alone. The evaluative belief that something is awful is a conclusion drawn from certain philosophies or premises about oneself and/or the world. In these premises we find the evaluation of self and others and the demandingness components.

A brief reminder about semantics before we continue. As we noted earlier, it is the *meaning* of the words the client uses that is important. When a client uses any of the words we will discuss—*awful, should, must,* and so forth—he may or may not mean them in the sense we will use. It is the job of the therapist to check out meanings.

Awfulizing. Awfulizing is believing that something is awful, terrible, horrible, catastrophic. As a result of such a belief, the individual experiences an extremely upsetting emotion, such as shame, guilt, anxiety, depression, or anger. Let us look at the meaning of the word *awful.* Awful, of course, means bad. But more than that, it means the worst thing that could happen—100 percent bad. We usually do not say that something is "awfuler" or "awfulest," but simply "awful." Ellis points out that it is irrational to believe that something is awful, because awful does not exist. Nothing can be 100 percent bad, because something worse could happen. For instance, if I thought that the worst thing that could happen to me would be to be eaten slowly by a school of piranha fish, dying after three days, that might be 99 percent bad—but 99.1 percent might be that they would take four days. Of course, we do not walk around with a calculator in our heads to compute the badness of an event in percentages, but we can do something similar; we can judge the relative badness of an event by asking what could be worse.

The first reaction of many people to the message "Nothing is awful" is that it implies that nothing should be judged as bad. Clients often arrive at that conclusion, saying, "You mean to tell me that it's all right to leave my children?" or whatever it is they are awfulizing about. Certainly, things that we judge to be extremely bad do happen: a loved one dies, a person is completely paralyzed after an accident, a nation practices genocide. The RET message does not imply that these or any other event should not be judged bad, because the message explicitly states that badness, as judged by each individual's value system, does exist. It is a matter of degree.

The clinical reason for helping clients make distinctions among gradations of badness, including awful, has been pointed out by Beck (1963, p. 329): "The affective reaction is proportional to the descriptive labeling of the event rather than to the actual intensity of a traumatic situation." If our goal is to help clients reduce and minimize extreme, perhaps incapacitating, feelings of anxiety, shame, guilt, and depression, then we will want to help them evaluate events with more perspective. Awfulizing allows for no perspective. As we say to clients, "I don't want to minimize your problem; I want to help you not to maximize it."

Occasionally a client is grappling with a problem that most people would consider quite bad; for instance, losing one's eyesight or facing death from cancer. When a client is facing such grim realities, the discussion of the difference between 100 percent and 99 percent bad can be useful. Also, when people label something as awful, they usually also believe that it therefore must not happen (demandingness, to be discussed later). The RET message is that very bad things will and do happen; that there is no reason why they must not happen, although there are many reasons why we hope that they will not; and that we would do better to accept the fact, change it if we can, and live with it if we cannot.

More typically, the events that clients label as awful are nowhere near the extremes we have been discussing—failing a test, being rejected by a friend, not giving a speech well, and so forth. Here particularly, conveying the relative nature of badness can be useful. To illustrate, a client once told one of us that it would be awful if his girl friend left him. When asked "Would it be worse if you wrecked your car on the way here?" he thought for a moment and smiled, "You know, it would be worse if I ran out of gas." To repeat Beck's words, "The affective reaction is proportional to the descriptive labeling of the event rather than to the actual intensity of a traumatic situation."

Demandingness. Demandingness means believing that certain things must or must not happen; believing that certain conditions, such as success and approval, are *necessary*. Horney (1942) aptly coined the phrase "the tyranny of the should" for this type of thinking. Demandingness implies that certain absolute laws of the universe must be adhered to and that the violation of these laws is unthinkable—*awful.* Demandingness and awfulizing go hand in hand: "I must not make a mistake. It would be awful if I did!" "Big businesses must not cheat the consumer. It is terrible that they do!" "Life should be easy. How awful when it's not!" There is no evidence that the "thou shalts" and the "thou shalt nots" are anything more than human fabrications. The fact that some prohibitions, such as those against murder and incest, are practically universal signifies only that such behavior threatens the social group and most societies have created these prohibitions for their protection.

By contending that there are no absolute laws of the universe, is RET espousing anarchy? Certainly not. To pursue this point, we digress to the issue of the RET conception of the basic motivation of the predominantly rational person (predominantly, because we do not conceive of any human's thinking as completely rational). If there are no needs, no absolute necessities, what, then, is a desirable goal for a human? What is desirable in most cases is to live. If we are to live, then it is also desirable to live happily. Living happily means maximizing pleasure and minimizing pain in life. Thus, the sensible or rational motivation is hedonistic.

To be sensible, this hedonism includes a long-term view of life, simply because life is an ongoing, long-term process. Thus, if I maximize my pleasure and minimize my pain today by not meeting my scheduled classes at school, particularly if I were to do that fairly often, the effect would quite likely be to maximize my pain and minimize my pleasure in the future—because I would get fired. The same reasoning applies to any number of behaviors, including social behaviors. It is often not sensible in the long run to cheat, steal, fight, and so forth, for such behaviors are likely to have adverse social or legal consequences. This discussion of motivation is similar to that of Combs, Richards, and Richards (1976), who present a perceptual theory of personality with the phenomenal self at the core. They posit as the basic motivation of humans a striving for adequacy; that is, maintenance and enhancement of the self. They state (p. 56): "Thus, each person seeks not merely the maintenance of *a* self, but the development of an *adequate* self—a self capable of dealing effectively and efficiently with the exigencies of life, *both now and in the future*" (last italics ours).

Sensibly keeping in mind potential long-term consequences of our behavior does not preclude the enjoyment of an activity for the sheer pleasure of the moment. Forgoing all short-term enjoyments would be just as irrational (detrimental to the goal of maximizing pleasure and minimizing pain) as living only for the pleasures of the moment. Simply, the pleasures of the moment are balanced against the potential negative consequences in the future, just as the pains of the moment (effort, work, deprivation) are weighed against potential benefits in the future. A choice is then made. If this process sounds calculating, it is. But calculation is not necessarily antihumanistic. Here is part of Rogers' (1961, p. 190) description of a fully functioning person: "An analogy which might come close to a description would be to compare this person to a giant electronic computing machine. Since he is open to his experience, all of the data from his sense impressions, from his memory, from previous learning, from his visceral and internal states, is fed into the machine. The machine takes all of these multitudinous pulls and forces which are fed in as data, and quickly computes the course of action which would be the most economical vector of need satisfaction in this existential situation. This would be the behavior of our hypothetical person."

Would the sensible, rational person behave altruistically? Yes, indeed. In order to maximize pleasure and minimize pain in the future, it would be highly desirable to live in a society that promotes the well-being of all its members. For if some members are oppressed, the oppression might spread to me. It is sensible, then, to strive for a society where no one is oppressed, where neighbor helps neighbor, and where people get along with minimal disruption to the well-being of others. Such a society perhaps has never existed, but for a rational hedonist it makes perfectly good sense and is worth striving for. If such a society is desirable, then it is highly desirable for individuals to live up to the values and norms implied. So the sensible person would *want* to be kind to others and not harm them—not *have to* by any absolute rule, but *want* to—because to do so flows naturally from one's own self-interest. Self-interest, therefore, is not selfishness, which implies a lack of concern for others. Concern for others is implied in self-interest. To be self-interested is to be concerned for one's own welfare, and, as just described, the welfare of others is often related to one's own welfare.

The RET point of view is that rational people will try to

live up to certain rules of conduct and to their own morals and standards; they will view such behavior as highly desirable and beneficial to their own well-being, but not as absolutely necessary to avoid damnation. Just as the rational alternative to "awful" is some degree of "bad," not "neutral" or "good," the rational alternative to "must" or "have to" is some degree of "want" or "prefer," not "I don't care."

Evaluation of Self and Others. The third component of many irrational beliefs is the evaluation of self and others. We will focus our discussion on the evaluation of self, but any of the arguments for the irrationality of self-evaluation can be applied to the evaluation of others. People are often reluctant to give up their self-evaluative beliefs because one translation of self-evaluation or self-rating is self-esteem. We have yet to have a client say "I have too much self-esteem and I want to get rid of it." Yet this is precisely what the RET therapist would like all clients to do.

Self-rating means the rating or evaluation of one's entire self, determining the total value of the person, in statements such as "I'm no good," "What a louse I am," or the reverse, "I am a worthy person." All these statements include an evaluative label applied to the total person. The effect of such thinking is to create, on the one hand, the debilitating emotions of guilt, shame, anxiety, and depression or, on the other hand, the self-enhancing emotions of pride and euphoria. Unfortunately, the self-enhancing emotions are derived from the same belief—that people can be worthwhile or worthless—that creates the debilitating emotions. Pride goeth before a fall.

The very idea of human worth, according to Ellis, is illogical because it is a case of overgeneralization—in effect, judging a book by its cover. When we make judgments of human worth, these judgments are usually based on some limited actions of the person, or the effects of these actions. At any given moment, when we attach a value label (good or bad) to a person, at best that label is a sum of all the pluses and minuses ascribed to the person's acts and characteristics up to that moment. Even if we could accomplish this feat, the future, with its potential for change, is ignored. Not all people show significant change, but since we cannot predict the future, it is not the fact of change but the potential for change that is important here.

When we engage in self-rating, we typically focus on some specific characteristic, behavior, or effect, evaluate it according to some standard of desirability or worth, and then apply this evaluation to ourselves. For example, a person may believe that it is undesirable or bad to make mistakes. In fact, in most instances it *is* undesirable or bad to make mistakes. Usually there are negative consequences, slight or great depending on the mistake. Indeed, we probably can list the unfortunate consequences and certainly justify our evaluation of "bad." But we cannot justify applying to ourselves the legitimate evaluation of the act and of its consequences: "I did a bad thing; therefore, I am a bad person." That is why self-rating is irrational or erroneous thinking, a case of overgeneralization.

RET therapists do want people to evaluate their actions and the effects of their actions. Clearly, some behaviors lead to more beneficial results than other behaviors do. The sensible person would want to make these judgments about his or her behavior in order to live more effectively. But RET therapists want to help people minimize their tendency to leap to *total* self-evaluation. A byword of RET is "Rate the act, not the person."

To do so is not easy. Ellis (1976) believes that irrational thinking is a part of our human heritage. The tendency to think irrationally, particularly to evaluate oneself, may have evolved because irrational thinking makes social control easier (Wessler, 1977). The idea that our brains are programmed for this type of thinking is supported in the literature of cognitive psychology:

> Yet a one-dimensional view is surprisingly close to the truth in characterizing many aspects of human judgment. This was pointed out by DeSoto (1961) in a paper called "The Predilection for Single Orderings." DeSoto noted that when subjects are asked to rate others in such diverse things as voice quality and intelligence, they tend to see those high in one quality as also high in others. . . . DeSoto argued that, even in everyday language,

> one can detect a tendency to act as though there were only one ordering of a group of people. Use of expressions like "Joe's tops" or "Joe's the greatest" avoids any hint that there may be any orderings on which Joe does not stand uppermost.
>
> DeSoto's experiments indicate that we have difficulty learning and remembering lists which involve different orderings of the same people. It is as though we stored a master list of people, just as we do the alphabet. New orderings might be tried out on a provisional basis, but it is easier not to store separate orderings on different dimensions. In this sense the overall list structure tends to distort our thinking [Posner, 1973, pp. 83-84].

Ellis (1973, chap. 2) proposes two solutions to this problem of evaluating human worth. First, since practically all ascriptions of human worth are based on factors extraneous to the person and on the erroneous thinking previously described, a reasonable conclusion is that we have worth simply because we exist. However, as Ellis points out, such a statement is a mere definition, although a useful one for many clients. We might just as flatly state that, because we exist, we are worthless. His second solution, the elegant solution, is simply not to rate oneself at all. Give up the notion of human worth. Accept the fact that there is no way to judge the worth of a human being. A graphic illustration of the self-rating process and of both solutions to the problem of human evaluation is shown in Figures 1-3.

The vertical dimension–labeled "Action, Effect, Characteristic"–can stand for any dimension that we evaluate as positive or negative, desirable or undesirable, good or bad. Taking the previous example of making mistakes, we can put this action on the vertical dimension and legitimately judge that not making mistakes is a positive action and that making mistakes is a negative one. The self or total person comprises a separate dimension, independent of the first dimension. When we engage in self-rating, however, we treat the two as correlated. As a result, we judge ourselves as good people when we do well and as bad people when we do poorly.

Figure 1. Illustration of the Process of Self-Rating; Two Related Dimensions

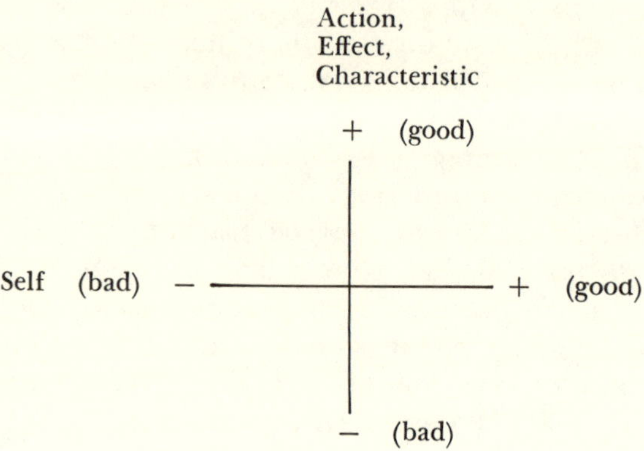

The first, inelegant, solution is to keep these two dimensions independent and uncorrelated; as a result, no matter where one's behavior falls on the vertical dimension, one's worth or goodness remains unchanged on the self dimension. Figure 2 illustrates this solution. A person's worth remains at *a* (because of his very existence), whether his behavior falls at *b* or *c* or anywhere else on the vertical dimension. In fact, the self dimension shrinks and becomes a point at the positive end of

Figure 2. Illustration of the Inelegant Solution; Self-Worth Is Invariant at *a*

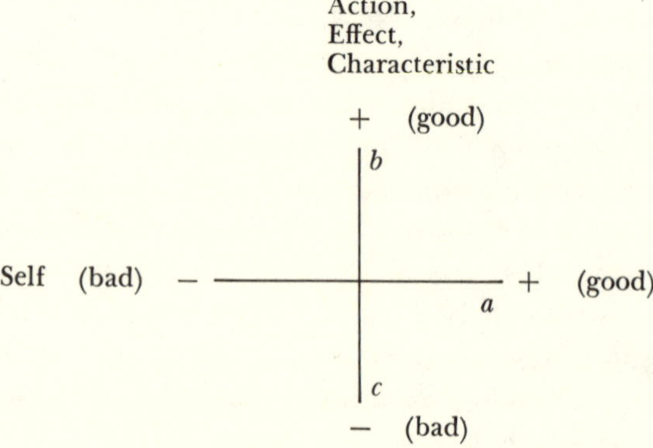

the previous self dimension. By the way, this is also Carl Rogers' solution of "unconditional positive self-regard."

Figure 3. Illustration of the Elegant Solution; Self Dimension Has Disappeared

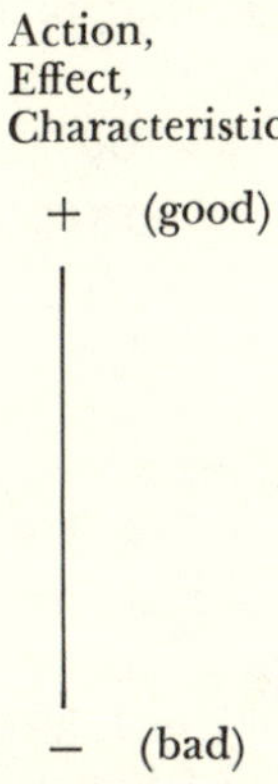

Figure 3 illustrates the elegant solution. Here the self dimension, including the invariant point in Figure 2, has disappeared. Thus, we continue to evaluate our actions, effects, and characteristics, but we no longer evaluate our self, our total being. According to Ellis, the elegant solution is an ideal that is worth striving for. Although never completely achieved, because of the nuances of human thinking discussed earlier, it can be approached; that is, global self-rating can be minimized, and, when self-rating does occur, a person can soon become aware of it and change his thoughts.

If a person gives up self-rating—and that does mean self-esteem—what is left? What is left is something quite important and something often lacking—self-acceptance. The desirability of achieving self-acceptance is not a value unique to RET. Self-acceptance is often discussed in the literature of humanistic theories and therapies. Often, though, this important concept is confused with self-regard or self-liking. As Combs, Richards, and Richards (1976, p. 263) state: "Acceptance of self should not be confused with 'liking.' Some experimenters, for example, have attempted to measure self-acceptance by asking subjects to indicate the degree to which they liked certain characteristics about themselves. But acceptance is no more related to liking than it is to resignation. It has to do with the admission of fact, the acknowledgment of existence, and has nothing to do with liking. . . . Liking and disliking have to do with judgments about self, while acceptance is nonjudgmental. It has to do with the consideration of evidence, not its evaluation."

Maslow (1970, pp. 155-156), in discussing people he considers self-actualizing, gives an excellent description of self-acceptance:

> They can accept their own human nature in stoic style, with all its shortcomings, with all its discrepancies from the ideal image, without feeling real concern. It would convey the wrong impression to say that they are self-satisfied. What we must say is that they can take the frailties and sins, weaknesses and evils of human nature in the same unquestioning spirit with which one accepts the characteristics of nature. One does not complain about water because it is wet, or about rocks because they are hard, or about trees because they are green. As the child looks out upon the world with wide, uncritical eyes, simply noting and observing what is the case, without either arguing the matter or demanding that it be otherwise, so does the self-actualizing person tend to look upon human nature in himself and in others. This is of course not the same thing as resignation in the Eastern sense, but resignation too can be observed in our subjects, especially in the face of illness and death.

The RET point of view is that self-acceptance can be achieved by rethinking and changing one's beliefs.

Emotions and Irrational Beliefs

Intensity of emotional response is *not* a characteristic that distinguishes between emotions derived from rational thinking and those derived from irrational thinking. It is true that the emotions derived from irrational thinking are quite often intense because of the extreme evaluation of awfulizing; however, we can also experience intense emotions that derive from rational thinking. Let us say that a person judges her relationship with her husband as very important. It is extremely satisfying to her, and she cares greatly about him. He dies. Let us say that the same person also cares about some fine china she owns. Her dishwasher malfunctions. Much of the china is broken. In both cases, because she has lost something she cares for or values, she will feel sad and perhaps also annoyed, frustrated, and disappointed. In *ABC* terms, we can illustrate both events with *A* (loss), *rB* (I didn't want to lose that/him), *C* (sadness). But in the first case, losing her husband, because of the high degree of caring and the great importance of the relationship to her, her sadness would be much, much greater (in fact, we would probably say that she was grieving) than her sadness at the loss of the china. Thus, emotions deriving from rational thinking may be quite intense, but the degree of intensity is related to the importance or desirability we attribute to the event.

Given the three components of irrational thinking, we can now see how they interact to produce specific irrational beliefs. Some combinations include only the first two components, awfulizing and demandingness. Examples of these beliefs are "The world should be fair," "Life should be easy," "Others must do what I want." All these ideas are followed by "and it's awful when that doesn't happen." Ellis refers to such thinking as low frustration tolerance. One result of such thinking is hostility—hostility at the world, at life, at others. When the belief is directed toward others, "You should do what I want" or "You must not hurt me," we may also find evaluation of others. The idea becomes "You shouldn't have done that and you're a rotten person because you did." Alternatively, if a person believes simply that it would be highly desirable if there were fairness in the world, if others acceded to one's wishes, and so forth, that person will feel annoyed and frustrated, but not hostile, when these events do not occur.

Another combination of awfulizing and demandingness without the self-rating component occurs when the events are one's own emotions. "My God, I feel anxious; that's terrible!" results in what Ellis (1979a, 1980) terms discomfort anxiety. Alternatively, the person who believes that it is not awful to feel in certain ways may feel concern when these events occur, but he will not add further anxiety to the event and will not dwell on the "bad" feelings, demanding that they go away.

When the self-rating component combines with the other two components, the most common ideas are these: (1) I need to be approved (accepted, loved) by all significant persons in my life *in order to be* worthwhile. (2) I need to be successful, to do well, *in order to be* worthwhile. Implied in each of these beliefs is that if the event does not occur it is awful. It is, of course, quite devastating to regard oneself as worthless. The result of either of these ideas is anxiety in anticipation of rejection or failure, or shame or guilt when rejection or failure is experienced. Alternatively, if a person wants to be liked or successful but does not believe that either is necessary for his worth, that person will feel regretful and disappointed, but not ashamed or guilty, when he experiences rejection or failure.

Much of what has been said to this point can be summarized in a table utilizing Freud's conception of anxiety as a frame of reference. Freud's categorization of anxiety is useful in illustrating that anxiety can come from many sources. Included in this table are the sources of anxiety as viewed by Freud and by Ellis and the emotion that occurs if the feared event occurs. These emotions are then contrasted with those that would occur if awfulizing and self-rating were absent and demandingness replaced by preferring.

Missing from this table is the emotion of depression. However, we can take any of the irrational ideas outlined in Table 4, add to it the ideas of helplessness and hopelessness, and the result is depression. To take just two examples: First, a person believes that life should be easy and nonfrustrating. On experiencing frustrations, if he believes not only that it is awful and should not happen but, in addition, that there is nothing he can do about it and that life will always be that way, he will

Table 4. Sources of Anxiety: Freud and Ellis.

Freudian Terms	*Freudian Source*	*Event Anticipated (A)*	*Ellis's Source[a] (iB)*			*Emotion if Event Occurs (C)*	*Emotion if Irrational Belief Absent*
			A	*D*	*S*		
Objective anxiety	Real world	Physical harm	no	no	no	Fear	Fear
		Frustrations	yes	yes	no	Anger	Annoyance, frustration
		Disapproval	yes	yes	yes	Shame	Regret[b]
Neurotic anxiety	Id	Loss of control	yes	yes	no	Panic	Regret
Moral anxiety	Superego: Ego ideal	Failure	yes	yes	yes	Guilt	Regret
	Conscience	Violation of prohibitions	yes	yes	yes	Guilt	Regret

[a]A = awfulizing, D = demandingness, S = self-rating.

[b]The reader may want to supply some label other than regret. The point is that some other emotional response would occur, but not shame, panic, or guilt.

experience depression. This we can call an angry depression. Second, a person who believes that she is no good because she has done the wrong thing, and also that she can do nothing to change her behavior and thus will always do wrong things, will be depressed—a guilty depression.

Anxiety, panic, anger, guilt, shame, and depression are the concerns of the RET therapist. All these will be discussed in more detail in Chapter Five. However, Table 4 also illustrates that, though a client may present several seemingly different emotional problems, underlying all these emotional problems are two or more common components of irrational beliefs.

3

Goals and Values of RET

Goals of RET

Simply stated, the goals of RET are emotional change and the acquisition of methods to maintain that change. As Ellis (1974b, p. 147) states: "My main goals in treating any of my psychotherapy clients are simple and concrete: to leave clients, at the end of the psychotherapeutic process, with a minimum of anxiety (or self-blame) and of hostility (or blame of others and the world around them); and, just as importantly, to give them a method of self-observation and self-assessment that will ensure that, for the rest of their lives, they will continue to be minimally anxious and hostile."

In order to change and maintain changes in *C* RET seeks to change and maintain changes in *B*. So we can alternatively state the goals of RET as achieving and maintaining attitudinal change, the kind of change discussed in the previous chapter. Thus, we are not speaking of behavioral goals, except to the extent that self-observation and self-assessment are behaviors. Even though RET can properly be termed a cognitive-behavioral approach, behavioral techniques and homework are used to bring about attitudinal change, which will achieve the goal of emotional change.

A mistake made by some beginning and even some advanced RET therapists is to focus on behavioral goals, to get caught up in the specific changes the clients desire: "How can I help them make new friends, improve a relationship, or get into graduate school?" The mistake is that by doing so we are indirectly focusing on *A*, situational changes: "If you do this and that, you are likely to get such and such." However getting such and such may not result in emotional change: even if the client gets such and such, he will still be plagued with certain ideas that will lead to distress if he loses such and such or does not get a similar such and such in the future.

A client may state the goal "I want to make more friends." If we assume that the client is not simply uninformed or unskilled about how to go about meeting new people, but is anxious around strangers, our primary goal as RET therapists is to help this client reduce his anxiety, not to help him make new friends. But even though our goal for him is anxiety reduction, we might suggest that he talk to five new people each day as his homework assignment. This would be a good risk-taking exercise (combined with didactic techniques) to help him overcome his anxiety about rejection, as we will discuss in Chapter Six. Our purpose is to encourage him to behave in ways inconsistent with his present attitude of "rejection is awful." If he does not experience rejection, then the following week we would probably suggest some behavior that is riskier or that is even almost guaranteed to result in rejection (for example, asking people to buy yesterday's newspaper or cutting into lines at a supermarket).

The many techniques discussed in Chapter Six are means, not ends. If our client's anxiety is reduced, he will be free to pursue the making of friends if he chooses to do so. That is his decision. Here is a further illustration:

During an initial session, a client presented the problems of guilt, anger, and depression and eventually said that he would like to improve his deteriorating marriage. He asked the therapist if she would like to see his wife. (The two of them were concurrently in marital counseling.) The therapist answered that she would do so if he thought that would help but that she really did not care about his marriage. She explained that her goals for him were to help him reduce his guilt, anger, and depression so that he could work toward improving the relationship in a more adaptive way—to tolerate the relationship if it did not improve or to end the relationship if he chose. On leaving the session, he told the therapist that he was somewhat shocked when she told him that she did not care about his marriage but that her explanation made sense. He continued in therapy for four months and made significant progress in reducing guilt, anger, and depression.

The crucial word in the examples just cited is *choose.* By minimizing anxiety and hostility, the individual is free to make choices in life—to make friends or not, to stay in or leave a marriage, to take or reject a job involving air travel. Freedom to choose is one of several important consequences of RET goals. To choose means to direct one's life as much as is possible within physical, social, and economic restraints. As we noted in the preceding chapter, self-interest is the basis of these choices. There are other related consequences of the goals of RET. One is risk taking. A person who does not blame himself or devalue himself for failing finds many options open to him. Easily willing to risk failure, he experiences life as an adventure, not a test. Other consequences of RET goals are tolerance (of self and others) and flexibility.

To describe the person who has achieved the goals of RET, we can borrow a term from Carl Rogers and call that person "fully functioning." Rogers (1961) describes these characteristics of the fully functioning person:

1. Openness to experience. "He is able to take the evidence of a new situation, *as it is,* rather than distorting it to fit a pattern which he already holds" (p. 115).
2. Trust in one's organism. "Out of this complex weighing and balancing he is able to discover the course of action which seems to come closest to satisfying all his needs in the situation, long-range as well as immediate needs" (p. 118).
3. An internal locus of evaluation. "Less and less does he look to others for approval or disapproval; for standards to live by; for decisions and choices. He recognizes that it rests within him to choose" (p. 119).
4. Willingness to be a process. "The individual is more content to be a *process* rather than a *product* . . . a fluid process, not a fixed and static entity; a flowing river of change, not a block of solid matter; a continually changing constellation of potentialities, not a fixed quantity of traits" (p. 122).

Values in RET

No value-free therapy exists. Therapists, depending on their theoretical orientation, will convey to clients certain values or standards of behavior—for instance, it is good to engage in introspection, or let anger out, or be helpful to others. Therefore, RET therapists also convey certain values to their clients. We will first discuss those values conveyed by all RET therapists, those inherent in the theory of RET. Later, we will discuss those values that may be unique to the individual therapist.

Human Nature. The RET therapist values the uniqueness of all humans. Although people tend to disturb themselves in common ways, as discussed in Chapter Two, when free of disturbance they are "exceptionally unique and individual in many of their traits, including their personality, their artistic ability, and their various likes and dislikes" (Ellis, personal communication). Valuing uniqueness, the RET therapist does not try to force clients into any particular mold. Each person is unique and is also fallible. We are mistake makers and, even with the "best" intentions, prone to error. Simply, no one is perfect. Individuals determine what is a mistake or an error in terms of their own value systems. Thus, a particular RET therapist may believe, for instance, that it is an error to have extramarital affairs. But all RET therapists value the right to err, the right to be wrong by any standard, for that is a fact of human nature; and they surely do not value or devalue the mistake maker, the unique human being, for any behavior.

The RET therapist also values a philosophy of hedonism: Go for the pleasures of the moment, but weigh those pleasures against their future consequences. The individual judges the consequences within his or her unique system of preferences and values. It might be better to forgo the momentary pleasure. Sometimes, however, it might be better to pursue the momentary pleasure; for if we lived only for the future, we might pass up a good deal of current enjoyment. Such are the choices we face. Further, being fallible in making any decision, we will discover occasionally that we have made the wrong choice.

Given this hedonistic viewpoint, it is natural (as well as inherent in the RET approach) that the RET therapist values freedom from extreme, sustained negative emotions—the basic goal of RET. Total freedom from such experiences is conceived of as an impossible, though valued, goal; one can, however, minimize and correct such emotional reactions. The RET therapist does not value freedom from *all* negative emotions. Indeed, the RET therapist *values* most negative emotions, because the experiences of sadness, regret, grief, and other such emotions indicate that we are living fully in the world. Living in the world as we know it implies frustration. We do not always get what we want, and when we do, we may experience loss. To give up negative feelings means to give up desire. To give up desire is to give up all possible pleasure. To give up pleasure, in the RET view, is to give up the purpose of life.

Responsibility and Decision Making. Unique, fallible hedonists who are mindful of the future, we make our way through life faced with continual choices. Shall I continue to sit here and write or shall I take a break? Shall I finish this chapter or give it up as a lost cause? Shall I continue to work as a psychotherapist or change careers? Choices and decisions are constantly there to be made—some major, some minor, many in between. In the RET viewpoint, they are a given. What is valued is taking personal responsibility for the decisions we make. RET therapists strongly encourage their clients to accept responsibility for their behavior and emotional responses. Consequently, they might say to a client, "You choose to feel miserable because you continue to believe that life should be fair, although you could work to change that belief. Furthermore, you would rather feel trapped by your parents' expectations than accept the consequences of behaving otherwise."

RET theory, then, is not deterministic. Humans have freedom of choice, although this freedom has its limitations. To quote Ellis (1978b, p. 307): "Deterministic theories see individuals as not responsible for their behavior, as the pawns of society, heredity, or both. Indeterministic theories put emphasis on self-direction and place control within the person. RET stands mainly in the indeterministic camp. But it sees choice as *limited.* It hypothesizes that the more rationally people think and behave, the less deterministic they act. But rationality itself has its limits and hardly leads to completely free, healthy, or utopian existences." Thus, RET theory allows for some freedom of choice. In this respect it is similar to existential approaches, which view humans as responsible for their lives and as creators of their existences within social, physical, and economic restraints.

Style of Life. RET advocates and values certain behavioral styles of living—styles implicit in the notions "It is better to have loved and lost than never to have loved at all" and "What's worth having is worth striving for." The first, "loved and lost," implies risk taking. RET therapists strongly encourage their clients to take risks, not risks that endanger survival but those that could lead to failure or rejection—at first, in areas less crucial than, for instance, on the job and in close interpersonal relationships. Then, as the person practices risking rejection or failure and acquires a risk-taking philosophy, which means that he or she no longer fears rejection or failure, that person is free to apply it in *all* areas of life as he or she chooses. Taking risks ties in with the hedonistic philosophy of RET. To maximize pleasure means getting, as much as possible, what we want. (We can get some of what we want without trying, but then we leave the result up to chance.) To try to get what we want means to risk failing. More succinctly, if we do not risk failure, we will hardly ever succeed.

Related to risk taking is the effort involved in taking the risks; thus, "What is worth having is worth striving for." RET advocates work, and hard work, within the therapy and in life. Although in some instances the process of striving can become pleasurable in and of itself, in many other instances the striving involves drudgery and discomfort. Work or effort almost always is required to achieve long-term goals. A conflicting philosophy is "I shouldn't have to do anything that is unpleasant or uncomfortable, and I'd sooner maintain the status quo than risk discomfort." In RET, we call the results of this philosophy low frustration tolerance. While anyone clearly has a right to live by such a philosophy, it can lead to unhappiness by blocking us from the goals we seek to attain.

Ways of Thinking and Knowing. Although we have been discussing ways of thinking—thinking about human nature, about the goals of life, about how to attain them—we are referring here specifically to *how* a person thinks and draws conclusions about himself and the world. Just as RET emphasizes a philosophy of living, it centrally features a philosophy of knowing. The humanistic stance of its founder is evident in that RET relies on the methods of science for knowledge about self, others, and the world. Unlike religion, science gives tentative answers in the form of hypotheses rather than dogmatic pronouncements or explanations. Hypotheses are tested with facts, which either support or refute them. Facts result from reliable observations of events, and new observations may lead to new facts.

Ideally, science is skeptical; it deals with probable rather than absolute truths, with relative rather than invariant laws.

Scientific theory consists of logically interrelated hypotheses which help to organize knowledge and empirical data. Theory permits the logical deducing of new hypotheses, which may be tested with additional empirical data. Of paramount importance in scientific theory are evidence and logic. RET—like science, on which it is modeled—is based on rules of evidence and logic. According to Kelly (1955), we do not have to teach people to construct theories of themselves or the world. Humans, by nature, do this. But, like Kelly, RET practitioners advocate that people construct more realistic personal theories of themselves, of other people, and of the world in which they live. This realistic view of things is an accepting, not an evaluative, view. Acceptance, which we discussed in the previous chapter, is one of the strongest values in RET. Briefly, acceptance is not synonymous with resignation. Acceptance is independent of, not the opposite of, disliking. The accepting attitude can be stated "That's the way it is, although I sure as heck may not like it" or, more poetically, by the often-quoted prayer of Reinhold Niebuhr:

> God grant me the serenity to accept the things I
> cannot change,
> the courage to change the things I can,
> and the wisdom to know the difference.

Religion and RET

The writings of Albert Ellis are purposely filled with the principles of ethical humanism. Ellis rejects all forms of religion and fully believes that moral or prosocial behavior can derive from the use of human reason to anticipate the consequences of individual actions. What is ethical, then, is specific to each situation, and there are no absolute rights and wrongs. In fact, the self-imposition of absolute rights and wrongs, combined with the necessity to live up to them, is precisely what leads to guilt, shame, anxiety, depression, hostility, and intolerance toward others and oneself. Philosophical humanism differs from humanistic psychology. The former is scientific and skeptical, while the latter, in its most extreme forms, is antiscientific and mystical.

Albert Ellis, a prominent humanist and atheist, has declared religion to be a main cause of neurosis and atheism a cure. However, only rigidly dogmatic and absolutistic forms of religion are incompatible with RET. Some Christian and Jewish clergy practice RET in pastoral counseling. They, of course, do not encourage clients to give up all religion but to reject orthodoxy and literal readings of religious writings in order to increase their self-acceptance and their tolerance of others and of life's realities, thereby increasing their enjoyment of life. Coming from Christian backgrounds, we are aware that much of the teaching in the New Testament is consistent with and reinforcing of the RET philosophy. Described in the New Testament are many instances of Christ's acceptance and forgiveness, an acceptance and forgiveness not exhibited by many Christian clients. There are strong messages about human fallibility; for instance, "He who is without sin among you, let him first cast a stone" (John 8:7). An RET therapist, atheistic or not, who works with Christian clients would do well to become something of a Biblical scholar to correct misconceptions of clients about the humanistic message contained in the New Testament. A client who had been in RET writes (Beaman, 1978, p. 18): "Though I have not actually confirmed it, I am postulating that all the concepts that form the basis of RET can be found in the New Testament. I have found that RET has led me to a greater understanding of my religion, and has enabled me to live my religion rather than just subscribe to it."

There are wide divergences among interpretations of religious tenets and messages within any major religion. The label "Catholic," for instance, tells us little about what a person believes. If a client is not going to give up religious beliefs, and most who are not already atheists are probably not going to do so, we can encourage a religious viewpoint that is not dogmatic, absolutistic, and rigid, but is humanistic and accepting of human frailties, a point of view found within most major religious movements.

Values of the Therapist

All RET therapists accept, teach, and attempt to live by the values we have been discussing. But each holds other values as well, and there may be wide individual differences among values held. One therapist values monogamy; another, many sexual encounters. One therapist values city life; another, suburban life. One therapist values neatness and order; another, casualness. The list of possible differences is practically endless, for we are talking about the individual preferences and values that, by definition in RET, are part of the uniqueness of each human being. A therapeutic encounter can be viewed as an encounter between two uniquely preferring individuals. This does not mean that we do not hold certain preferences in common with our clients, and we do so to a greater extent the more similar our socialization has been. But it does mean that we are accepting of differences and do not try to persuade our clients that our preferences are somehow better than theirs. Our goal as therapists is to help our clients free themselves, so that they can better obtain the satisfactions that they desire. If clients want to reevaluate their goals in life, and sometimes that may be desirable for them, that is their choice and something they are fully capable of doing for themselves after they have achieved or approached the goals of RET. The therapist who is not accepting of the client's preferences and aspirations is not practicing RET.

What about the client who wants to injure someone or behave in other ways that most of us would consider antisocial? For instance, a client of one of our colleagues was seriously considering beating up a professor who, he believed, was treating him unfairly. Here we can distinguish between the client's desire for fair treatment—a preference we share—and his demand that his preference be satisfied and the related idea that evildoers should be punished. We would attempt to show this client that if he actually harms the professor he is not acting in his own self-interest, because negative consequences to him probably will result from that action. Presumably, this client wants many other things for himself as well as fair treatment. Then we would explore with him the irrationality of his demanding and damning. A less extreme example might be a client who does not want to work for a living. As long as the client does not exhibit ideas suggesting that he is not only unique but somehow special, ideas such as "The world owes me a living" or "Life should be easy," we can see no reason to try to convince him that our preference for gainful employment, deriving from our acceptance of the work ethic, is in his interest.

To sum up, values not only enter into RET but are actively taught. That is, the values of RET are taught; the therapist's personal values and preferences are *not* a part of therapy. When tempted to influence a client to hold our own personal preferences, we have found it useful to check this temptation by asking ourselves "Is it in my client's interest, and, in fact, do I really want my client to be just like me?" Unless we are somehow special, more than unique, the answer is obvious.

4

Initiating RET

Much of the work of RET is done by the client. The client is encouraged to put effort into the therapy between sessions—by reading, thinking, and doing things that are difficult, if not uncomfortable. Our long-term hedonistic viewpoint suggests that people are more likely to do the immediate work and to experience the immediate discomfort if they are convinced that it will benefit them in the long run. An important task of the therapist, then, is to show the client how the work of therapy will be beneficial to him or her. If we can do so, then we are working as allies with the client in the change process. If we cannot do so, then we are neutrals or adversaries; and neither of these relationships is conducive to change.

Presenting Problems

The large majority of problems people present in therapy can be analyzed with two concepts. The first is frustration tolerance. A person with low frustration tolerance lives for the immediate gains of any situation. Little delay of gratification is tolerated; discomfort and anxiety are adamantly avoided. The second dimension we call arousal. Under arousal we subsume anxiety, shame, and guilt, those emotions created by awfulizing, demandingness, and self-rating. These two dimensions lead to three typical presenting problems, as illustrated in Figure 4. For

Figure 4. Typical Presenting Problems and the Ideal Outcome

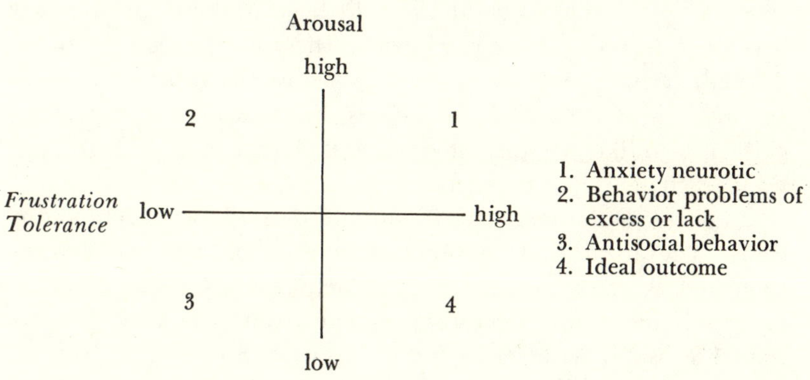

purposes of discussion, Figure 4 illustrates "pure" types. Actual individuals may fall anywhere in this two-dimensional space. Here are descriptions of each type:

Anxiety Neurotic. Anxiety neurotics want to rid themselves of their emotional problems; are strongly motivated to work at their therapy; and, because they have relatively high frustration tolerance, will work diligently at their therapy. Their goals merge easily with our goals, and problems of establishing a working relationship are usually minimal.

Behavior Problems of Excess or Lack. Clients presenting behavior problems either want to stop some disturbing habit, such as overeating or excessive drinking or compulsive handwashing, or they are disturbed because they are unable to do certain things, such as speaking up for themselves. In either case, excess or lack, the behavior has resulted in anxiety reduction and short-term comfort. These individuals can be difficult to work with, particularly if their frustration tolerance is very low; for, despite all good intentions, they often do not carry out homework assignments, because to do so would be uncomfortable and not easy.

Antisocial Behavior. Individuals with low frustration tolerance and low arousal may engage in behaviors considered antisocial. Because of the short-term hedonism implied in low frustration tolerance, these individuals pay little attention to the consequences of their actions, the goal of which is to bring immediate comfort or excitement. Lacking the high arousal characteristic of persons in quadrant 2, little guilt, shame, or anxiety is present to control their behavior. These persons are the most difficult to work with, because they are usually referred to therapy by others (relatives, the courts, hospital or prison personnel) and, unlike persons in quadrants 1 and 2, usually do not want to change their behavior.

Ideal Outcome. This quadrant defines our therapeutic goals. The ideal may never be achieved, but it can be approached, which means that we can help persons in quadrants 1, 2, and 3 move into quadrant 4. Thus, our goal with 1 is to reduce arousal; with 2, to reduce arousal *and* increase frustration tolerance; and with 3, to increase frustration tolerance. Of course, with 3 we could also attempt to reduce antisocial behavior by increasing arousal in the form of guilt. This, however, probably will not work and, even if it did, would not benefit the client (although it might benefit society.)

The Therapeutic Alliance

The process of therapy is a partnership: two persons working together to achieve a common goal. This goal involves change on the client's part. Not all persons who come to a therapist can benefit from psychotherapy. Some persons' problems may be primarily physical, not psychological. Others—for instance, some of the clients in quadrant 3—may be defined as having problems by other people. In this case, the therapist's initial task is to show the client how change would be beneficial to him or her. Actually, if the therapist were able to accomplish this task, a good deal of the work of therapy would be completed, for if this person comes to view change as being desirable, he or she would already be shifting to a longer-term hedonistic viewpoint, away from the short-term hedonistic viewpoint implied in low frustration tolerance. Other clients, however, usually those in quadrants 1 and 2, are distressed by behaving in what they consider self-defeating ways or by experiences of severe or chronic emotional upset. They want to change, and we share that goal. One of the first tasks of RET is goal setting.

But beware of becoming too model-bound. Some RET practitioners we have supervised are so intent on convincing clients that thoughts cause feelings that they neglect the clients' concerns, hopes, and expectations for therapy. Some clients are not ready immediately to specify a problem and analyze it according to the *ABC* model of the emotional episode. Such clients benefit from expressing their feelings and their ideas about their problems. Before they will work on problems or their own belief systems, they want to complain, whine, emote, and generally say what concerns them. We find it more effective to let them do so than to force them into rigid uses of the *ABC* model. However, we would not ordinarily devote more than a half a session to such expression of feelings.

In addition to whatever temporary, palliative benefits the client derives from discussing his or her problems at length, the therapist can learn enough to begin to form a picture of the client. That picture or conception is tentative, but it can serve as a guide to therapeutic interaction. The picture is formed from client statements that reveal beliefs, as well as views of self, of others, and of the nature of the world. It consists of implicit irrational demands, unrealistic expectations, and interpersonal strategies and styles. In other words, much of what can be learned about the client through dialogue can be obtained from listening. Of course, the therapist's listening is a very active kind. For, in addition to letting the client ventilate and to forming tentative hypotheses about the client, the therapist can communicate understanding, undamning acceptance, and the expectation that the client can change.

Occasionally, a therapist will want to help a client with

practical problems before working with the client's emotional problems. A client seen by one of us had a job decision to make immediately after the first therapy session. Much of the therapist's working with the client consisted of clarification of alternatives, consequences, values, and expectations. There was very little therapy directed toward emotional change, although the therapist was forming impressions about the client and her problems. When her fears and anxieties were discussed in the second session, both client and therapist could quickly get to the heart of the matter. The therapist knew during the first session that, although he was helping her with a nonpsychological, but real, problem, the client was too distracted to benefit from the usual RET approach at that time.

With some clients, then, we may choose not to leap too rapidly into the business of emotional change. If clients want to describe in some detail how they view their problems, we let them. If we judge that some immediate counseling would be beneficial, we provide it. In practically all instances, however, we would devote no more than one session to such endeavors.

In setting goals with clients, we want the client to be as specific and concrete as possible. Some goal-setting questions are "What would you like to change?" "How would you like to act differently?" "What are you now doing that you would like to stop, or what are you not doing that you would like to start?" If a client mentions only a vague, abstract goal—such as "I want to be more self-confident"—a question that can bring that goal down to concrete reality is "How will you know when you have changed?"

Our goal as therapists is to help clients to emotional change. Quadrant 1 people generally share this goal. Quadrant 2 individuals, however, due to their low frustration tolerance, may want "easy" solutions. For instance, a woman may have as her goal the elimination of her anger, whereas in talking with her we judge that her major problem is lack of assertion due to guilt over the expression of both anger and annoyance. Our goal for her would be the reduction of the guilt. In the next chapter we will discuss in detail many of the specific problems that clients bring to therapy. The point here is that, before proceeding any further with therapy, the therapist will want to reach an agreement with the client about goals.

Once goals are specified and agreed on, we have still further work to do before we proceed. If, for instance, a client says that she wants to feel less anxious around people and we hear a "should," an "awful," or "I am no good" and leap in and start disputing that idea, the client might well be taken aback and become defensive, because she has no idea what we are talking about and may perceive our words as a personal attack. With clients presenting emotional problems, our first task after goal setting is to show them that they create their emotions by their own thoughts. Clients who are motivated to reduce their emotional upset will work at assessing and changing their thoughts *if* they understand that by doing so they will achieve their goal of emotional change. So we had better agree with clients not only on goals but also on the means of achieving them. Without this merging of goals and agreement on the means of achieving the goals, which is the therapeutic alliance, little therapy can take place.

Expectations for Change

A very important task in the initial session with many clients is creating expectations for change. Clients who attribute their miseries to external causes—who believe that *A* causes *C*—have little chance of benefiting from any form of counseling or therapy, except perhaps some limited benefits from skill-training approaches (Försterling, 1980). They are not likely to work at gaining personal insight or toward changing their thinking, acting, and emoting. With such clients, the *ABC* model is especially useful. It is a model that people can understand, *and* it pointedly shows them that external events do not directly cause feelings, emotions, or actions.

A second self-attribution relates to the stability of a personal characteristic; that is, trait (stable) versus effort (variable). For instance, a woman who does poorly on an examination can attribute the reason to her low intellect (stable) or to not studying enough (variable). People generally do not change attitudes, including self-attitudes, that are based on "human nature" or inherited characteristics (Levy and House, 1970). If a person believes, "I'm hot tempered because I'm Irish," he is not likely to believe also that he can control his temper and virtually eliminate his anger by revising his philosophy of living. A person who believes himself "crazy" may also feel that change is not possible. We recommend that therapists transform hopeless statements by clients to ones that are more realistically hopeful (see also Bergner, 1979). Thus, one of the therapist's tasks is to encourage self-attributions of internal causation and variable personal characteristics. Therapist statements to the effect that "change is possible if you work at it" influence the client to make attributions that promote change. Ellis does this when he tells a client to "go work on it," one of his favorite ways to end a session.

RET theory, according to Ellis (1977e), further conveys hope for change by proposing internal-variable attributions about rational and irrational thinking. RET theory assumes that humans are biologically predisposed to think *both* irrationally and rationally. Given the tendency to think irrationally, people easily teach themselves emotionally disturbing philosophies about themselves and the world. However, since people also have the tendency to think rationally, the assumption conveys the principle that people can change, that they are not unilaterally programmed by their parents, passively conditioned by society, or unconsciously fixated at a critical point in their development. That they largely teach themselves irrational thinking means that they can also learn more adaptive ways of thinking.

We now consider methods that can be used to prepare the client for therapy, particularly ways in which to present the *ABC* model and to convey the idea that change is entirely possible, given time and effort. Of course, there are other ways to present such expectations. Most intriguing are the methods of indirect suggestion of Erikson, Rossi, and Rossi (1976) and Bandler and Grinder (1975). These approaches, many points of which can be effectively combined with RET (see Chapter Ten), recommend that the therapist imply that change is already taking place and that it began when the client chose to come to the therapist.

Conveying the *ABC*s

One of our first tasks is to let the client know what we are going to do and why we are going to do it; we also obtain the client's agreement that whatever it is we are going to do is sensible. We call this "setting the stage." Usually, we begin to set the stage as soon as we have two thirds of an emotional problem, the *A* and the *C*. Sometimes the problem is not all that evident or easily identifiable, so setting the stage often mingles with assessing problems. With that fact in mind, let us proceed under the assumption that we have a clear *A-C* connection, as will be true with such problems as explicitly stated test anxiety, fear of rejection, or guilt over the violation of one's conscience.

We will use the example of a woman who is quite anxious about speaking up in groups and who tells us that she is afraid she will say something stupid and that others will not like her. She wants to overcome this fear. If we immediately ask her what it means to her to be rejected and begin showing her the errors of her thinking, it is likely that she will be confused by such quick interventions. It is good practice to take a few minutes to set the stage for exploring irrational ideas. Actually, a few minutes are usually all that is required at this point, although many reminders may, and probably will, be called for as therapy progresses.

Direct Explanation. One way to convey to the client how we will proceed is simply to explain the approach by giving a brief lecture on the *ABC* theory of emotion. The more philosophical issues of demandingness and evaluating human worth will come later, as the client's beliefs are explored. Here we simply want to set the stage for exploring those beliefs. An important point about the *ABC* theory to underscore is that, although we may not be able to change *A,* and we certainly cannot change our past experience, we *can* change our beliefs. There are at least two good reasons to emphasize this fact. First, it can give the client a sense of power or control, as we mentioned previously, in that there is something she can do to reduce her anxiety. Second, it begins to convey the idea that, with work and effort, *she* will do the changing; the therapist cannot do it for her.

The lecture might be preceded by a question such as "Do you know what causes your anxiety?" Quite often the answer is "no" or "I'm not sure." In that case we are set up for our explanation. Sometimes the answer will be "yes," with the client's conception coming from some other point of view, such as psychoanalysis or classical conditioning. For example, the client may say, "Yes, my parents were very strict and would not tolerate what they thought were stupid statements on my part." A possible response to that could be "That may be how your anxiety started, but you continue to be anxious. You continue to be anxious because you've learned to think some pretty upsetting thoughts about appearing stupid. What we feel is determined by what we think."

At the end of the explanation, we will get the client's reactions to our presentation (if we have not done so along the way). If the explanation has made sense to the client, we are ready to explore her problem further. Presumably, she will now expect exploration of her thoughts and beliefs. In fact, at this point we usually say something like "So, you see, we will be spending a lot of time looking at what you believe and getting some ideas of how you can work at changing those beliefs." If, however, when asked about her reactions, the client says something like "I'm not sure I think anything when I'm anxious," we may choose one or more further methods to attempt to show her that beliefs underlie her anxiety.

Contrasts. One way to illustrate that it is *B,* not *A,* that leads to *C* is to contrast the way she feels in groups with the way some other people feel, or with her feelings at home at some other time or in some other situation. Here are some examples:

1. *T:* Do you know others who are not so anxious in groups?
   C: Yes, I guess I do.

T: Doesn't that indicate that it's not the group but how we view the group that creates anxiety?

She might say "yes" here or something like:

C: It means they've been successful. People like them. They have a lot of confidence. I don't.
T: And, therefore, they have different ideas about what it would mean to say the wrong thing.

2. *T:* Were there times when you weren't so anxious about speaking up in groups?
C: Yes, when I was in high school.
T: What is different between now and then?
C: I guess I wasn't so concerned then about their liking me.
T: And now you are. You see, then you didn't think of it as being so important, but now you believe it is crucial.

3. *T:* Are there times in a group when you don't feel so anxious?
C: Yes, sometimes it doesn't seem to bother me so much.
T: Can you think of anything that is different about those times?
C: Well, sometimes I am really tired. I say, "The hell with it." I just want to go home.
T: Yes, and you're thinking something else when you are anxious.

How Would You Feel If... Here we can set up a hypothetical situation, given a belief different from the one that the client presumably holds. For example, we can ask our client, "How would you feel if the next time you met with that group you were thinking, 'Well, if they don't like me, too bad'?" If the client responds, as many do, "I guess I wouldn't feel so anxious," we have made our point. A possible result of this method and the methods of contrasts is that the client may get the message that if she just does not care she then will not feel anxious. Not caring, of course, will eliminate the anxiety; however, as we have pointed out previously, our goal is not to have the client give up all caring or concern. Even so, if the notion of not caring is conveyed at this point, it is not that important, because we presumably will have many more sessions to disabuse the client of this misconception. Our main concern here is to convey the idea that one's thinking determines one's feelings.

Homework. Even after all the preceding methods have been tried, some clients still will doubt that they are actually thinking anything when they are feeling upset. As Beck (1976) points out, sometimes a person's thoughts can be so overlearned that they become automatic. Just as an experienced driver does not think about the steps involved in driving a car, a person may not be aware of thinking certain thoughts. But, just as an experienced driver *could* become aware of the action of stepping on the brake, so can a person become aware of her automatic thoughts. This explanation can be given to our client as a rationale for homework involving the monitoring of her thoughts. There are two variations here: one for the client who gets anxious in the course of her life; the other for the client who gets anxious only in specific situations, which are usually avoided.

In the first case, we can ask the client to write her thoughts (or speak them into a recorder) whenever she is anxious and to bring the results to the next session. The *ABC* format is useful here. She can write what she is feeling (*C*), in what situation (*A*), and what she is thinking (*B*). This assignment is actually the beginning of the *ABCD* (*D* for disputing) written homework that is used as a change technique (described in Chapter Six). The purpose of the assignment at this point is for the client to become aware of what she is thinking when she feels anxious.

The second variation is to suggest that she actually *do* something about which she is likely to feel anxious. If, for example, she rarely enters into a group situation and then rarely speaks up, she could be asked to meet with other people, to talk with them, and then to listen for what she is thinking. Often, just the suggestion of doing something risky is sufficient to evoke the upsetting thoughts right at that moment in the session. Later we will want to encourage the client to take similar risks, but then the purpose will be to change her cognitions concerning rejection. At this stage, we want her to become aware that her thinking relates to her anxiety.

Usually we ask the client to do some reading between sessions to supplement and enhance the orientation of looking for and changing irrational thinking. A frequently recommended book is *A New Guide to Rational Living* (Ellis and Harper, 1975), written specifically for the nonprofessional. Paul Hauck has written a number of problem-oriented books—for instance, on depression (1973), anger (1974), and anxiety (1975). We also recommend *Humanistic Psychotherapy* (Ellis, 1974b), written for a professional audience but appropriate for many clients as well. Whatever the choice, the reading can serve a number of purposes. First, it may persuade the client that thoughts are indeed important in emotional reactions. Second, less time is needed in sessions for explanation, and more time can be spent in discussing issues that are unclear to the client and, of course, moving ahead with the change process. Third, it can be the first step for the client in actually thinking about and working on her therapy between sessions.

We hope that by the end of the first session our client will understand that emotions are created by her thinking and that she can minimize upsetting emotions by becoming aware of her beliefs, which underlie these emotions, and changing those beliefs. In essence, we are ready to begin therapy proper. Meichenbaum (1977, p. 151) points out the importance of this initial stage, which he calls the educational phase: "The scientific validity of a particular conceptualization is less crucial than its face validity or air of plausibility for the client. . . . Naturally, any conceptualization must be offered with clinical sensitivity. The purpose of providing a framework is not to convince the client—perhaps against his will—that any particular explanation of his problem is valid but rather encourage him to view his problem from a particular perspective and thus accept and collaborate in the therapy that will follow."

Setting the Stage for Time and Effort

Not unreasonably, clients often want to know how long they can expect to be in therapy. This question sometimes comes up later in therapy, when the client may state, "OK, I see I am thinking that I would be a crumb if I were rejected. But I've believed that all my life. Will it take another thirty years to change that idea?" Given the fact that the client understands that the goal is to change certain beliefs, we have found the following analogy helpful:

T: Changing beliefs is somewhat similar to learning a new language. You've spoken English all your life. Let's say you want to learn to speak German, and you want to speak it well. How long do you think it would take you to do that?

People give varying answers, but we will continue with an answer of "A year, maybe."

T: What would you have to do to accomplish that?

C: Well, I'd study pretty hard, maybe even go to Germany or get myself around people who speak German.

T: That's right. You'd have to work at it, but, as you say, you'd probably be adept at German after a year. If you work at your therapy—and it does take work—the same could hold true. So it may take a year—maybe more or less—to alter your thinking enough to be relatively unanxious, but it won't take another lifetime.

Two other points can be made with this analogy: (1) The work of therapy can begin to pay off before the year is up, just as studying German will do so. (2) The work will actually last a lifetime if one is to *maintain* the gains made in therapy. This analogy, then, serves two purposes. It conveys some idea of the length of therapy without setting a specific date, and it illustrates that work and effort will be required on the client's part.

Some clients respond to the time question with "I could

never learn German." Usually, if asked, "You mean that if you really wanted to learn German and worked very hard at it, studied hard, you couldn't?" the client will admit, "Well, if I did that I guess I could. But it would take a long time." Then we can go from there to "Therapy can take time too, *and* it will take a good deal of effort on your part." In such cases, we are likely to be dealing with a client with very low frustration tolerance. Finally, for the holdout who steadfastly says he could not learn German, the following approach will usually work: "Unfortunately I am unable to do this, but if I could guarantee you a million dollars for learning German, could you?" Almost everyone says "Yes."

Setting the Stage for Techniques

Just as it is important not to leap into therapy proper without explaining its rationale, it is also important to explain the rationale behind any specific technique—even something as simple as changing the subject. Kahn and Cannell (1957), in their discussion of the forces affecting a respondent's willingness to cooperate with the interviewer, state (p. 54): "There is always the possibility of a sudden increase in opposing forces. Perhaps the factor most frequently responsible for such a shift is the introduction of new material or a new kind of question." Explaining the rationale is also important when we are asking the client to do something—for instance, to talk to an empty chair, pound a pillow, or call out the stops on the subway. If we make such requests without explanation, the result can be confusion, defensiveness, or compliance for the sake of compliance on the client's part. On the therapist's part, indulging in techniques without explaining the rationale to the client sometimes leads to willy-nilly use of techniques that are not thoughtfully considered and either have little to do with the established goals of therapy or are harmful to the attaining of those goals.

In RET we often ask clients to do something that they do not want to do. Few people want to get rejected, to act silly, or to make mistakes intentionally. When we make such requests, it is important to convey how such actions will be beneficial to the client. We want our clients to agree that such actions can help them.

By explaining the rationale and by obtaining the client's agreement that the action would be worth a try, we create a different set of circumstances than if we just say, "Do it." If the client then says, "I won't" or, after the fact, "I didn't do it," we now have a power struggle. Admittedly, a client who agrees that it would be a good idea to engage in a certain activity and that he could benefit from it in the long run still may say, "I can't" or, after the fact, "I didn't do it." But the direction taken in this instance is different. We can say, "You agreed that it would be a good idea. What kept you from doing it?" as opposed to the less constructive "Why didn't you do what I told you to do?" In the former case there is still a power struggle or conflict, but now it is an *intra*personal conflict instead of an *inter*personal conflict.

There are exceptions to the rule of explaining the rationale for techniques, just as there are exceptions to all rules. At a particular juncture in therapy, we might decide to startle the client in an attempt to evoke a particular reaction. For instance, a client may say that other people's hostility does not bother him, whereas we have good evidence that in fact he would feel upset by hostility but religiously avoids any confrontation. To attempt to evoke his response to hostility, we might suddenly shout at him in an angry manner. If we had explained our motives and our action in advance, the technique probably would have been ineffectual. So there are occasions when we may not want to explain the rationale of what we are doing, but these occasions are rare, and it would behoove us to explain the rationale afterward.

Keep in mind that RET, and presumably all therapies if they are to be effective, is a collaborative venture. Clients need information to decide whether or not to collaborate in their therapy. One explanation, however, is rarely sufficient to keep the client focused on cognitive change. For one reason or another, including years of conceiving the emotional problems differently, many clients easily stray to attributing the cause of their emotional problems to the situations they are in or to past events. At these times it is important to *continue* to set the stage, which may mean going back to the beginning and explaining again the *ABC* theory or using some of the other methods discussed here. In short, setting the stage may occur throughout therapy and not just during the first session.

5

Assessing Client Problems

We know some therapists who are sympathetic to the RET approach yet who make statements like "Joe Jones is not a candidate for RET." Such statements reflect the idea that RET is a *technique* useful for clients who are verbally sophisticated and aware of their self-defeating ideologies. In our experience, such clients are not all that common. More typical are clients who are not aware of *C* or who have multiple and interacting *ABC*s or who present problems that are indirect results of irrational thinking. All these individuals are candidates for RET. However, much of the work of the therapist goes into assessing the problem with the client and conveying the problem so defined in terms understandable to the client.

There are many ways to define problems. For example, Mary wants a raise but is afraid to ask her boss for it. She might believe that her boss—whom she describes as cold, blunt, and quick to anger—is the problem. Or she might view her problem as anxiety—fear of authority figures—or as a lack of assertiveness. As RET practitioners, we would agree with Mary on two of her three interpretations. Her boss is not the problem, but anxiety and lack of assertion are. We define problems in terms of emotions or behaviors, not in terms of other people (or other activating events). But "emotional problem" (anxiety) and "behavioral problem" (lack of assertion) are shorthand expressions for the fuller problem. Since RET is a "depth" therapy, we want to treat the underlying cause, not the symptoms which are the emotional or behavioral manifestations of that cause. The underlying cause is faulty thinking or beliefs, which lie at or just below the surface of awareness.

But we will not define Mary's problem simply as *B,* with little notice of the triggering *A* or the resultant *C.* Mary presumably is thinking irrationally when she feels anxious about the anticipated angry response of her boss, but for Mary the *A* and *C* also exist and indeed were what brought her into therapy. So we consider the total emotional episode. *A* is not the problem. *B* is not the problem, although it is tempting for us to think so. *C* is not the problem, although it leads to a shorthand label such as "anxiety problem" or "guilt problem."

Given the example of Mary and using the *ABC* model, we can now begin to define "the problem." Actually there are two. For Mary the more general problem, and the one we are more concerned with, is the *BC* part of the *ABC* model. Mary believes certain ideas that lead to her feeling anxious around authority figures. It is "the problem" for Mary because she feels anxious about confronting her boss and *any* other person she defines in the same manner. So our first definition of the problem is the *BC* part of an *ABC,* with *B* standing for irrational, not rational, beliefs.

The second definition, *less* important for our goals with Mary but *more* important in our actual work with Mary, is the full *ABC.* However, for this discussion we will now change the notation to a_1BC (a_1 standing for Mary's boss; a_2, a_3, to a_n standing for any number of other triggering *A*s for Mary's anxiety). We do so for two reasons. Each reason relates to a common error made by beginning RET therapists. The first error, as mentioned before, is to focus almost entirely on the client's belief system, nicely disputing ideas of demandingness and self-worth, but not tying the beliefs to the client's life. The a_1 reminds us to do that. Mary is anxious around her boss. The second error is to focus almost exclusively on the a_1BC that Mary presents. We hope to minimize this error by our lowercase usage of *a* for the activating event. With exploration we probably can determine that Mary has similar anxieties (*BC*s) with a number of other people (a_2, a_3, . . . a_n); and we are trying to help Mary resolve her problem of anxiety not only with her boss but also with similar people now and in the future. Perhaps more important, as we shall describe in more detail in the next chapter, this conception of Mary's problem opens up a wide variety of homework possibilities, so that she can confront authority figures without jeopardizing her job. If, for instance, she perceives a store manager as an authority figure, we can encourage her to practice going up to store managers and telling them that they have shoddy merchandise. So the problem we are seeking is a *BC.* The format in which we shall be looking for it is an *aBC.* (For the sake of convenience, however, we will now return to uppercase *A,* just as we will use *B* to stand for *irrational* beliefs.)

One of the first tasks for the therapist is to discover with the client whether such problems exist. Such problems will be readily apparent in many clients; in others, they will be more difficult to assess; in still others, they will be nonexistent. For instance, a woman's husband may accuse her of having an anger problem when she expresses her annoyance toward him. In exploring this concern with her, the therapist may discover that in fact she has no anger problem or any other problem related to irrational thinking. She probably does have the problem of living in a relationship that is not satisfying to her. Here she has many options. She can attempt to improve the relationship, accept the relationship as is, or leave the relationship. The therapist would work with her in helping her explore the various options and send her on her way. No attempt would be made to change her belief system, for the good reason that her beliefs are rational and therefore not problematic for her.

This example raises two important points for the therapist to keep in mind. First, do not assume that all, or even any, of the problems presented by a client involve faulty thinking. Second, do not decide too easily that the problems presented by a client do *not* involve faulty thinking. These two points can be summed up in a single statement: Do not assume, but explore.

Let us return to our hypothetical client with her presenting problem of anger. Again, we may discover that she seldom expresses or even feels anger but that her annoyance has been defined as anger. However, in exploring her relationship with her husband and what she might do about it, we find that she would like to leave him but is afraid to, or that if she stays with him and he does not change his accusing ways she will feel inadequate, or that when he accuses her of being angry she feels guilty. In each of these instances, we have a potential problem for RET. If, as suggested here, we discover a problem that is not the client's presenting concern, our task becomes at this point to show the client *how* it is a problem for her. In other words, we want the client to agree that this indeed is a problem for her and that it is worth the effort to work at changing in this area. We are back to the issue of the therapeutic alliance. In this case we would be attempting to have the client redefine her goals for therapy.

Identifying the *ABC*s

Before trying to help a client change specific irrational beliefs, we first want to find out what those beliefs are and have the client recognize what they are. The *ABC* format is very useful here. The general rule of thumb is: Start with *C,* tie *C* to *A,* get *B.* This order is not invariable, as we shall see; however, it is probably the most common order in identifying the *ABC*s of a problem, since many clients readily present problems such as "I feel anxious about . . ." or "I feel guilty about. . . ." However, clients who are in great distress may not present a tidy problem to be fashioned into a neat *ABC* and then on to *D* (disputing). Several overlapping and, to the client, overwhelming problems may be outlined. Or everything may seem like a problem, and nothing specific is mentioned. The responsibility of the therapist, then, is to untangle the web of problems for the overwhelmed client, or to make concrete the vague, nonspecific problem of the greatly distressed person.

It is preferable to begin with goals. A good question is "How would you like to be different?" or, more concretely, "How would you like to be different in six months" (or some other period of time)? "What would you like to do that you don't do now" (carefully avoiding the phrase "can't do now")? "What do you now do that you would like to stop?" These are simple questions that invite goal setting. Responses to the questions may be too abstract. The answer "I'd like to have a better life" may be heartfelt, but it is too vague to let us know how to proceed. So we ask, "What would be different if you had a better life?" or "How would you know if you had a better life?" In general, we strive to get the client to say what different feelings he or she would like to experience and what different actions he or she would like to engage in. Conversely, we are concerned with habits to be abandoned, phobias to eliminate, and realities to accept.

To illustrate, a client stated in an initial session that he had a "heavy problem." His father and brother had died within the past year, and his younger brother had just been hospitalized with suspected terminal cancer. Several minutes passed as he told his story, and it seemed clear that allowing him to talk about these difficulties was in order before seeking clarification. Finally the therapist asked, "And what is *your* problem with all this?" The answer was "I don't think I'm strong enough to be the last surviving adult male in my family." And then "I don't want to have to live up to this macho image I'm supposed to have." We quickly formulated the goals of not having guilt over his "weaknesses" and not feeling shame when others discovered them. The basic thrust is to evoke from the client the problem in an *ABC* format. There is no one right way to do this. An understanding of RET theory is the important guide in evoking the problem.

Probing Techniques. Following are some methods that can be used by the therapist in identifying with the client a specific *ABC.* Let us assume the client has told us, "I get very anxious in groups."

1. The client presents an *A* and a *C.* If a person is anxious, ashamed, or otherwise greatly disturbed by an event, that emotion is related to some perceived negative aspect of that event. Particularly when the emotion is anxiety, when the happening has not occurred but is anticipated, the *A* may be presented in broad descriptive terms, such as *groups, tests, giving a speech.* Take the example of "groups" given by our hypothetical client. Many things can happen in groups: a member is accepted or rejected, speaks wisely or stupidly, appears assured or nervous. "Groups" is simply too broad. Some possible probes are:

- What about groups is scary?
- How would the group have to be different for you not to be scared?
- Is it just groups that are scary, or something about groups?
- When you think about being in a group, what do you think might happen?
- What runs through your mind when you think about being in a group?

The last question will probably evoke information about *A,* not *B.* Most clients will answer such a question with responses like "I'm afraid I may say something stupid," "I keep wondering what they are thinking," "They all seem so assured." These responses, of course, are not *B* statements. Beginning RET therapists often assume incorrectly that a "What do you think about . . ." question will prompt an irrational or a rational idea for an answer. We will say more about probing for *B* later. The point to keep in mind here is that many of those same probes can yield excellent information about *A.*

If probes similar to those just mentioned do not turn up some specific negative event, such as being rejected, we might try some leading questions or probes. For example, the client might say in response to our earlier probes, "I don't know, I'm just anxious in groups." On the assumption that fear of rejection and fear of failure are so common that one or both might afflict our client, we can then directly ask:

- Do you think you're afraid that they won't like you?
- Might you be afraid that you will behave stupidly?
- Often people who are anxious in groups are afraid that they won't be liked or won't do well. Do you think that that might be the case with you?

Or we can take the reverse approach:

- Are you afraid that people are going to like you?
- You're afraid that you're going to do well?

If the client says "no," we have narrowed the field to "Then maybe you're afraid that you won't be liked (do well)?" But if the client indicates, following the direct or indirect probes, that she actually is afraid of doing well or being accepted, we would then return to our initial nonleading probes to discover the negative connotations held by our client:

- What about their liking you is scary?
- What might happen if they did like you?

Now we want to get *B*. What we are looking for are the three components of irrational thinking: awfulizing, demandingness, and evaluation of self and/or others. Possible probes are:

- What does it mean to you if they don't like you?
- What would you tell yourself about their not liking you?

Sometimes clients answer these questions by stating how they would feel rather than what they think; for example, "If I thought they didn't like me, I'd be depressed." Possible responses are:

- Yes, that's how you'd feel. But what would it *mean* to you if they didn't like you?
- Right, you'd feel depressed. But remember, how you feel is determined by what you think. You're thinking some pretty depressing thoughts. What might they be?

If we get an answer that contains only one of the three components of irrational thinking, we will continue probing until we have obtained at least two components. Unless the emotional problem is anger or low frustration tolerance, where the components are awfulizing and demandingness, we will also press for the self-rating component. Our purpose is to obtain the full irrational idea, because it is that complete idea we will want to help a client change, such as "It's awful that they don't like me because I need their approval to prove that I'm OK" rather than simply "It's awful that they don't like me." About this we can ask:

- Because . . . ?
- And what would be so awful about that?

Or the client might say, "I need their approval." We can then ask:

- What do you need it for?
- OK, you need it. But what if you don't get it?

Or more directly:

- Would it mean anything about you if you didn't get it?
- What would it tell you about yourself if you didn't get it?

Sometimes the answer is a further elaboration of *A*. In this case, we will continue probing for *B*. For example, the client might say, "If no one liked me, I'd be alone." We can continue with:

- And what would be so scary about being alone?
- And what does being alone mean to you?
- What if you were alone?

Such probing may continue step by step through a series of contingencies until we reach *B*. For example, the following series might be obtained:

- If no one liked me, I'd be alone.
- If I were alone, I'd have to take care of myself.
- If I had to take care of myself, I might not do well.
- If I didn't do well, I might have to go on welfare.
- If I went on welfare, I'd be a rotten person.

If at this point the therapist misunderstands or forgets the distinction between *A* and *B*, he or she might be tempted to think that "I might have to go on welfare," for instance, is an irrational belief, stop the sequence at that point, and begin disputing that *A* idea.

2. The client presents a *C* with no *A*. These are usually cases of chronic anxiety or depression. The client may say, for instance, "I feel anxious all the time and don't know why." Possible probes are:

- Are there times when you feel more anxious than others?
- Have you always felt anxious?
- When you notice you're particularly anxious, what runs through your mind?
- Has anything happened that might be related to the anxiety?
- Do you feel anxious right now? (If so, what are you thinking?)

In such cases, any probing we do may not turn up a specific event as an *A* for the anxiety or depression. The emotion itself may be the important *A*. For instance, the major problem for the person might be feeling anxious about feeling anxious or feeling depressed about feeling depressed. If that seems to be the case, we then pursue the *ABC* with *C* as a feeling and *A* as another feeling; for example, "What do you tell yourself about your depression?"

3. The client presents an *A* but no *C*. Some clients present as problems situations with which they are dissatisfied. They may speak of broad dissatisfaction or frustration without specific emotional overtones. Some examples, ranging from the global to the specific, are "Life is dull and uninteresting," "I'm unhappy with my career," "I'm not getting along with my roommate." Some of these individuals may have no problem of irrational thinking and may benefit from counseling in the sense of providing information and exploring the alternatives for change. Other persons, even given information and opportunities to change undesirable situations, will not do so, because to do so may lead to anxiety, guilt, or some other undesirable feeling that they are adamantly avoiding. Thus, such an individual is avoiding the *C* of the *ABC* we are seeking. Our task, in any given case, is to determine whether this avoidance behavior is true for our client.

Let us say the client tells us, "Life is dull and uninteresting." We would first explore with the client in what way life could be more zestful. Of a multitude of possibilities, let us say he responds, "I love to travel and can't afford to get away." Now, there are a number of things he might do to be able to travel more. He might, for instance, spend less money on other things or get a higher-paying job (which might involve further training or schooling) or a job involving travel (a job as a guide, a ship's steward, a salesman, or the Secretary of State). So we begin exploring the options with him. Particularly if we hear "Yes, but . . ." from him, we have a clue that he is blocking himself from change. We will pursue this example down two possible routes. First:

C: I guess I could save more money if I lived in a cheaper apartment.

T: Well, how about that?

C: I'm not sure I could do that. Where I live is really nice. I'm not sure what my friends would think.

T: You're concerned that they might look down on you?

C: Yes, I'm afraid they would.

T: So, maybe your fear of their looking down on you keeps you from getting some of the things you want for yourself in life.

C: I guess that's right.

A second possible route:

C: I'm not sure I could get a better job.

T: Have you tried?

C: No, I haven't yet.

T: Well, how about beginning to look for a new job?

C: I could, but I'm not sure I want to.

T: What would stop you from looking for it?

C: I'd be afraid that if I got a better job I might not do so well—get fired. At least I know I'm doing OK on my present job.

T: So a fear of failing locks you in.

C: Yes, I guess that's right.

In these examples, the client is easy to work with and readily agreeable. In actual practice, it may be more difficult to evoke from the client certain fears that are at the core of dissatisfactions in life. As another example, let us take a less global problem, "I'm not getting along with my roommate."

T: How aren't you getting along?

C: Well, she stays up to all hours, and half the time she has friends in—guys. It's hard to study and it's certainly hard to get to sleep.

T: She knows this bothers you?

C: Sure. She should know. I've told her.

T: Very often?

C: Well, a couple of times anyhow.

T: How about letting her know in no uncertain terms you'd like her to change her habits?

C: You mean threaten her?

T: Sure, why not?

C: I couldn't do that.
T: What would stop you?
C: I'd be scared.
T: Scared of what?
C: I'd be scared she'd get mad.

Then on to *B*.

If a person is dissatisfied with a situation but does not take action to change that situation (assuming he or she is aware of possible remedies), we will look for the "stoppers"—the feelings he or she is avoiding. Some possible probes are:

- How would you feel if . . . ?
- What stops you from . . . ?
- What keeps you from . . . ?
- Why don't you . . . ?

These probes are intended not to get the person to carry through on a particular action but to get her to see that there are actions available and that she avoids such actions for fear of suffering some dire emotional consequences. As is probably evident by now, persons presenting such problems are usually low in frustration tolerance.

Simulated Situations. With some clients, verbal probes will not elicit any of the components of irrational thinking. Such clients may respond to our verbal probes with "I don't know what I think" or "I don't think anything." There are still several options open to us. Many problem situations can be simulated within the therapy session. One way to do so is through the use of imagery. The client who is anxious about being in groups, for instance, can be asked whether she can imagine herself walking into a room full of people. If she says she can, we can then ask her to describe the situation. After she does so, we can ask her how she is feeling. (Not only are we attempting to tie *A* to *C*, but we are checking on the vividness of the imagery for this client.) If she answers "anxious," we then ask her what she is thinking. If the client describes the situation in a bland way, we can try to embellish the scene for her in ways that are presumably threatening; for instance, "Picture yourself saying something and everyone laughing at you" or "Picture everyone ignoring you."

We can also simulate distressing situations through role playing or by having the client carry out some relevant action that will elicit the upsetting emotion, often anxiety, and the related irrational thoughts. For example, a person who is afraid to tell others how he feels could be asked to do so to the therapist, who can role-play an appropriate other: spouse, boss, teacher, or the like. Similarly, a client who is afraid that others will think badly of her could be asked to dial a number at random and to tell the person who answers that she is conducting a survey on the use of contraceptives. Or a client who complains about procrastinating and not doing the writing he wants could be asked to write a brief summary of his political views. In all these instances, we would ask, "How are you feeling; what are you thinking?"

Homework. Perhaps during the session we have not succeeded in eliciting from the client any specific *ABC.* We still have not exhausted all of our possibilities, because, assuming the client will return, we can use between-session homework in this quest. Risk-taking homework may be particularly appropriate for clients who avoid the distressing situation and therefore do not feel anxious and are unaware of anxiety-producing thoughts. These clients can be encouraged to put themselves in the avoided situations and to notice and write down their thoughts leading up to and during the situation. One of many possible examples is a woman who avoids confrontation. She could be asked to purchase an item at a store and then return it. Though risk-taking homework is an important exercise in helping clients change irrational thinking, as we shall discuss in Chapter Six, the goal here is for the client to become aware of her irrational thinking. As stated in Chapter Four, the mere suggestion of taking risks is often sufficient to elicit the irrational thinking at that moment in the session.

Written homework can take a variety of forms and serve a variety of purposes. One useful purpose, especially at the beginning of therapy, is to enable the client to become aware of what he is thinking at times of emotional distress. The *ABC* format is useful here. The client suffering from anxiety can be asked to write down what has just occurred (*A*) each time that he feels anxious (*C*) and then to write what he was thinking at the time. He is then to bring his notes to the next session, presumably now aware of what he is thinking to create his anxiety.

Some clients are unaware of what they are feeling or are in a fairly constant emotional state. One example is a person who often comes home from work with headaches but is not aware of feeling tense during the day. A second example is a person who is anxious all the time but is not aware of situations in which she is more anxious or less anxious. The goal of written homework in these instances is to tie *A* to *C*; that is, to enable the person to become aware of emotional changes and their relationship to the environment. Once this *A-C* connection is made, then *B* can be explored. We might ask the client to keep an emotional diary for the week, particularly to note changes in feelings and then to indicate what was going on when he noticed the change.

Typical Problems

Ellis, in giving demonstrations of RET, often amazes and even unsettles some members of the audience by the speed in which he evokes the *ABC*s with a volunteer who has given hardly any background information or details about the activating event. To questions like, "How can you leap in so quickly with so little background from the client?" Ellis typically responds, "Although people are all unique in many ways, and although they often have different kinds of emotional problems, the ways in which people create their problems are nauseatingly similar." This similarity arises from common ways of thinking (awfulizing, demandingness, and rating of self and others), which lead to relatively few emotional problems (anxiety, shame, guilt, anger, hurt, and depression) as well as fairly typical combinations of these emotional problems. Here we will review a number of typical presenting problems, starting with fairly simple problems (one *ABC*) and moving to more complex problems (multiple *ABC*s).

Emotional Problems

Shame and Guilt. Although the presenting problem is more likely to be anxiety (to be discussed next), often what people are anxious about is the *anticipation* of doing something that would make them feel ashamed or guilty. Some people who are guilt ridden or shame ridden also become depressed. (Depression also will be considered later.) Here we will look at the single problems of shame and guilt. Although they constitute two distinct problems, we consider shame and guilt together because they result from the same type of ideation and, as far as we can tell, produce the same type of arousal. Both involve doing something considered bad, stupid, or wrong. The difference is the locus of evaluation—external for shame, internal for guilt. Shame comes from receiving the disapproval of others; guilt, from receiving one's own disapproval. In both cases, the conclusion is "I'm no good."

When people say that they feel guilty, often they are actually feeling shame; that is, if no one would ever know about their mistake, failure, or misdeed, they would not feel bad at all. A good way to check out whether the emotion is shame or guilt is to ask, "How would you feel if I could guarantee that no one would think badly of you for failing?" or "How would you have felt if absolutely no one had been around to see you make that mistake?" Distinguishing between shame and guilt has some importance in the course of therapy. For one thing, if shame, not guilt, is the emotional problem, shame-attacking exercises (discussed in Chapter Six) are particularly appropriate. Because we usually do not want to ask a client to violate his own standards or ethics (as we would ask him to do things that others would not approve of), dealing with guilt occurs primarily on a cognitive, rethinking level (If you behave badly, does that make you an evil person?). However, if we err by construing the emotional problem as guilt rather than shame, no great harm is done, since in either case we would be attempting to help the client work toward self-acceptance, not self-evaluation. Moreover, in the course of therapy, the importance of others' evaluations will arise, and our error will be corrected. Finally, some people may experience both shame and guilt.

To summarize, the *ABC*s of shame and guilt are:

A: Doing something that others disapprove of.
B: I need their approval. Because they think badly of me, that proves I'm worthless.
C: Shame.

A: Doing something that I consider wrong.
B: I shouldn't do wrong things. Because I did, I'm no good.
C: Guilt.

Anxiety. Anxiety, a common presenting problem, relates to events that have not occurred and is the emotion felt in anticipation of some dreaded occurrence. For instance, if we change the *A* presented for shame to "*What if* I do something that others don't like" and the *B* to "*If* they think badly of me, I'm worthless," the *C* becomes anxiety. Similarly, we can change the *ABC* for guilt to that of anxiety by inserting "What if. . . ." Although there are several sources of anxiety, as illustrated in Chapter Two, the ideas underlying shame and guilt are probably the most common sources of anxiety. Ellis groups the anxieties related to shame and guilt together under the heading of "ego anxiety," which he distinguishes from "discomfort anxiety" (Ellis, 1979a, 1980). Discomfort anxiety results from a variation of the low frustration tolerance philosophy, to be discussed next, with ideas such as "I must be comfortable" and "What if I get anxious; wouldn't that be awful." As we shall see, discomfort anxiety is a prime contributor to panic reactions.

Emotions Resulting from Low Frustration Tolerance. Low frustration tolerance (LFT) is not a feeling but a philosophy, which can manifest itself in several ways: impatience and anger, self-pity, panic, depression, and various avoidance behaviors. The general idea is that "Life should be easy and go the way I want. If not, it's awful and I can't stand it." Here are some emotional consequences of that theme.

1. Anger derives from demandingess and awfulizing directed toward perceived frustrations. We experience frustration when we do not get what we want; we experience anger when we do not get what we want *and* believe that we *should have* and therefore it is *awful.* Therefore, unlike the well-known frustration-aggression hypothesis (Dollard and others, 1939), we say that frustration leads to anger (then perhaps, but not necessarily, to aggression) only if the frustrated person believes something *should not* have happened. The source of frustration can be external or internal, so anger can be directed at other people, the world in general, or oneself. An example of anger directed at oneself is a person who recognizes that it is her own behavior that prevents her from getting some of the things she wants and who says to herself, "If I'd only speak up, I could get what I want. I didn't speak up. I should have, damn it!" If negative self-evaluation also enters, the anger becomes analogous to guilt.

A major source of frustration is transgression against valued personal rules (Beck, 1976). While most instances of rule breaking lead to negative feelings, whether the emotional consequence is annoyance or anger depends on one's belief system. Annoyance comes from a rational preference that people's conduct follow the rules; anger and rage, from an irrational demand that the rules be followed and a condemnation of the transgression. Believing, even implicitly, that one can function as a rule maker for others, for the world, or for nature or God is grandiose to say the least. It is important to keep in mind and to convey to the client the distinction between annoyance and anger. If anger is a problem for the client, our goal is to help him minimize the anger, not to lead him to enjoy or be indifferent about frustrations, which by definition lead to annoyance because we do not like or want what is happening.

2. Self-pity comes from the variation of LFT thinking that leads to the conclusion "Poor me, because of the mistreatment I receive." Self-pity is perhaps the counterpart of self-righteousness, seen in many forms of anger. People often express self-pity when they say that they feel hurt. *Hurt* (although

people may use the term to refer to other emotions) occurs when some perceived injustice to oneself occurs—being falsely accused, being ignored or rejected, not being appreciated—followed by an idea similar to "I don't *deserve* that, and woe is me! I should get what I deserve." Hurt may be expressed behaviorally by pouting, sulking, or whining. These behaviors are often labeled "passive-aggressive," which shows another similarity between hurt and anger.

When a person presents a problem of hurt, he also may feel shame, particularly when the *A* is rejection. One belief, then, would be something like "Because I have been rejected, that proves I'm no good," leading to shame, followed by the thought (perhaps as a protection against this blow to self-esteem) "No, I am really a good person and do not deserve this. Poor me." One final similarity between anger and hurt: Self-righteous anger also may serve as protection against the loss of self-esteem involved in guilt and shame.

3. Panic, which results from a need to be in control of one's feelings, derives from a variation of LFT thinking, expressed in ideas such as "I must feel good," "I mustn't feel anxious," "I must always feel calm, cool, and collected." Given such thinking and given the fact that the individual begins to feel discomfort, the ultimate result is likely to be an anxiety attack. The discomfort becomes the *A,* followed by the *B* of "My God, I'm losing control; I must feel comfortable!" The resulting anxiety in turn becomes an *A.* Now the cycle continues with the *B* of "My God, it's getting worse. I've got to stop this," leading to more anxiety, which in turn becomes an *A,* and so on, until the person experiences a full-blown anxiety attack.

Depression. In addition to the ideational components involved in the other emotional problems discussed, depression involves the components of helplessness and hopelessness, which are added to self-pity or self-downing or both. For example, when a person who believes that she needs the approval of others is rejected, she may think not only "What a louse I am" (shame) but also "And there's nothing I can do about it; I'll never be any good." At least three routes can lead to depression: guilt or shame, self-pity, and the comfort trap.

Guilty depression, or shameful depression, occurs when the individual has done something that he feels guilty about or ashamed of. Added to his negative self-evaluation are the ideas of helplessness and hopelessness. In this type of depression, unlike the others we will discuss, there may be little LFT involved. If that is the case, the focus of therapy would be almost entirely on the guilt or the shame, for this individual feels helpless and hopeless about ever achieving worth. But the person experiencing this type of depression may also have ideas like "Life is too hard" or "I can't live with myself" or "I can't stand it," which we would not want to ignore.

Depressions resulting from self-pity may occur after some loss, such as the death of a loved one or the loss of a job. Assuming the individual does not feel responsible for the loss (in which case we would have a guilty depression or a combination of the guilty and the self-pitying depressions), if the person is feeling depressed, he is thinking something like "How could this happen to me? I've lived a good life, and I didn't deserve that. There's nothing I can do about it. I'll never get a replacement. Life is rotten!"

Finally, some depressed clients believe that they are trapped in a miserable situation and see no way out of the trap. Low frustration tolerance, particularly discomfort anxiety, is the primary component of this depression. With such clients, suggestions that they do something to change their lives are likely to evoke the "Yes, but . . ." response, which most often means "Yes, but it is too hard" or, more to the point, "Yes, but I'd be uncomfortable." To avoid the discomfort, often anxiety, this type of person will not take steps to change her life. However, she does not realize that she is *choosing* not to risk discomfort. Because she sees no choice, she therefore believes that there is nothing she can do (helpless) and that her life will never change (hopeless). She is trapped, not by life's circumstances but by her choice of the comfortable, easy alternative. The need for comfort is the major problem here. We point out very directly to these clients that "You've got a choice. You want some things for yourself in life and you also want to feel comfortable. Unfortunately, you probably can't have both. Up to this point, you've been choosing comfort. Is that what you want most for yourself?" Just helping the client see that she is *choosing* to do or not to do certain things and that she is not a pawn of fate can help to lift her depression. Other problems, then, such as shame or guilt, may well come to the fore.

Behavioral Problems

Here we will discuss what we called in Chapter Four behavior problems of excess or lack. People with these problems seek therapy because they are doing something they do not like or are not doing something they would like to do. In practically all such cases, there are emotional problems combined with LFT. We can view the behavior as avoidance behavior, which enables the client to avoid negative feelings, especially anxiety, guilt, or shame. In discussing these problems, we will illustrate how various *ABC*s interact with each other and with behavior. Three of the most common behavioral problems are unassertiveness, procrastination, and self-indulgence.

Unassertiveness. Assertive behavior, when expressed, derives from the person's *preferences*—the person likes or does not like something and expresses that fact. Aggressive behavior, when expressed, derives from the person's *demands*—the person believes that certain things *must* or *must not* happen and expresses that fact. Thus, the distinction is the one we have made between annoyance and anger. The person expressing anger intends to harm in some way the object of his anger. Assertive behavior is behavior simply directed toward obtaining what one wants. Although what one wants may conflict with what others want, the intent of assertive behavior—unlike the intent of aggression that may follow anger—does not include the desire to harm, upset, or cause unhappiness to others. Thus, except in cases of extreme aggression, we differentiate assertive and aggressive behavior not by their impact on others but by their intent.

A person who lacks assertive behavior will usually not obtain some, perhaps many, of the things she wants. Dissatisfaction may lead a person to seek therapy. Here is a fairly simple case where LFT interferes with assertive behavior.

A: Not getting what I want.
rB: I'd like to get what I want.
C: Frustration (followed by at least two possibilities):

Possibility 1:

A: Frustration.
iB: Life should be easy, not frustrating.
C: Anger, which may lead to aggressive behavior.

Possibility 2:

A: Frustration.
iB: It's too hard; I'll never get what I want. Poor me.
C: Depression, which may lead to doing nothing.

In both possibilities, there is first the rational belief "I'd like to get what I want," leading to frustration, followed by a new set of *ABC*s, with frustration as the *A*.

Some people seek assertiveness training because they recognize that they have difficulty in expressing themselves to others, particularly in expressing their desires. Here is one example:

A: Friend makes a request.
rB: I don't want to do it.
C: No strong emotion.

If I say "no,"
A: Friend may not like me.
iB: That would be awful; I need her approval.
C: Anxiety.

A: Anxiety.
iB: I must feel comfortable.
C: More anxiety, avoidance, say "yes."

A common presenting problem that is often a variation on unassertiveness is anger combined with guilt and shame. For example, a woman comes to therapy because she says she is short-tempered with others, often with her family, and is feeling guilty because of losing her temper. Her goal is to gain control of her temper. Here is an example:

1. *A:* My husband doesn't consider my feelings.
   rB: I don't like that. I wish he wouldn't do that.
   C: Annoyance.

2. If I confront him,
   A: He may not like me for that; he might leave me.
   iB: That would be awful; I need his approval.
   C: Anxiety.

3. *A:* Anxiety.
   iB: I mustn't feel bad; I must feel comfortable.
   C: More anxiety, avoidance, no confrontation.

4. *A:* No confrontation.
   iB: I should have spoken up. I'm not liberated, and that means I'm a crumb.
   C: Guilt.

5. *A:* Guilt.
   iB: I mustn't feel bad; I must feel comfortable.
   C: Anxiety.

6. *A:* Conflict (between 3 and 5).
   iB: He shouldn't do that to me.
   C: Anger, yell, shout.

7. *A:* His anger (a response to her yelling and shouting).
   iB: How awful; he doesn't love me; I need his love.
   C: Shame, fear of losing him, resolve not to say anything in the future.

So our client remains quiet about her likes and dislikes for a while. Her husband continues to ignore her (possibly, though not necessarily, because she does not tell him and he is unaware of doing so) until she finally allows herself to feel annoyed and starts the cycle again at point 1; or she begins to tell herself that he *must* consider her feelings and starts the cycle at point 1, but this time with anger instead of annoyance; or she expresses the anger and short-cuts the cycle to point 7, where this expression is followed by shame and a resolve never again to show anger.

Although this is just one specific example of an assertiveness problem, it illustrates the possible complexity of interactions among the various *ABC*s and behavior. Assertive behavior is often impeded because the individual avoids behaviors that could lead to guilt or shame. We chose this case also to highlight the relatively common case of a person who is in a no-win situation (of her own making). If she speaks up, she risks rejection and shame; if she does not, she feels guilty. What she will do probably will depend on whether the guilt or the anxiety over rejection is stronger.

Procrastination. Procrastination almost always involves LFT. The short-term discomfort of engaging in a task is avoided in spite of the potential long-term benefits of completing the task. Almost any behavior can be the object of procrastination, including assertive behavior ("Next week I'll tell my husband that I want him to be more attentive") and self-indulgent behavior ("I'll diet tomorrow"). Procrastination can be a problem in areas related to school or work—a student not studying or writing a paper, a manager not writing reports, a composer avoiding his piano, or a placement counselor not calling clients. The client presenting a procrastination problem may simply have a problem in low frustration tolerance:

A: Work to do.
iB: It's too hard.
C: No arousal but avoidance of the situation.

However, since our procrastinating person has sought therapy, other elements may well be involved. For example:

1. *A:* Work to do (and I may not do well at it).
   iB: If I fail, that would be awful; I'd be no good.
   C: Anxiety.

2. *A:* Anxiety.
   iB: I must not feel anxious.
   C: More anxiety, avoidance.

3. *A:* Avoidance (thus, possible failure).
   iB: If I fail, that would be awful; I'd be no good.
   C: Anxiety.

4. *A:* Anxiety.
   iB: I must not feel anxious.
   C: More anxiety, work.

Whether the person works or avoids the work depends on whether the anxiety at 3*C* is greater than that at 1*C* (the avoidance-avoidance conflict). The result is a person whose behavior is motivated by the avoidance of anxiety. If the anxiety over failing is strong enough (for a student, perhaps the night before an exam), he will do the work. But if it is not (perhaps a week before the exam), he will avoid the anxiety engendered by doing the work.

Self-Indulgence. Self-indulging behavior brings us momentary, short-term pleasure or relief. Since we are not solely long-term hedonists, self-indulgence is a part of life, and a rather pleasant one at that. However, some individuals habitually and compulsively engage in self-indulging behavior that has detrimental long-term results for them. Such individuals, if they recognize the detrimental long-term consequences, may seek therapy in order to change that behavior—for example, to stop smoking or heavy drinking, to lose weight, or to give up gambling. Low frustration tolerance is probably involved in all such cases and is combined with some other source or sources of emotional upset to lead to a vicious cycle of upset-relief-upset-relief, and so on. Here is one illustration:

A: Possible rejection.
iB: I need approval; it would be awful to be rejected.
C: Anxiety.

A: Anxiety.
iB: I must feel comfortable.
C: More anxiety, eat (relief, gain weight).

A: Overeat.
iB: I shouldn't overeat; what a weak crumb I am.
C: Guilt.

A: Guilt.
iB: I must feel comfortable.
C: More anxiety, eat (relief, gain weight).

And so on. Whether the behavior is smoking, eating, drinking, gambling, or whatever depends on the individual's past learning history; that is, on what behavior for that person has become associated with relief of discomfort. A second example:

A: No one likes me; I have no friends.
iB: Life shouldn't be lonely; poor me.
C: Self-pity, spend money on clothes; debts pile up.

A: Spend money on clothes.
iB: I deserve nice things.
C: Satisfaction, but . . .

A: Debts.
iB: I'm swamped under; I'll never get out of debt; what a fool I am.
C: Depression.

A: Depression.
B: I should feel good; poor me.
C: Self-pity, spend money on clothes; more debts.

In many cases of self-indulgence, the self-indulging behavior serves not only the relief function illustrated above but also a self-protective function, so the behavior is doubly reinforced. By "self-protective function" we mean that the behavior or its results can be used in a rationalization to protect the individual from coming to the devastating conclusion "I am a rotten, worthless person." Here are two examples of this self-protective logic that can reinforce self-indulgent behavior: first, overeating; second, procrastination, which is also a form of self-indulgent behavior:

1. I need to be liked to have worth.
   People don't like me because I'm fat.
   If I were thin, they would like me.
   Therefore, their rejection proves nothing (while I'm fat).
2. I need to be able to do well in school to have worth.
   To prove I can do well requires hard work and study.
   I don't do that; I study at the last minute.
   Therefore, if I fail, it's not because I can't do well; it's because I have poor study habits.

Sometimes the reinforcing behavior serves a self-enhancement function rather than a self-protective function. Here is an example of a compulsive spender:

I need to be liked and loved in order to have worth.
There is nothing likable about me.
If I have nice clothes, cars, and other possessions, people will like me for that.
Therefore, I *must* have those things.

Multiproblems and Where to Begin

Given a clear conception of the client's problem, we are almost ready to move into the change process. Before doing so, we need to convey our understanding of the client's problem or problems, so that we can determine whether the client understands and agrees with our conception. In conveying to the client how we view the problems, we might outline on paper the various *ABC*s and their interactions, such as we have done in this chapter. For the therapist as well as the client, this procedure can eliminate the confusion that often results from a purely verbal description and can serve as a sort of "road map" to guide the therapy.

If the problem appears to be a simple *ABC,* we simply begin to help the client rethink the *B.* However, for clients who present the interacting multiproblems, such as those we have just illustrated, our problem is deciding where to start. We cannot simultaneously focus on ideas underlying guilt, anger, and shame. We can deal only with one at a time. As we proceed, we can point out similarities in thinking underlying the various problems; for instance, "Your guilt comes from demanding that you be perfect and never make mistakes. Your anger is very much the same. You generously impose your standards on others and demand that they, too, be perfect." Then we proceed, "Now let's take a close look at your guilt" or, alternatively, "Let's take a close look at the anger." How do we make this choice?

The simplest way to choose where to begin is to let the client make the choice. After conveying to the client how we view the problems, and after checking to see whether the client understands and agrees, we ask, "Where would you like to start?" Occasionally we ourselves might choose the starting point, particularly when we believe that the client is unaware of or attributes little importance to his underlying problem. Two relatively frequent examples come to mind: first, unassertiveness combined with anger; second, fear of rejection combined with low frustration tolerance.

The client who wants to become less prone to anger may reveal that she becomes angry after letting others take advantage of her (for fear of rejection) and then feels ashamed of her anger-induced behavior (because of others' disapproval). If the client convinces us that the anger occurs relatively frequently and thus probably is getting her into significant difficulties with, for instance, her boss, we will work with the client directly on minimizing the anger. Otherwise, we believe it is best to acknowledge the anger but to point out that the anger is secondary or a result of a different problem—in this example, the fear of rejection. There are several reasons for our choosing not to work with this client on overcoming anger. First, if the client were not so fearful of rejection, and would therefore allow herself to behave more assertively, she would be more likely to get what she wants and would experience less frustration. Second, if we agree that anger indeed is a problem for her and then work with her to change the demands that she places on others, we may well just reinforce her idea "I must not feel or express annoyance" and will be counterproductive in our attempts to have her become more able to express her desires. We would explain these reasons to the client.

If a person presents the problem of fear of rejection combined with low frustration tolerance, perhaps as in a case of agoraphobia, we would begin with the low frustration tolerance. In fact, in all multiproblems where discomfort anxiety is a strong factor, it is usually best to begin work in that area. The rationale for this choice is that, until the need for comfort is reduced, the client will probably not change any other irrational beliefs because he will participate only halfheartedly in his therapy; for to do otherwise involves work, discomfort, and in many cases some anxiety, all of which this client strongly avoids. Again, we would explain our rationale to the client.

So we choose to begin with the problem that we judge is the major source of interference with the client's long-range goals. The problem may not be the client's presenting problem. If we have no basis for making this decision, then we let the client choose. But if we choose to begin in an area that is not the client's presenting problem, it is particularly important that we convey our reasons for doing so. If we want progress to take place in therapy, it is important for us to explain to the client and obtain his agreement that change in the area of our choice would indeed be beneficial to him. Otherwise, we will be working at cross-purposes and will not have a working therapeutic alliance.

Assessment of the problem does not occur once and for all. As the number of sessions increases, we gather more information about our clients, and that information may change our initial conceptualizations of their problems. Even if our conceptualizations do not change, some clients tend to forget what they were in the first place, returning to a focus on A, or perhaps do not see how a problem in irrational thinking pervades many situations in their lives. For instance, a client who has difficulty expressing himself to his parents, who has few friends, who does not speak up in groups, and who does not return unwanted purchases may view each of these difficulties as separate and independent. Each week he may bring in a new "problem," and each week it may be shown to him to be an instance of a fear of rejection. Going through the *ABC*s of problem assessment with a client who is continuing in therapy can serve several valuable purposes. For the client, it is a means of teaching him a method to assess his own problems, so that he can be more aware of his irrational thinking when it occurs, as it will throughout life. For the therapist, it is a means of checking out initial assumptions made about the client's problems in thinking. Our assumptions may be wrong.

6

Changing Irrational Beliefs

Many clients, after their problems have been defined for them in *ABC* terms, will say, "OK, now I see that I believe such and such. What do I do about that?" or "How can I change it?" Good questions. Our answer is "You change it in the same way that you change any other belief: by looking for the evidence for it. If there isn't any good evidence to support it, you give it up—just as you gave up your belief in Santa Claus." Other clients will not ask such a direct question. In this case we set the stage for change by saying, "You see that your belief of such and such is what creates problems for you. Now, let's work on changing that idea. The way we can change any belief is by looking for the evidence for it. If there isn't any good evidence to support it, give it up." Then we start exploring the evidence for the client's belief.

Looking for empirical evidence for irrational beliefs, finding none, and substituting alternative beliefs for which there is good empirical evidence combine to form the foundation of RET change techniques. These comprise the first group of techniques we will discuss. However, the RET therapist uses many techniques to help the client achieve belief or attitude change. The therapist here can be compared to a teacher. The effective teacher is one who provides a variety of learning experiences and who does not just lecture (in this case, provide the client with disputes) but actively involves the student in his or her own learning by a variety of outside assignments and in-class discussions and simulations. As therapists, we also use a variety of outside assignments (homework) and in-session discussions and simulations.

Before we begin our discussion of change techniques in RET, the reader may want to pause and think about ways to help anyone change a particular attitude or belief. Any ethically acceptable technique or method that aids in changing attitudes or beliefs is appropriate in RET. We will discuss a large number of specific methods commonly used by RET therapists, but these methods do not form an exhaustive list. In fact, the list of techniques becomes almost limitless when appropriate variations are made to tailor the language and concepts to the intellectual, educational, and cultural background of individual clients. A general approach that can occur throughout the therapy is to offer encouragement. RET has a reputation as a tough approach to therapy. Certainly, we do not advocate coddling clients who can stand on their feet or suffering along with people who can help themselves. However, even though we accept no nonsense from clients and actively confront them with their irrationalities, we can still offer encouragement. An attitude of "I know you can do it" on the part of the therapist helps in most cases.

We will discuss change techniques in three broad categories: cognitive, imaginal, and behavioral. Although some techniques are used solely within the therapy session and some others solely outside the session as homework, most can be useful in both settings. We will conclude with some general remarks on using creativity and flexibility in RET.

Cognitive Techniques

Cognitive techniques are those techniques that rely solely on verbal interchange between therapist and client (within sessions), between the client and himself (written or thinking homework), and between author and client (reading and listening to tapes as homework). The purpose of the interchange is to help the client rethink irrational ideas and discover alternative ways in which to view himself, others, and/or the world.

Asking the client to look for the evidence supporting (or not supporting) his beliefs is called challenging or disputing. A simple model for challenging clients' irrational beliefs consists of the following: (1) The therapist states the client's irrational belief (perhaps on the basis of the therapist's inferences rather than words spoken by the client); the client confirms that she has this belief. (2) The therapist asks the client what evidence or proof she has to support the belief; why is it true? (3) The client's reply will be another belief. If the belief is rational, the therapist stops disputing; if it is another irrational belief, steps 1 and 2 are repeated. Here are two brief examples:

T: So you believe that you would be worthless if you flunked out of school. [C nods.] Where is the evidence that you would be worthless if that happened?

C: My parents would sure think so.

T: How would their thinking so prove you were worthless?

C: I guess it wouldn't.

And:

T: So you believe that you would be worthless if you flunked out of school. [C nods.] Where is the evidence that you would be worthless if that happened?

C: I would feel like I was no good.

T: You mean that, because you would *feel* rotten, like you were no good, that would prove you were worthless?

C: I guess so.

T: Does that make sense—that a feeling proves an idea correct?

C: No, it doesn't.

T: OK, what other evidence do you have that you'd be worthless?

Asking for evidence is the most direct manner of challenging irrational beliefs. However, there are times when a less direct approach seems better. For example, some clients are not especially persuaded by evidence or have not produced any noticeable changes as a result of intellectual disputing. In addition, some therapists prefer to work experientially rather than didactically or when working didactically prefer to involve the client in the learning process rather than simply to use him as a foil in a one-sided debate. Some of the methods we will discuss here involve didactic explanation to point out alternative ways of thinking, but most are in the form of questions or problems that indirectly challenge irrational beliefs. We want the client to do the work of rethinking, instead of merely accepting the word of the therapist that an idea is irrational. We want the client to *understand how* that idea is irrational. We will take each component of irrational ideas—awfulizing, demandingness, and evaluation of self and others—and present some ways in which the client can be taught to rethink those elements.

Awfulizing. A useful method of disputing the notion of "awful" with most clients is to point out that they are misusing the term. We discussed the logic of this approach in Chapter Two, pointing out that by "awful" we usually mean the worst thing that can happen. What the client has labeled "awful" is not the worst thing that can happen, though it might certainly be bad, even very bad. This misuse of the term *awful,* then, can lead to a high degree of emotional upset. Here are two examples of helping the client understand that she is making the error of inexact labeling (Beck, 1963). First, a didactic approach:

T: When we say "awful," we mean the worst possible thing that can happen, don't we? How can your failing a test be awful? I can think of worse things that can happen to you.

Second, an evocative approach:

T: You say failing the test is awful. What do you mean by "awful"?
C: I mean it's very bad.
T: Yes, it is for you. Do you use "awful" whenever bad things happen?
C: Not necessarily. But this is really awful.
T: Meaning very bad?
C: Certainly.
T: How would you feel if you told yourself, "Failing the test is very bad–not awful, but very bad"?
C: I'd still feel lousy.
T: As lousy?
C: No, I guess not.
T: Well, I'm not trying to make you happy you failed the test, but do you see that using the label "awful" makes you feel even worse?
C: Yes, I guess it does.
T: Many bad things can happen to us, and to label them "awful," meaning the worst, is a mislabeling that only serves to make us feel worse.

This interchange may continue for some time.

In this example, we are attempting to point out not only the erroneous use of a label but also the emotive effect of using that label, since the client usually wants to change the emotion, not the label. When the client sees the connection between the label and the emotion, she presumably will want to work to change that label. During attempts at changing *B,* we constantly remind the client that *B* causes *C.* However, the recognition that "awfulizing" contributes to upsetting emotions will not, in and of itself, lead a person to change her belief that an event is awful. In fact, this recognition may lead to a second problem if the client has learned nothing else; for example, "There I go again thinking 'awful.' I *mustn't* do that." We want our clients, first, to *realize* that awfulizing (believing that bad things are awful) constitutes an error in labeling; second, to *understand* the difference between bad, very bad, and the worst; and, finally, to make these distinctions in everyday life and to correct themselves when they do not.

A general approach that can be used with awfulizing, and with the other components as well, is "inductive disputing." Instead of starting with the premise that nothing is awful, we can take a learning-by-discovery approach. For instance, we can ask the client what outcomes he anticipates would be awful. Then, taking each outcome in turn, we ask the client how he would cope if that anticipated "awful" outcome occurred. Each coping strategy can be explored and suggestions offered when the client cannot imagine how to cope. After all possibilities are considered, we ask the question "How can your anticipations be so awful if you can think of ways to cope with all of them? Anything you can cope with cannot be awful!" This approach relies heavily on addressing the client's inferences (interpretations—Step 4 in the emotional episode) and might at first seem like "empirical disputing" rather than something more elegant. However, the goal remains attitude change.

Awfulizing is practically always one of two or three components of any particular irrational idea. Often we may choose to ignore the awfulizing and help the client dispute the demandingness or the evaluation of self and others, judging that the awfulizing will be discontinued as the client begins to give up demands and ideas of specialness or human worth.

One kind of awfulizing that usually deserves a direct attack is awfulizing that leads to discomfort anxiety, typically expressed as "I must feel comfortable; it's awful when I don't." Here there are often related ideas: "I can't stand it." "I can't function." Our attempt here is to show the client that he is engaging in mislabeling, both with "awful" and with "can't"; that anxiety or discomfort is not an awful but, rather, an unpleasant feeling that can be and is tolerated. Here, again, we try to get the client to see the difference between unpleasant or bad and awful. For the "I can't," we point out to the client that indeed he can—can stand it, can perform, can function. Here are some ways to proceed:

C: I get so uptight that I just can't stand it.
T: What do you mean, you can't stand it?
C: I mean I just want to get out of there; I can't stand the way I feel.
T: I still am not sure I know what you mean by "I can't stand it."
C: I can't take it.
T: But you are taking it; you're enduring it; it's not killing you.
C: Yeah, but I don't like it.
T: Certainly, but that's different. Do you see how?

And:

C: When I get so anxious I just can't function.
T: You mean you can't do anything?
C: I can't.
T: Have you tried?
C: Yes, I get all confused and mess up.
T: So you mean when you get anxious, you can't do anything very well.
C: That's right.
T: Not being able to do well is different from not being able to do anything, isn't it?
C: Yes, I guess it is. But it's awful not to do well.
T: So you see you *can* function anxiously.
C: OK, I can. But I can't stand failing.

Then we could pursue the awfulizing or the meaning of failing.

One client entered therapy for the problem of speech anxiety and later was not only giving speeches when required on her job but seeking out opportunities for doing so. When she was asked what she had learned in therapy that was helpful to her, she said, "What really helped was when you said, 'You can do it anxiously.' That had never occurred to me." Her old idea, of course, was "Because I am anxious, I can't do it." "I can't" will crop up again and again with many clients in therapy: "I can't speak up." "I can't get up in the morning." "I can't stop drinking." "I can't quit my job." The "I can't" usually covers more important issues that keep a person from changing—fears of failure, disapproval, or discomfort. However, in order to get to these problems, it is important for the person to see that in fact he can do what he thinks he cannot. The simple approach here is to translate "I can't" to "I won't." For instance:

C: I can't speak up when I'm with strangers.
T: Do you mean that you won't speak up?
C: OK, I won't.
T: Now, that's different. What keeps you from speaking up?

Or:

C: I can't speak up when I'm with strangers.
T: Don't you mean that you won't speak up?
C: No, I just can't.
T: Let's say I could give you a million dollars if you did. Then could you?
C: For a million I guess I could.
T: Then you can; you are able to.
C: Yeah, but I would be so scared.

As we get the client to see that "cannot" is an erroneous label, we usually will find underlying beliefs involving demandingness and self-rating, as well as awfulizing.

Demandingness. Here our overall goal is to help clients understand that they are escalating their desires and preferences to absolute imperatives. We might, for instance, ask clients how they would feel if, instead of thinking in imperatives ("I must do well"), they were to think in terms of preferences ("I want to do well"). Often clients will say something like "Well, I guess I wouldn't feel so anxious," to which we respond, "See, it is the 'must,' the 'got to,' that creates the anxiety." A more elaborate and general approach, which we learned from Edward Garcia, goes like this:

> Let's say there are two ways of viewing the world. We'll call them the "desiring philosophy" and the "requiring philosophy." [Here we take a sheet of paper, draw a line down the middle, and label one side *desiring* and the other side *requiring.*]
>
> With each philosophy there are certain thoughts and certain feelings that go together. [Now we draw a line across the middle of the page and label the top portion *thoughts* and the bottom portion *feelings.*]
>
> In the desiring philosophy, we think in terms of wants and desires. [We write down *desire* and *want.*] Can you think of other such terms? [Usually the client will mention some others—such as *prefer*—and we add these to the list. We usually add *love* if it is not mentioned, saying, "Some things we want a little; other things we may want very much." Some clients mention words like *need,* to which we say, "Now that's a necessity, a requirement, so it goes over here, under the 'requiring' heading."]
>
> Under the requiring philosophy, we also have certain other thoughts besides *need.* Can you think of others? [We end up with such terms as *must, should, ought,* and *have to.*]
>
> Now, let's look at the feelings. Let's say you *want* a new car and can't get one for some reason. How would you feel? [Many clients will say, "disappointed," "frustrated," "sad," or "annoyed," and we write down their response. If a client says something like "angry" or "depressed," we try again and say, "Now you only *want* that car; would you really feel depressed?" Most clients will say something like "No, I guess not; I'd feel unhappy, though."]
>
> Now, let's take the same car, but this time

> say you believe you *need* that car, have to have it. *Now* if you don't get it, how would you feel? [Most often we get answers like "worse," "awful," or "*now* I'd feel depressed," and we write the response down.] You see the difference in the two philosophies? Same car, different feelings. [To complete the example, we will fill in other feelings under both philosophies, such as annoyance, sadness, frustration, and disappointment under "desiring" and depression, anxiety, shame, guilt, and anger under "requiring," pointing out that the latter emotions come from thinking in terms of demands.]

This exercise often helps clients see more clearly that *B* (in this case beliefs involving demands) leads to *C*. It does not help the client *change B,* and the client erroneously may conclude, "I shouldn't say 'should.' " But once the client has the idea that demandingness leads to unwanted emotions, we can begin to help the client rethink the demands.

The imperatives people hold can be classified by whether they refer to oneself or to others. In the first case the subject is "I." A few such imperatives are:

- I should do well.
  should love my parents.
  must be liked.
  have to be on time.
  must behave like an adult.
  must not make mistakes.
  must be comfortable.

The subject of the second set is other people or the world:

- Others should treat me fairly.
  must be nice to me.
  have to do what's right.
  should do what I expect.

When the subject is "I," the imperatives generally are statements of the conditions under which the person considers himself worthy or adequate. The most useful approach here is to help the client rethink notions of self-worth, for if the client begins to see himself as worthy under all conditions or gives up the attempt at self-rating, the rules are unnecessary. After having the client see the difference between preferring and demanding, we usually can get to the self-worth belief fairly easily by asking such questions as "OK, you do want others to like you, but why is it necessary?" or "You say you need others' approval. What if you don't get what you need?"

The second set of imperatives, those with others as the subject, may also involve notions of self-worth, such as "Others should be nice to me, because if they were, that would prove I'm a good person." However, many of these imperatives are unrelated to self-worth and are simply ideas about the nature of the world. After making sure that the client wants to change the emotional consequence, our approach is to point out that it would be nice if the world were the way we want it to be (predictable, fair, and pleasing to us), but it simply is not consistently so. Demanding that it be so will not make it so. Here are some examples of attempts to get these points across to the clients:

C: Goddamn it, I get so angry when people treat me unfairly!

T: You believe that people should treat you fairly?

C: Yes, I do!

T: Where did you learn that?

C: I don't know.

T: I don't know either. I know of no commandment that says, "Others shall treat me fairly," do you?

C: No, but are you saying people should walk all over you?

T: Not at all. I am saying that no matter how much we may want people to treat us fairly, there's nothing written to say they should. And the fact of life is that some people simply won't treat us in ways we consider fair.

C: But I don't like it.

T: Exactly. And you probably never will. But not liking something and demanding that it not exist are two very different things.

Our second example deals with the "reverse golden rule":

C: I try so hard. I'm nice to everybody I meet, and it seems people just don't care.

T: Are you saying that if you are nice to others they should be nice to you?

C: Yes, they should.

T: That's very interesting. A lot of people have that silly idea.

C: Silly? What's silly about that?

T: The "should" part is silly. Where is it written that others should be nice to me?

C: Well, they should, shouldn't they?

T: It would be nice, and in fact often people are nice to us if we are pleasant to them. But there is no guarantee that this will be so. I think what you have done is to confuse the golden rule.

C: What do you mean?

T: The golden rule and other moral codes tell *us* what to do. Doesn't it say, "Do unto others as you would have them do unto you"?

C: Yes.

T: It doesn't say, "Others should do unto me what I do unto them."

C: I guess it doesn't. But can't I expect people to treat me well?

T: Certainly. But expecting and getting are two different things, and expecting and demanding that we get what we expect are two different things.

In pursuing the demandingness with a client, we often make explicit the possibly unstated idea of specialness. Let us continue with the above example:

T: Look around you. Do you see people who are nice to others always receiving gratitude or liking in return?

C: No, they don't.
T: Then why should you be different?
C: How do you mean that?
T: If others are sometimes rebuffed, what makes you so special that you should never be rebuffed?
C: Well, nothing.
T: But that's the implication: "Somehow I am special. Unlike all other human beings, I deserve good treatment."
C: I don't mean that.
T: But unfortunately–unfortunately for how you feel–you do mean that when you say, "It shouldn't happen to me."

Self-pity, as expressed in "Poor me, it shouldn't happen to me," combines elements of demandingness and specialness. Self-pity is a component of hurt and of certain depressions. As in the above example, both the self-pity and the demandingness can be attacked. As a result, the client can be led to see that his general rule of "Life should be easy," for example, is irrational and his specific rule of "Life should be easy for me" is even more untenable.

Evaluation of Self and Others. The idea that people have worth or do not have worth is probably the most difficult one to change (see Chapter Two). When a client says, for example, "If I am not successful, that means I am a bum," often our first approach is to get him to define his terms, in this case "bum." Our goals here are for the client to see that by "bum" he means worthless and that his idea of "bum" is a pure and simple definition, one that can be changed. For example:

C: If I don't succeed, that means I'm a bum.
T: And what is a bum?
C: Why, ah . . . a bum, someone who is no good.
T: So you're saying that if you fail you are no good.
C: That's right.
T: How does that follow?
C: Well, it means I won't make it in the world. I'd have to take a lesser job or not even work.
T: And that would make you a bum?

C: Yes.
T: How?
C: It just would.
T: It just would if you define yourself as a bum or worthless if you weren't working. What if I said you're a bum because you *are* working?
C: I'd say you're crazy. That doesn't make sense.
T: How is that different from what you are doing?
C: Well, it doesn't make sense.
T: But it's the same. You're a bum if you work. You're a bum if you don't. They are both definitions, not facts.

The point here is that, in self-rating, one or more criteria of behavior or outcome are used as measures of human worth. The criteria are arbitrary. In the above example, we reversed the scale for our client, with success redefined as worthlessness. We can also apply the client's scale to others: "What if I fail? What if I do a lousy job as a therapist? Does that make me a bum?" Most clients will say "no." Or we can ask, "You know others who are not successful. Are they bums?" Again most clients will say "no." The question then becomes "So what makes you a worthless bum—the one and only?" We can also use other criteria that are not those of the client to illustrate the arbitrariness of rating human worth by any criterion. For example:

T: Let's say I believe that if I can't dance well I'm a bum. Does that make sense to you?
C: No. But that's different.
T: How so?
C: Well, it's not really important.
T: Ah, it may not be to you. But it's important to me.
C: OK, but I wouldn't think you're a bum.
T: What would you think of me if I couldn't dance well?
C: Just that you can't dance well.
T: And if you failed, you would be just a person who has failed, not a failure or a bum.

How about those clients who would say, "Yes, you would be a

bum"? We would probably compliment the client on his consistency and try another approach.

A most useful and general approach is the "fruit basket," which goes like this:

> Let's use our imagination [picking up some object, such as an ashtray or a tissue box] and say this is a basket. Now, let's put some fruit in it [taking bits of paper or simply pretending to hold some object]. Here is a luscious peach, juicy and just right, and we put it in the basket. Here is an apple—filled with worms [making noises of disgust]—and we put that in. But here is a lovely bunch of grapes—delicious—and we put them in, too. Oh, but look here. Here's a banana that's been in the refrigerator for several years—all black and rotten—in it goes. And we continue to fill up the basket in the same way. Now, the question is: Is this a good basket or a bad basket?

Answers vary. The one we want is that it is neither. It is just a basket. Other answers are examples of evaluating the basket on the basis of its contents: "It is good," "It is bad," "It is both good and bad." Let us take one of these answers and follow it through:

C: It's bad.
T: And why is it bad?
C: Because it has bad fruit in it.
T: So when you say "bad," what are you describing?
C: Well, the fruit.
T: But I asked about the basket.
C: Oh, I guess it's just a basket, then.

Or, instead of this last response of the client:

C: But the bad fruit will spoil the basket.
T: Let's say all the fruit becomes spoiled; would that make the basket bad?

C: No, I guess it wouldn't–just the fruit.

T: So the basket is just a basket, no matter what kind of fruit it has?

C: That's right.

T: How about thinking of yourself as a basket and your potential failure as the bad banana?

We can use the basket example also to illustrate that overall evaluations of the container (self or others) are erroneous in that they are tied to one point in time and that change can and often will take place. For instance, we can remove some of the fruit and change the composition of the contents. But when we label the basket by its contents, we imply that that is the way it is.

Here is another inductive approach that can be used to teach about human complexity and the futility of evaluating oneself or others. The therapist asks the client to measure the office desk (or chair or any other convenient piece of furniture). This is an impossible task because objects cannot be measured; only their properties or characteristics can be measured. Clients often try, however, by estimating the length, width, weight, and so on. The therapist accepts none of the answers because they are not the desk. The whole may or may not be different from the sum of its parts, but one thing is certain–the whole is not any one of its parts. After clients understand that desks are too complex for measurement, they are invited to make the same analysis about humans.

Moving from baskets and desks to humans, an example we occasionally use is that of Nathan Leopold, who along with Richard Loeb committed the "Crime of the Century" in the 1920s by kidnapping and killing a young boy. Years later, Leopold was pardoned as a changed person, became a social worker, married, and spent much of the rest of his life doing good works. After telling or reminding the client of Leopold's story, we ask, "Now, was Nathan Leopold a good man or a bad man?" Again we get a variety of answers. The one we are looking for is "He was neither. He was a man who did both good and bad things." Leopold is an extreme case (which makes him a good example) and leads to a discussion of human fallibility:

T: Isn't that what all humans do, some good, some bad things, some successful and some unsuccessful things? Aren't we by nature fallible and imperfect?

C: Yes, that's true.

T: But aren't you saying, "I need to be perfect. I must never make a mistake"?

C: You're right.

T: Doesn't that deny your humanity?

C: Yes, it does. I must be superhuman.

T: Right, because you are in essence saying that if I am human, make mistakes and fail, I am a no-good bum.

A more general approach for demonstrating to the client that he is overgeneralizing, evaluating an action or an outcome as bad and then evaluating himself as bad, is to illustrate the process of self-rating by drawing for the client our Figures 1, 2, and 3 in Chapter Two. The vertical dimension can be labeled anything to which the client has attached self-worth—approval-disapproval, unselfishness-selfishness, intelligence-stupidity, and so on—and therefore can be tailored to each client.

An approach that is frankly paradoxical is to ask the client, "What stops you from being perfect?" This ploy directly focuses on the client's conditions of worth. The subsequent discussion, though, indirectly challenges the unrealistic assumption that humans can attain perfection and the irrational belief that one must be perfect. When done well, this approach can take a great deal of time as the therapist seriously discusses what the client can do to attain perfection. Bit by bit, the plan can be constructed until it is so enormous that its very size makes it seem absurd. Should the client object, the therapist can reply, "Don't give up. I'm certain we can help you toward your goal of perfection."

Most of the approaches we have mentioned can be used, with slight modification, to help people overcome their rating of others as well. For whether the rating is applied to oneself or to others, there are certain messages contained in these approaches. These include: All persons are fallible. It is irrational, not sensible, to rate an entire person. Rate the acts, not the person.

Our goal is to help the client *understand* the philosophical principles underlying these messages. Therefore, it is important to include techniques to test out this understanding. When a client says, for instance, "I know it is irrational to think I'm a bum," we had best pursue that statement. The client simply may be parroting back our words or words he has read with little or no understanding. With a statement such as that just given, a good question is "*How* is that irrational?" If the client does not understand how, then we begin again.

Challenging is very much a part of RET—challenging the client to think and defend his ideas. This includes challenging rational ideas, for if the client cannot defend them, it would indicate that he does not understand them or very strongly believe in them. For instance, a client might say after a few sessions, "OK, if I fail, I'm not a bum." Here are a few challenges:

- Why not?
- But I think you're a bum.
- OK, you're not a bum. What would make you one?

Another good way to get the client to challenge his own thinking as well as to test out his understanding is to reverse roles. We can say, "Let's try something different. I'll be the client and you be the therapist. Let's see if you can convince me that I am thinking irrationally." Then we can present either the same problem with which the client is struggling ("If I lose my job, that would prove I'm no good") or a similar problem involving self-worth: "If I'm a poor dancer, that would prove I'm no good." Not only does the role reversal give the client an opportunity to challenge another's irrational thinking but it provides us with a sampling of the client's thinking, which allows us to assess his understanding of the idea that we are all fallible human beings whose value cannot be judged by what we do or the results of what we do. Here is an example of role reversal with a client who does not either understand or strongly believe that it is an error to judge the entire person on the basis of his or her actions.

T: [acting as client] If I fail, I'd be a bum.
C: No, you wouldn't.
T: Why not? I think I'd be a bum.
C: Well, you wouldn't be.
T: What would I be?
C: I guess you'd be a failure—but not a bum.
T: But I don't want to be a failure.

In the above example, the therapist labels herself as a "bum" and a "failure." We can profitably discuss with clients both the effect of applying such labels to oneself and the irrationality of doing so. The effect, of course, is that one will feel like a bum if he believes he is a bum. The irrationality is, again, the overgeneralization from evaluating one's acts to evaluating one's self.

Some individuals have difficulty in understanding that a label applied by others is simply a label and not a fact; for instance, "If others see me as a bum, how can I see myself any other way?" The following example can be useful here:

T: What if others thought you were a bulldozer? Would that make you a bulldozer?
C: No, of course not.
T: Let's say because they thought you were a bulldozer, you believed you were a bulldozer and you started chugging around, kicking dirt here and there. Would *that* make you a bulldozer?
C: No way—weird, maybe, but not a bulldozer.
T: Now, if people thought you were a bum and you believed you were a bum, would that in fact make you a bum?
C: Well, I guess not. But that's harder.
T: Sure it is, but it's the same thing. Calling a person something does not make that person into that thing. "Bum" is simply a verbal label, one with bad connotations, but a label nevertheless.

And we might want to point out at some time that if he acted like a bulldozer it would simply mean he was *behaving* weirdly, not that he *was weird.*

Homework. Homework is an integral part of RET. Clients are encouraged to work on their therapy daily. Within the realm of cognitive techniques, we will discuss reading, listening, writing, and thinking as homework.

Reading, appropriate throughout therapy, is particularly appropriate at the beginning of therapy. It can serve to explain the RET approach to clients and to reinforce and enhance the presentation of the new ways of thinking we are trying to teach. If the client does the reading suggested, this also ensures that she is doing some thinking about herself and her problems outside the session. There are a number of articles and books appropriate for reading homework. Perhaps the most commonly assigned book is Ellis and Harper's (1975) *A New Guide to Rational Living,* which explains the approach and has chapters relating to a large number of irrational ideas.

By listening homework, we mean listening to tapes. Ellis, for instance, has recorded a number of talks on the philosophy of RET and various problems that people have. These recordings can be used to supplement or replace readings. Another valuable use of the tape recorder is for the client to record the therapy sessions and listen to them one or more times between sessions. Some therapists, in fact, require their clients to do so as a part of their therapy.

Written homework can take a variety of forms. It is most often used to give the client specific practice in recognizing and disputing irrational beliefs. It also serves as a check, when the client brings it to the therapist, on his understanding of the distinction between *A* and *B* and the difference between rational and irrational beliefs. Here we use the *ABCD* format, with *D* standing for disputing. Included in *D* are questions such as "What is the evidence for . . . ?" and the answers to those questions. A typical procedure in this kind of homework is for the client to observe when he feels anxious, guilty, or some other undesired emotion during the week and then to identify and write *C,* his feeling; *A,* the activating event; *rB,* his rational belief about the event; *iB,* his irrational belief about the event; and *D,* his disputes of the *iB.*

Another variation on written homework is to ask the client to write down all the ways he can think of to dispute a particular irrational belief—one that he clearly holds. Still another variation is to ask the client to write an essay contradicting that belief. This variation leads us into thinking homework, where the client is assigned the task of thinking about and disputing a particular irrational idea. For example, Criddle (1974) has listed a number of questions that clients can use to challenge the more common irrational ideas. Spending twenty minutes a day challenging irrational ideas is a good thinking homework assignment. Again, a tape recorder can be used here. The client can think out loud and relisten to his own irrational ideas and his disputes. Rule (1977) had clients humorously exaggerate their beliefs and write or tape-record them in order to increase their self-awareness and self-acceptance through self-modeling.

Most RET therapists encourage their clients to do some form of cognitive homework every day. However, some clients—often those with a very low frustration tolerance—will not follow through. In Chapter Seven, we will discuss some ways of working with such clients. Here, however, are some general rules that will enhance the probability of clients' doing homework, be it cognitive, imaginal, or behavioral:

1. Get the clients' agreement that homework is important for them, since cognitive change will take place only very slowly, or possibly not at all, if the only time and work spent on therapy is during the sessions.
2. Ask clients what they would like to do that week. If they do not know:
3. Suggest an assignment and have the client agree to it, or give several suggestions and have the client choose one or specify an alternative.
4. Whatever the choice, make it concrete and specific. Instead of "Dispute your irrational ideas this week," try, for example, "Take your idea that 'If I fail, I'm no good,' write down as many disputes as you can think of, and then spend twenty minutes a day disputing that idea." Or, if the homework is behavioral, instead of "Talk to strangers this week," try, for example, "Talk to at least one stranger each day."
5. Do not overload or overwhelm clients with homework as-

signments. One good assignment carried out is better than a number of equally good assignments not done. Clients can always do more than what is assigned.

6. After clients have agreed on a specific assignment, have them repeat it. Otherwise, some clients will return the next week and say that they forgot or did not understand.
7. As a matter of course, or certainly with clients who show a pattern of not following through on homework, have them write the assignment down.

Imaginal Techniques

We utilize relatively few techniques involving imaginary situations, because RET places heavy emphasis on behavioral homework (discussed in the next section). However, there are several imaginal approaches that can be useful.

Time projection (Lazarus, 1971) can be helpful to combat awfulizing and ideas of hopelessness in the person who is depressed or anticipating a loss. The client is asked to imagine scenes in which positive events are occurring in the future—a day, a week, a month, or a year. Lazarus (1968, pp. 84, 87-88) gives this rationale: "Depression may be regarded as a function of inadequate or insufficient reinforcers. . . . Once the patient can imagine himself sufficiently freed from his oppressive inertia to engage in some enjoyable (or formerly enjoyable) activity, a lifting of depressive affect is often apparent." This technique also shows the client that he is not helpless, that he can cope with life and obtain some pleasure. Scenes can be provided by the therapist (based on knowledge of what is or has been enjoyable to the client); for example, "Imagine yourself enjoying a good novel" or "Imagine yourself having lunch with friends." Clients who are afraid of some impending loss can be asked to imagine what they would be doing at various times in the future following the loss. Let us take the example of a client who is afraid of losing her job and says that "It would destroy me."

T: Let's imagine that you, in fact, have lost your job. You go to work tomorrow, and your boss tells you you're fired. Can you imagine that?

C: I sure can.
T: Tell me what you are doing and how you are feeling.
C: I feel awful. I don't know what I'd do. I'd go home and be miserable. I wouldn't do anything. I'd feel like dying.
T: OK, let's say it's a week later. What would you be feeling and what would you do?
C: I'd still feel miserable.
T: Would you be doing anything?
C: Well, I guess I'd start checking the ads and checking with some agencies.
T: OK, let's say it's a month later. What would you be feeling and what would you be doing?
C: I can see myself starting another job, so I guess I'd feel OK.
T: So if you lost your job, it wouldn't destroy you.
C: I guess it wouldn't.

Use of time projection in this manner can help put the feared event into perspective—bad, yes, but not awful—and show the client that she would cope and that she has misused such terms as *destroy*.

Maultsby (1975) has developed an approach called rational-emotive imagery (REI). In Ellis's version of REI, the client imagines a scene that he has reported to be upsetting—for instance, getting criticized or making a speech. When the client says that he is able to do so, he is asked to tell how he is feeling. Let us say he imagines getting criticized and says, "I feel ashamed." He is asked to continue imagining the scene but to change his feelings from shame to concern. If the client reports that he is able to do so, we ask, "What did you do in order to change your feelings?" The client is likely to report some change in thinking, such as "Well, I thought to myself, 'It's not that terrible to be criticized.' " REI thus can be used to show the client that *B* leads to *C,* or it can be used as homework in preparation for entering an actual situation. A variation on REI might be called positive rational-emotive imagery. Clients are guided through the imagining of a scene in which they feel and act as they want to. In other words, the client rehearses positive emotional and action goals and is encouraged to stick with realistic assumptions and rational beliefs about the scene. The in-session exercise then is assigned as homework.

Hypnosis can be effectively used in RET. Several studies of what Tosi and Reardon (1976) call "rational stage directed hypnosis" have been reported. In effect, irrational beliefs are replaced under hypnosis with rational ones, following several steps or stages from awareness through internalization, and clients can be led to imagine more successful coping, as in REI.

Clients who are anxious about certain events can be asked to imagine the worst thing that could happen and simultaneously combat the irrational thoughts. For example, a client with speech anxiety may tell us that the worst thing would be to block and forget what she was going to say. Further, let us say that in such a situation the client would think, "My God, this is awful. What a fool I am." We would ask this client to imagine herself standing there, forgetting what she was going to say, but thinking, "Well, I did it; I forgot. That's too bad, but it's not the worst thing in the world. And it doesn't mean I'm a fool; I'm just a person who is blocking. Even if I appear foolish, I'm just a person appearing foolish for the moment, not a fool. OK, now what am I going to do about this?" When we suggest imagining the worst to clients, often they will say, "But I don't want to imagine myself doing poorly; I want to imagine myself doing well," to which we reply, "But you are not *afraid* of doing well. Our goal is to overcome the fear. Also, it is unlikely that you are always going to do perfectly well. Then what?" The purpose of this technique is to have clients practice disputing irrational ideas in the presence of an imagined *A*. The next step is to practice disputing irrational ideas in the presence of a real *A*, which means they are asked to seek out the feared situation.

Behavioral Techniques

Here we will discuss techniques that engage the client in some activity, an activity that is feared and/or avoided. Our goal is not to have the client simply engage in a feared or avoided act, but to have the client *change* the ideas underlying the anxiety or low frustration tolerance. The use of *in vivo* homework, in which clients act on their rational beliefs and take risks that promote new attitudes, has been an important feature of RET since its inception. Several theoretical bases can be cited for this practice. Desensitization is one; the reinforcing aspects of successfully attempting something new is another. The theoretical base that seems most compatible with the cognitive emphasis of RET theory is cognitive dissonance theory (Festinger, 1957) and its later derivatives and elaborations. Briefly, it is postulated that people are motivated to maintain a consistency or equilibrium among the cognitive components of their attitudes (knowledge and evaluation) and their behavior. A change occurring in one part of the system leads to dissonance—which is uncomfortable—and an adjustment will be necessary in other parts of the system for a return to equilibrium and comfort. However, people usually maintain the status quo and thus avoid dissonance—by ignoring, avoiding, or explaining away information that is incompatible with their attitudes. But, when a person behaves in a way that is inconsistent with one of his beliefs, *and* cannot justify the action (rationalization) or attribute the reasons for engaging in the behavior to external causes, the resulting dissonance will be resolved by a change in cognition.

For example, in one study (Zimbardo and others, 1965) subjects were induced to eat grasshoppers. Subjects who were given a "cold," impersonal invitation reported liking the experience better than subjects who ate in response to a "warm," friendly invitation. An explanation for this seemingly illogical finding is that the subjects could not justify doing something unpleasant under the "cold" experimental condition for any reason other than that they really liked to eat grasshoppers. Thus, one way to get people to change their attitudes is to induce them to act as though they already held those attitudes. This is the rationale for assigning behavioral homework to clients and shows why it is important to work with them to increase the probability that they will actually carry out the assigned task. But if we become overzealous in encouraging behavioral homework, to the point of telling the client to do it, the status quo of the client's beliefs can be preserved by "I did it to please my therapist."

Behavioral homework assignments, when willingly carried

out, threaten the status quo of the individual's belief system and thereby bring about or strengthen cognitive change that has been discussed in therapy. Bard (1973) found that persons who attempted to teach other people the principles and the value of rational living decreased their own irrational thinking. From our perspective, behavioral homework is a central feature of RET because it gets desirable overt changes started and confirms the cognitive changes we view as essential for overcoming disturbance. To coin a cliché: The proof of the thinking is in the doing. The best homework assignments grow out of therapeutic discussions of problems and are action assignments that are discrepant from the individual's typical behavior and belief system, especially beliefs about the self.

We will discuss these behavioral techniques under three major headings: risk-taking exercises, shame-attacking exercises, and antiprocrastination exercises. Before we do so, role playing or behavioral rehearsal—a technique that can be used for a variety of purposes—deserves a mention. (For a thorough discussion of this technique, see Rimm and Masters, 1979.) We discussed role playing, in the context of role reversal, earlier in this chapter; and we will note some uses of role playing in the remainder of this chapter. Here we mention only as a reminder that this technique can be used to help clients acquire and practice interpersonal skills.

Risk-Taking Exercises. Here we ask the client to take risks. We ask clients to risk obtaining whatever they fear, usually rejection or failure in some form. Risk refers to the occurrence of an undesired outcome, as defined by the client, the probability of which ranges from practically zero to practically 100 percent. Some behaviors are viewed as more risky than others. If rejection is the undesired outcome, it is more risky to ask a stranger on the street for a date than to ask a stranger in a singles bar. Both are risky, but rejection or refusal is less likely in the singles bar.

The severity of consequences also varies from situation to situation. Being disliked or rejected by a sales clerk in a store may in fact lead to no other consequences than the dislike, whereas being disliked or rejected by one's boss may lead to getting fired. We do not encourage risk-taking exercises or shame-attacking exercises when the outcome seems likely to lead to severe consequences, such as being arrested, losing one's job, losing one's spouse, or being dropped from school. Now, of course, we cannot predict the future. If we encourage an unassertive woman, for example, to tell her husband, "Gee, honey, I'd like it if you would put the cap on the toothpaste," a seemingly innocuous request from our point of view, he *may* become furious and threaten to leave her. We therapists had better be aware of that *possible* consequence and openly discuss the risks with our client.

A major error made by some beginning therapists is to suggest and encourage behaviors on the client's part with no consideration of the risks involved. We recently have heard therapists tell their clients, "If you surprise your husband on his birthday by taking him out, he'll love it" and "If you are open about your feelings, it will be better for everyone and your relationship with your family will improve." These statements are false, of course, for they are absolute predictions of others' reactions in the future. They become true statements and, in fact, risk-taking exercises if the therapist replaces "will" with "might" or even "will probably, but may not, and in fact the opposite might occur."

How do we go about assigning risk-taking exercises? First of all, we do not suggest—in fact, we discourage—behaviors that may well lead to undesirable consequences. For instance, a client may say, "I'm fed up. I'm going to tell my boss that he's asking way too much of me," to which we might say, "OK, but you might lose your job. Are you prepared for that?" Second, we keep in mind that we are working with the client to change *B,* not the specific behavior in a specific situation. If a client does not speak up to her husband and does not tell him what she likes and dislikes—for fear (*C*) of his rejection (*A*), because of (*B*), "it would be awful and I'd be no good if he hates me"—other *A*s probably also trigger the same *B,* as suggested by our use of lowercase *a* in Chapter Five. Often, we can easily find these other *A*s by asking the client, "Are there other people with whom you have the same difficulty?" It would be most unusual if she said, "No, only my husband."

It is important to tailor risk-taking exercises to the client.

In other words, what is risky for one person is not necessarily risky for another. The ideas for risk-taking exercises usually arise from problems the client is discussing. For instance, a client might be saying how difficult it is for her to contradict her mother-in-law. Keeping risk-taking exercises in mind and viewing the hesitance to contradict her mother-in-law as a specific instance of a fear of another's anger and disapproval, we might ask, as mentioned above, "Are there other people with whom you have the same problem?" More specifically, if we have a particular risk-taking exercise in mind, we might ask, "How about a stranger? Would you be anxious about disagreeing with a stranger?" If we find that contradicting a stranger would indeed be difficult, we could suggest, "How about striking up a conversation with the person sitting next to you on your train tomorrow, then disagreeing with that person?" We might find that for our client striking up the conversation itself would be difficult, so we might suggest striking up a conversation with a stranger each day, saving the disagreement until later.

In a sense, we use graded exercises with our clients, although we do not formally work out a hierarchy from least anxiety provoking to most anxiety provoking. If we assign an exercise the client considers too anxiety provoking, he probably will not do it and thus will not benefit from the exercise. If we assign an exercise with little risk to our client, he probably will do it, but he will not benefit as much as from a riskier exercise. The logic here is that we *want* our clients to experience the undesired outcome—failure, rejection, anger, or whatever outcome our clients have been religiously avoiding. The riskier the exercise, the more likely the undesired outcome. In assigning risk-taking exercises, we always explain the rationale for the exercises. Once clients understand the rationale, they presumably understand our comments when we say, "I hope you get rejected this week" or "Hey, that's good. You got rejected (and you survived)."

How do we find the "optimal" level of risk taking with our clients? We do so by suggesting an exercise that the client probably will consider too difficult. We have found that clients will then choose a somewhat less difficult one. For example, when asked what risks he would like to take this week, a client might say, "Well, I'd like to speak up more in class. I never do." We could then suggest, "How about asking five questions in each of your classes this week?" He might say, "Oh, I don't know if I could do that. How about if I ask one question in each of them?" In a sense, we have a compromise between asking one question in one class and asking five questions in all classes. The client chooses. Some clients readily agree to and carry out the assignments suggested, which shows that our expectations of them were too low—another reason for suggesting exercises that *we think* are too difficult for the client. Another approach to assigning risk-taking exercises is to propose ones suggested by the discussion occurring during therapy session. Taking the example we have just used, after discussing the fear of talking in classes, we might say, "It seems you don't speak up in class for fear of saying the wrong thing and consequently looking stupid. Why not for homework this week ask at least five questions in each of your classes and risk looking stupid?"

Some clients will say that they would not know what to say or do in asking questions in class, in striking up a conversation with a stranger, in asking someone for a date, and so forth. Here is an instance where role playing or behavioral rehearsal can be useful. The client can practice with the therapist, who can model appropriate remarks, who can play the role of a rejecting person, and who can also model rational thinking, such as "There's someone I could talk to. But what if he doesn't want to talk to me? Well, if he doesn't, he doesn't. I can survive it. It wouldn't be the end of the world. I can accept myself even so. It might be interesting to see what happens."

Some clients tell us that they see the value of risk-taking exercises but "can't do it" because "I'd be too scared." In such cases, as with shame-attacking exercises, we have sometimes gone with them to an appropriate place—the street, a store, or a train station—and done the exercise ourselves, so that the clients could observe the outcome. In every case, the clients have then done the exercise themselves and were usually less hesitant to carry out other exercises on their own. Another reason for holding a therapy session away from the office is that the topic of discussion—for instance, rejection—becomes more immediate and more real. Instead of talking about what it *would be* like to experience rejection, we can talk about what it *was* like. Instead of the client's reflecting on what he *would* tell himself if he were rejected, we can talk about what he *did* tell himself. The therapy becomes more salient and less intellectual and abstract. For certain clients, especially those who engage in intellectual defenses, this can be very helpful.

We do not have to leave the office in some instances to achieve this immediacy. We can simulate feared situations in our office surroundings. For instance, a client presented as one of her problems a strong hesitance to return phone calls, something that was a part of her job. When she and the therapist discussed this hesitance, it became evident that she was afraid of saying the wrong thing and that, consequently, the person she was talking to would not like her. The therapist suggested that she take the phone, dial a number at random, and talk to whoever answered. After she and the therapist discussed at some length her responses of "I can't" and "it would be silly," she agreed to do so and came up with the idea of taking a survey about interest in skiing. She made the call and then made a number of others as homework. Knaus (1975) describes this technique as "rational-emotive problem simulation," a technique that has wide application, limited only by the inventiveness of the therapist.

Shame-Attacking Exercises. Shame-attacking exercises (Ellis, 1969a) have a higher probability of obtaining rejection or disapproval than risk-taking exercises have. For example, as a risk-taking exercise, we might ask a client to walk up to a stranger on the street and attempt to begin a conversation; as a shame-attacking exercise, we would ask him to walk up to a stranger on the street and break into song. Shame-attacking exercises are directed specifically to overcoming the emotion that occurs when others disapprove of us, given the idea "I must be approved in order to be worthwhile." More to the point, the exercises are directed toward overcoming the *fear* of disapproval; just as the person with a fear of snakes avoids snakes at all costs, many people avoid actions or appearances they consider shameful. Thus, a person may be socially inhibited because she is afraid of saying the "wrong" thing; she may be compulsively proper because she fears what others would think; she may even fail to form her own opinions and values because she fears that others will not agree.

In assigning a shame-attacking exercise, we are asking a client to do something that he would not intentionally consider doing and that—on those rare, accidental occasions when he has behaved in that manner—led to shame, humiliation, mortification. For instance, a man who always *has* to appear impeccably dressed discovers that his fly is open. In shame-attacking exercises, it is not important that people in fact think badly of us (for most often we do not know what others are thinking); it is sufficient that we *think* that they think so. Here are some examples of shame-attacking exercises:

- Calling out the stops on a subway, train, or bus.
- Calling out the time while walking through a department store.
- Facing the rear in a crowded elevator.
- Dressing in a silly or inappropriate manner, such as a woman wearing jeans to a fancy restaurant or a man wearing his tie around his forehead.
- Trying to sell yesterday's newspaper.
- Wearing a sign displaying one's "weakness," such as "I am anxious."

Shame-attacking exercises are assigned in the same way as risk-taking exercises. That is, the rationale is explained to the client, and the client is asked to think of something that would be shameful for him or her. What one person considers shameful, of course, may not seem shameful to another; therefore, these exercises, like risk-taking exercises, should be individualized and not come from any set list, such as the one just given, although lists can be useful in explaining to the client what shame-attacking exercises are. Given the idea and rationale of shame-attacking exercises, clients can be quite inventive in thinking up their own. For instance, these have come from our clients: lying on the floor of an art museum and photographing the ceiling; getting into a trash container on a street and saying "thank you" to people depositing trash; playing a piano badly in a music store. Particularly with shame-attacking exercises we have this injunction: Do not do anything that would get you arrested or fired from your job. For instance, walking down the street nude may be a shame-attacking exercise for someone, but in all likelihood many other behaviors that are not illegal could serve the same purpose.

Together, shame-attacking exercises and risk-taking exercises are perhaps the most important form of homework in RET. By engaging in the feared behaviors and experiencing the feared outcomes, the client has a first-hand opportunity to become aware of and change his or her evaluations of these consequences. It is one thing to say, for instance, "I know it is not awful to be laughed at"; it is another to experience the laughter and to actively combat the idea that it is indeed awful. We are remiss as therapists when we do not encourage clients to engage in such behavioral homework.

Antiprocrastination Exercises. Some clients come to therapy complaining specifically about procrastinating: "I can't get myself to write my thesis," "I never seem to be able to get my work done on time," and so on. Some clients may present other problems, but in the course of therapy we may discover that they are procrastinating, postponing, or not doing the homework they have agreed to do. Procrastination will be maintained by low frustration tolerance or discomfort anxiety, deriving from ideas such as "I must be comfortable," "Things should come easy," and "I shouldn't have to do hard things." As illustrated in the preceding chapter, the person who is procrastinating may also have other emotional problems, which interrelate with the low frustration tolerance.

Some cognitive methods of helping the client rethink and dispute such ideas were presented earlier in this chapter (see also Ellis and Knaus, 1977). Here we will focus on behavioral homework, keeping in mind that discussions about such homework with the client would be in the context of the irrational ideas underlying the procrastination. What type of homework would we assign, for example, to a person who is not getting his work done on time and therefore must work late and on weekends to get it done?

Often a beneficial first step is to suggest that the client keep a diary, in which he notes what he was doing at various periods during each day, including perhaps where he was doing it and what he was thinking at the time. The diary can help both the therapist and the client get a fairly clear picture of how he spends his time. Given this record (the client may have a fairly clear picture without the diary), we can ask what behavioral changes would seem reasonable for him in order to get his work done on time. For example, he may spend most of the morning talking with others before he settles down for his work. (Even this example is not so simple. This person may not be doing his work because of difficulty in breaking off conversations, for instance, rather than reluctance to do the work.) He may say (or we might suggest), "This week I'll just say hello to the others when I arrive and get right to my work."

Usually such suggestions are rather obvious to the client, for that is exactly what the client has not been doing. Along with assigning the homework, however, we want to explore with the client the ideas that may keep him from making the change, pointing out his short-term hedonistic philosophy. We may also point out that he is misusing principles of behavior modification; that is, he has arranged for the reward (talking to others) to come before the behavior (doing the work). He would be wise, therefore, to reverse the sequence, rewarding himself for a morning's work by having lunch with his friends, penalizing himself for not doing the work by eating alone. Also, drawing upon principles of behavior modification, we would explain that the reward of keeping his job lies somewhere in the future. Short-term rewards and penalties will be much more effective in helping him change his behavior.

In discovering with clients effective rewards and penalties, we follow the methods used in behavior therapy. Our clients often seem to have a difficult time thinking of an effective reward. To be effective, a reward should be not only reinforcing for the individual but also fairly immediate. A trip to Europe may be highly reinforcing, but it is not a reward that can be administered each day. Perhaps one of the most useful and accessible rewards to be used in therapy follows the Premack principle (Premack, 1959), which essentially states that behaviors with a low frequency of occurrence can be reinforced by desirable high-frequency behaviors. For example, if our client enjoys reading at bedtime each night, the reading at bedtime can be used as a reward for his doing the neglected work and can be withheld when he has not done it.

After a discussion of rewards and penalties, our clients often choose specific penalties and ignore rewards. Penalties can be effective, particularly when the client views the short-term penalty as significantly more onerous than the short-term discomfort or anxiety of engaging in the desired behavior. For instance, a client, a black woman, wanted more companionship but would not bring herself to talk to new people. She had a good intellectual understanding of her problems—that she feared rejection, that she feared discomfort, and that she was choosing immediate comfort rather than facing and overcoming her anxieties. Despite this understanding, and even though she agreed to attempt the risk-taking homework of talking to a stranger each week, she would invariably return without having done so. After she and the therapist discussed and rediscussed her discomfort anxiety and after she tried out various rewards and penalties that were not effective, she agreed that, if she did not talk to at least one new person that week, she would send fifty dollars to George Wallace's campaign fund. Before she returned the next week, she had talked to five strangers.

In-session simulations also can be used. If a person says, "I can't get to my writing," the person can be asked to write during the session. If a person says, "I can't make telephone calls," the person can be asked to do so during the session. If a person says, "I can't get started on a diet," a box of cookies can be set out during the session. In-session simulations like these primarily serve a diagnostic function. However, as stated earlier in this chapter, the feelings and ideas associated with the avoided behavior become more salient and immediate when simulations are used, and heightened awareness of these feelings and ideas is an important first step in changing them.

We will conclude this section and the entire presentation of behavioral techniques with a reminder. Behavioral techniques are used in RET to diagnose and change irrational ideas, thereby helping people acquire a philosophy of self and the world that will enable them to choose whether to engage in any particular behavior. It is sometimes easy to be caught up in trying to help the client change a specific behavior, especially when the client views it as crucial. For instance, the man who gets his work in late may actually have been told that he will be fired in a month if he does not change. Or a student may come to a counseling center a week before finals and say he has not been able to study all semester. If we focus solely on specific behavioral changes that will enable the man to keep his job or the student to stay in school, we will simply provide short-term solutions to presumably long-term problems. We may decide to take this approach, but then we also point out that the client is likely to face similar crises in the future if he changes only this specific behavior.

Creative RET

Now that we have discussed a number of techniques that can be used to help people change irrational thinking, it may appear that RET—with its emphasis on rational thinking, logic, evidence, semantic accuracy, and personal philosophies of living—is primarily a straightforward logical approach. While we are not thoroughly convinced that the difference between the right and left cerebral hemispheres is as well established or has as many implications as its proponents claim, the distinction can be a useful one in therapy. The left brain is the hemisphere that appears to operate linearly, using verbal and mathematical symbols and leading to analytic and logical thinking. The right brain is the hemisphere that supposedly functions nonlinearly and nonverbally, using images and patterns (as opposed to discrete information) and leading to creative divergent thinking. (For a thorough discussion of left and right brain differences, see Watzlawick, 1978.)

Referring to the literature on the effectiveness of direct persuasion on attitude change, Zajonc (1980, p. 159) concludes: "This approach has been the least successful in attitude change. Even the most convincing arguments on the merits of spinach won't reduce a child's aversion to this vegetable. Direct persuasion effects have been so weak that researchers have instead turned to more pernicious avenues of attitude change, such as insufficient justification, persuasion through distraction, the foot-in-the-door technique, or the bogus pipeline." From cognitive and social psychology, Zajonc marshals a variety of evidence suggesting that, unlike other steps in information processing, affect (appraisal, *B,* or Step 5 of the emotional episode) is processed in the right hemisphere. His theory is an intriguing one for therapists who want to help clients change appraisals.

Most examples of disputing irrational ideas have a decided left-brain quality as clients are challenged to prove the validity of their evaluative conclusions, and the emphasis on problem solving suggests fairly linear thinking, converging on an optimal solution. The fact is that most of the therapy part of RET, in contrast to the assessment part, can be viewed as directed to the right brain. For this reason, we encourage therapists to bring their own creativity and divergent thinking into the therapeutic process.

When a client who shows insight or intellectual understanding of a problem does not change (that is, continues to act on irrational premises rather than rational ones), the therapist had best "talk to the right brain." One way to do this is through risk-taking or shame-attacking experiences. Watzlawick (1978) describes a compulsive graduate student who overcame his perfectionistic philosophy and resultant behavior by deliberately acting imperfectly and making mistakes. Watzlawick did not cite this as an example of RET homework, but indeed it is, as we have just discussed.

Another way of going beyond mere intellectual acknowledgment of irrational belief systems is to use vivid images—for instance, through cognitive rehearsal (Raimy, 1975)—to pierce the barrier of habitual, automatic irrational thinking. For example, a woman who is afraid to go to a disco with her husband is asked to imagine the scene and describe her anticipations. She fears ridicule for her awkward dancing (she also fears her husband's displeasure if she does not go with him to the disco). But mostly she fears the discomfort of experiencing the anxiety when (she supposes) people laugh at her. The client is asked how long people will laugh and replies, "about ten seconds." She is asked if they will laugh simultaneously or in sequence, orderly taking turns. *She* laughs at the image of their taking turns. She is asked to imagine the worst: each of thirty people will laugh in turn for ten seconds each, for a total of 300 seconds or five minutes. Can she bear her discomfort for five minutes? She imagines that she bears it. The next step is to do it—the behavioral and experiential homework for which she has just now rehearsed in imagery. She succeeds and spontaneously uses the imagery technique to help her face other situations that she might otherwise have avoided.

Mottoes, stories, parables, witty sayings, poems, aphorisms, and jokes have been used by RET practitioners. Rational songs (Ellis, 1977b) with memorable lyrics can alter the views one has of self and of the world, including other people. Personalized statements can have the same effect. In one group, two men had anger problems. Each understood intellectually that his anger was due to his demands and to blaming others when they did not meet his demands. Also, each could repeat intellectual disputes quite adequately, but for each the anger remained. One responded well when the therapist labeled him Robert the Rule Maker, saying that it reminded him that he had no special right to make rules for everyone, especially his wife. Since rule making was very dissonant with his self-image of being helpful and understanding, kind and considerate, the label helped him reduce his demands, his blaming, and his anger. The other responded to the therapist's making for him a name tag bearing his "true identity"—GOD.

There are several advantages to working creatively with clients rather than relying on a set of techniques. One is that personalized interventions are more likely to be recalled and applied in everyday life. Second is that it keeps therapy from becoming stale and mechanical. Robert would not have responded if he had been given the GOD name tag, he said; and

"GOD" said that calling him "Joe the Rule Maker" would not have reached him (it simply lacks the alliterative impact of the double *r* sounds). Third, it keeps the therapist interested, as people's problems are very similar.

Perhaps the most frequently overlooked form of right-brain tactics consists of therapeutic use of wit and humor. We know of no foolproof way to train therapists to have keener wits and highly developed senses of humor, but we urge people who have them to use them with clients, taking care to direct humor at the client's irrational ideas and not at the client. Exaggeration, in the manner of Dr. Seuss, is often effective. Puns are good, too. Clients may remember an outrageous pun a good deal longer than a well-reasoned explanation of how human complexity makes self-rating illegitimate. Most humor is spontaneous, but occasionally one spontaneously thinks of an idea that bears repeating. Once, when working with a perfection-demanding client, one of us said, "You're trying to be too perfect to be human. You're trying to create a new species—*homo angelicus.*" The Latin may have been corrupt, but the phrase hit the target, bringing a laugh from the client, and he was left with a memorable image. We have used it since, at times with similar impact.

Ellis's (1977a) statement that emotional disturbance largely consists of simply taking ourselves and things in general overseriously is worth repeating. Our attempts at humor, even if they do not always succeed, show the client that *we* do not take things overseriously, including our sense of humor.

We cannot report all possible "right-brain" tactics, and it is not our intention to furnish a list of specific interventions. Rather, we hope to stimulate responsible creativity in therapy. RET is not merely a collection of techniques, or a pugnacious way of interacting with clients. It is an outlook on life that says that nothing in the natural or social world is awful or terrible, although humans may create terror in their minds by their evaluative thoughts; that humans are neither saints nor sinners; that reality can be acknowledged and tolerated even when it seems exceedingly grim; and that there are no absolute rules for living.

It is not necessary to use RET jargon with clients, or to lecture them about the *ABC* theory. Indeed, we recommend against these practices. It is important for therapists to use whatever tactics they can competently and ethically employ to help clients alter their outlooks on themselves, other people, and conditions of the world.

7

Assessing Progress and Overcoming Obstacles

Psychotherapy is a process that eventually comes to an end. Sometimes therapy ends for external reasons; for instance, the therapist or the client might move from the area. Occasionally, it ends because the client desires to stop although the therapist may judge that further therapy would be beneficial. Ideally, therapy ends by mutual agreement that the client's goals have been achieved. An important part of therapy, then, is assessing the progress that the client is making toward the achievement of his goals. If we build into our approach methods of checking on what progress our clients are or are not making, termination simply becomes an agreement between therapist and client that sufficient progress has taken place and that the client has acquired the skills to maintain and continue the progress on his own.

Therefore, when a client states that she has changed in some desired way, perhaps is feeling less anxious, our questions are: What is the nature of that change? Has the client made the kinds of attitudinal changes that we, as therapists, have as the goal of her therapy? To answer these questions, we look for two types of evidence: (1) evidence that the client has changed attitudes—not that he has *eliminated* irrational thinking but, rather, that he has *minimized* irrational thinking to the point where it occurs less frequently and for a shorter period of time; (2) evidence that the client has acquired coping skills to deal with irrational thinking when it recurs. Some reported changes in feelings and/or behaviors may have resulted from factors other than attitude change. Take, for example, a client, once fearful of rejection and needing approval, who describes herself as no longer distressed. Several possible changes may have occurred. One possibility is that there simply has been a change in *A*. For example, she may have found a new lover (*A*) through no real effort on her part, which has led to a change in *C,* feeling happy, without a change in *B,* "If I did not have this lover, it would be awful and I would be no good." However, even if there has clearly been a change in *A,* a new lover in this case, that does not rule out an attitude change at *B.* In fact, acquiring the new lover may have occurred at the same time as, or even because of, a change at *B.*

One way to try to check out what changes have occurred is to review the progress that has taken place and then to ask the client to account for that change. Let us say our client had presented the problem of feeling anxious around others, particularly members of the opposite sex, and had been feeling lonely and depressed. Later on, the client is no longer feeling lonely, in fact has a new lover, and is quite happy. Is she ready for termination? Here are some examples of questions that can be asked:

- You're feeling differently now. How is that different from when you started therapy?

- Are you doing anything differently now than when you came into therapy?

These and similar questions ask the client to specify changes that have occurred. Particularly if the client reports feeling better without also reporting changes in behavior, we might suspect that no philosophical changes have taken place. Our client may have acquired her new lover, for instance, because *he* was attracted to her and because *he* took the initiative in beginning the relationship. Although behavioral changes are not always criteria for successful therapy (a person may have previously engaged in many activities anxiously and now can do the same things with little or no anxiety), such changes usually indicate that attitudinal changes have taken place. We view skeptically the client who says, "I no longer believe I would be worthless if no one liked me," but who still does not speak up in groups, confront others who are annoying, or initiate conversations.

Continuing to search for evidence, let us say our client reports feeling better and/or behaving differently. Our next question would be similar to these:

- What has happened for you to change?
- How do you account for that change?

These are open-ended questions which allow the client to attribute a variety of reasons for that change. If we hear something like "Well, now I have John, and when I came here I had no one," we would be skeptical. If we hear no evidence of attitudinal change, we can try some more leading questions:

- How have *you* changed?
- In what way are *you* different now?
- Did *you* do anything to lead to this change?

If the client does not state changes in attitudes by this time, we have good reason to doubt that such changes have taken place.

A recent example of a behavioral change reported by a client to her therapist in her seventh session went something like this:

C: I didn't get so angry with Joe this week when we were working together.
T: What was different for you?
C: Well, whenever he would get irritable, I just left for a bit and cooled off. Usually I'd stay and try to calm him down, and I'd just get more angry myself.

In the session the therapist did not pursue the matter further, perhaps thinking that his client's anger had not changed but that she simply was handling it differently. However, she *was* handling it differently, and the question becomes: What accounts for that change? A possible pursuit of this question could go like this:

T: So your leaving instead of trying to talk him out of his anger was different?
C: Yes, it was.
T: And it helped you feel less angry.
C: Yes, I quickly got over it.
T: In the past, why do you think you stayed?
C: Well, I couldn't stand his being angry with me.
T: And this week, what was different?
C: Well, I thought, "If he's angry, he's angry. I'm sorry, but talking him out of it doesn't work."
T: And why would you have had to talk him out of it?
C: So he wouldn't be so upset with me.
T: And what did you tell yourself this week when he was angry?
C: Well, I said to myself, "So he's angry. That's not the end of the world. And it's not my fault."

This example shows also that some further work remains to be done by this client; for, although she countered her previous awfulizing, "That's not the end of the world," she also handled her response to his anger by changing her conception of *A*, "And it's not my fault," which, although possibly true in this case, leaves the question of what if it were her fault? The logical next step is to ask that question, which is an example of anticipating the occurrence of the problem in the future.

Anticipating problems that could occur in the future is another method of checking out attitudinal changes. We want to do this with clients who in fact report attitudinal change in the present: "Well, I have John now, and I no longer believe that I would be worthless if I were alone." Anticipating problems for the client is using the "What if . . ." technique. Knowing what situations have given the client difficulties in the past, we can anticipate their recurrence:

- OK, now, I'm not suggesting this is going to happen, but what if you lose John?

Or if the client has had a fear of failure:

- What if you get fired?

Or if the client has been afraid that she would do a poor job as a mother:

- What if your kids grow up to hate you?

Clients who have made attitudinal changes usually handle such questions with equanimity, while clients who have not made such changes may show distress. The distress indicates the desirability for further therapy. Our task is to point this out as clearly as we can and show the client that, although a short-term solution has been achieved (for instance, John), problems similar to the presenting problem are simply latent and can recur, given the proper circumstances.

In checking on progress, we use open-ended questions because we do not want to put words in our clients' mouths. If we did so, we would not know whether the attitudinal changes then expressed were actual changes or merely the parroting of our words. If clients cannot, on their own, express changes in awfulizing, demandingness, and evaluation of self or others, they probably have not changed these philosophies. If a client can express such changes, we would still want to check out the client's understanding. A good way to do so, as mentioned in

Chapter Six, is to challenge the client's rational beliefs. For instance, when our client said, "Well, I have John now, and I no longer believe I would be worthless if I were alone," we could respond with "Why not?" or "When would you be worthless?" If she answered the first question with "I don't know," or if she answered the second question by supplying a condition, more therapy remains.

We cannot emphasize enough the importance of probing the basis for clients' rational beliefs. For example, in his third therapy session, a client said that he was going to remind himself each morning that he "was not a shit." While the therapist agreed that that was an excellent idea and that he might try a sign on his bathroom mirror to that effect, she said, "OK, I agree you're not a shit—a worthless person—now, you tell me why you are not." He responded by listing his desirable qualities, primarily his good nature with others and his intellect. In typical RET style, the therapist pointed out that he could lose both of these attributes by suffering brain damage in an auto accident on the way home that night and asked, "Then why wouldn't you be a shit?" He was stumped and, after further discussion, agreed to do more reading and thinking for his homework, so that he could answer the question. Without the understanding of *why* he could never be worthless, his reminder of "I am not a shit" could be helpful, but much in the same way that whistling in the dark is helpful.

How about those clients who indicate that they have indeed made attitudinal changes? Under the assumption that we do not completely eliminate irrational thinking but, rather, minimize its occurrence, we would want to find out *how* the client has achieved that change. Our purpose here is twofold. First, we want to ascertain that the client is not using superficial coping devices, such as "I don't care if I fail" (for how about the times she may well care?) or "It's irrational to think I'm a worm" (with no understanding of *how* it is irrational) or "Feeling guilty won't help me" (which is probably true but does not attack the thinking behind the guilt). Second, assuming that the client has found effective and valid means of challenging her beliefs, we want to have the client become openly aware of what she has done in the past to combat irrational thinking, so that she can use these strategies in the future, when the old patterns of thinking recur. We want to help people learn to cope with problems of living, since they will not solve these problems once and for all. Here again, review and anticipation are useful.

Review:

- What did you tell yourself to get up the courage to meet John?
- When you didn't get that job you wanted, how did you keep yourself from feeling so lousy?

Anticipation:

- Suppose John leaves you. What can you tell yourself to make it a bit easier?
- What if you find yourself getting depressed again, which you probably will. What can you do to get yourself out of it?

If the client has effectively challenged and reduced irrational thinking and is aware of the means by which she did so, anticipation of future problems can be used to good effect, both to give the client further practice in disputing irrational ideas and to reinforce the fact that problems will occur, whether they are anticipated or not.

Lack of Progress—Client Variables

Psychotherapists of any persuasion know that not all clients make the progress desired. Although the therapist often contributes to lack of progress when it occurs, clients do present certain difficulties and have certain characteristics that may interfere with the progress of their therapy. Specifically, progress (that is, the reduction of the intensity and duration of dysfunctional emotions created by irrational thinking through changing that thinking) can be impeded because clients do not present emotional problems appropriate to this goal or have different expectations about how change takes place.

Lack of an Emotional Problem. The sensitive RET practitioner recognizes that some problems simply will not yield to RET or to any other form of verbal psychotherapy. Psychosis, for example, is either demonstrably physical in origin—the organic syndromes—or most likely has a physical, biochemical basis—the functional psychoses. RET is intended for reducing neurotic disturbance, although one need not be diagnosed as neurotic to have neurotic problems. RET can help persons diagnosed as psychotic with their neurotic problems, but RET will not eliminate the psychosis. Furthermore, some psychotic individuals are so severely disturbed that psychotherapy is not indicated.

Other nonemotional problems are practical problems in living. It is probably clear by now that RET practitioners cannot get misbehaving spouses, children, parents, bosses, neighbors, and the like, to mend their ways to suit clients' preferences. We can and do suggest ways of influencing other people's behavior, such as better communications, frank discussions, disclosure of personal wishes, and negotiated mutual reinforcement agreements. We coach parents on better ways to discipline children, children on ways to cope with teachers, and so on. We advocate and sometimes teach intelligent ways of trying to get what one wants (or, in RET terminology, to change *A*).

One set of practical problems has to do with personal finances. The grim fact of many people's existence is that they barely have enough money to support themselves and may not have enough to create as many options as they would like. While the RET practitioner can help them accept this unfortunate situation and perhaps work out some plans to change it, RET by itself cannot make a difference in the family's fortunes. One of us supervised a therapist who worked at a community mental health clinic. One of this therapist's clients, a single parent, was concerned about her finances and the support of her young child. The therapist wisely refrained from talking as though the only problem were self-disturbing irrational beliefs; in fact, the woman was quite rational in her thinking about her impoverished state. But why, then, was she seen by a therapist instead of by someone who could help her with her personal finances? The social system defines many problems as psychological when they are not. Likewise, prisoners or convicted criminals may be referred for counseling when they have little intention or desire to change. Let us make sure that we are dealing with *emotional* problems when we are attempting to use RET with our clients.

Involuntary referrals constitute a special case. Some clients may indeed be right when they say that they have no emotional problem. A convicted thief may not experience guilt for his crime and may not have committed it out of fear, hostility, depression, or some other emotional state. An adolescent, court referred for runaway behavior, may have emotional problems but may see the cause in the home situation and the solution as escape. In these examples neither client wants to change. What can the therapist do? As with any client, the therapist can try to find ways in which the client *wants* to change. Sometimes this is possible. For example, if they are given information about how change takes place in therapy, some clients who are not voluntary or self-referred can be helped to discover emotions and behaviors that they might want to change. They may not know about the importance of identifying specific issues to work on with the therapist, and they may lack a working definition of "problem." For example, one of the authors was consulted by a 13 year old who had had considerable psychotherapy beginning at age 6 or 7. Her past experience with therapists was that they either "played games with you" (although she knew she was a little too old for that) or "listened and sometimes told you how you really felt about your mother and father." After a few exploratory, rapport-building sessions with her, it became clear that she did not know that the therapist expected her to bring up problems for discussion. Wanting to give her more responsibility than she had had previously, the therapist explained that the task of therapy was to learn ways to solve problems, including those that may occur in the future. Therefore, she was asked to bring in three problems for discussion each week.

"How do I know if I have a problem?" she asked. "Good question," replied the therapist, pleased with her insight and initiative in speaking up. "A problem is first of all anything *you* think is a problem. Second, it is usually something you are doing that you would rather not do, like an annoying habit. And third, it is when you'd like to do something that for one reason or another you aren't doing." Armed with this definition, she returned for several sessions with enough *A*s for easy entry into her belief system. An unexpected benefit was that she now had more or less objective criteria for defining a problem and therefore a way of sorting out those problems her mother said she had from those that were truly bothersome for her.

Some clients who are involuntarily referred exhibit problems deriving primarily from a philosophy of low frustration tolerance. These are *some* of the individuals referred by schools, agencies, and courts or *some* of the inmates of penal or detention institutions. In all probability, these clients will not desire personal change. If we are to engage in psychotherapy with these individuals, our task is to convince them that change is in their best interest—not in our interest or in the interest of the court, relatives, or society. Our task is to show these clients that their impulsive behavior, engaged in for the pleasure, excitement, or relief of the moment, is likely to lead to undesirable consequences in the long run. If the client has some long-term goals—a career, for instance—that he or she is sabotaging by impulsive behavior, we have an entrée. However, many of these individuals have not developed or have given up on long-term goals, except perhaps survival. Our task is much more difficult here, for the first step is to help these clients develop some long-term goals that they can value *and* have some reasonable hope they can achieve. In our therapy sessions we may not be able to accomplish this with our clients. In our opinion, they are most likely to develop values and goals over time if they identify with one or more valued persons through observational or social learning (Bandura, 1969). To work with such clients is not easy. The therapist who chooses to do so had better have a very high frustration tolerance. If the therapist could convince these clients that change would be beneficial to them, then much of the work of therapy would be completed. If these clients came to view change as desirable, they already would be shifting to a longer-term hedonistic viewpoint, away from the short-term hedonistic viewpoint implied in low frustration tolerance.

Our final set of recommendations concerning the problem of clients who do not identify any emotional problems is to work toward a molar or holistic understanding of such clients. It is very easy to misuse RET and to work only on problems brought up by the client. If we have a useful theory or model of a particular client, we can deduce emotional problems that this person might have. As with any model, the deductions had best be tested against reality for goodness of fit. Once again, we are stressing the assessment phase of RET. Since there is no formal assessment procedure in RET, we cannot give systematic rules to follow other than our suggestions in Chapter Five. We urge therapists to listen and use all their remaining senses, because nonverbal cues, although elusive, are rich sources of information. They will want to listen especially for self-descriptive words, unusual uses of words, rules or philosophies of living, and other clues to the individual's belief system. Bit by bit, a mosaic *representing* this particular client is formed. The mosaic will be only suggestive at first and may never be completed. But by probing for information, we can test our hypotheses about the client.

Experienced RET practitioners can discover belief systems and create mental mosaics of people by simply listening to what they say. Even a poor session of RET can produce data bits for the mosaic. Albert Ellis, when working with clients whom he has frequently seen, at times closes his eyes and listens to them present new problems. After a few minutes, he may break his silence by saying, "I'm going to take a flier. It sounds like you're saying to yourself. . . ." Listening and inferring, then *testing* these inferences, are active processes. Spontaneous remarks sometimes produce the best clues. One of us recently supervised a therapist who role-played an attractive female rejecting the client by saying, "I'd never go out with you. You're the world's biggest jerk!" The client responded by saying he would feel "flabbergasted against the wall" at such a remark. The therapist continued teaching social skills via role playing, but we were struck by the richness of this malapropism. Had he been our client, we would have quickly formulated a hypothesis based on this spontaneously expressed idea. Our hypothesis was that he felt surprised, caught off guard, and helpless. Thus, instead of rehearsing him more carefully to anticipate her rejection and be prepared for it, we would have led him into a discussion of getting caught unprepared. If our hypothesis was confirmed, we would ask him to discover that being caught unprepared is not awful (unless he defines it as such) and that his need for certainty was more salient here than either his fear of disapproval or his lack of social skills. We would suggest that he adopt experimentally the motto "Leap before you look."

Client Expectations. What clients expect from therapy and from their therapists may be at wide variance with their therapists' expectations. We will discuss four relatively common expectations that clients hold: that others must change in order for oneself to change; that one must delve into the past in order to change; that one must have a warm, friendly therapist in order to change; and that the therapist will magically bring about desirable changes in one's life, with little or no effort on the client's part.

The expectations about therapy that a client holds had better be discussed openly from the outset, as we noted in Chapter Four. But even after careful explanation of the *ABC*s by the therapist, many clients who do present emotional problems would rather, by and large, have someone else bear, or at least share, the responsibility for their problems. Although our discussion will center on marriage partners, the same principles hold for other family members. Children may attribute the source of their disturbance to parents and want the therapist to see the parents. Parents may want children seen. Whatever other messages they may be giving us (such as "If you think I'm disturbed, you ought to see my relatives" or "You'll understand that I can't change once you see those I live with"), our clients want us to change an important source of activating events in their lives. Typically, a married client (or one in a close nonmarital relationship) may blame his spouse or attribute the major portion of the problem to the spouse. At times this may be realistic, for the spouse may indeed be disturbed or may regularly act in ways that displease the client. Then comes the plea to the therapist: "You talk with her." Can therapists succeed in inducing change in the spouse when the client has not? If the therapist could, would it be a good idea to do so? In short, shall the therapist see the spouse?

There are certain advantages in conducting a session with the spouse. First, we may get some information that will help in the task of persuading the client to change irrational thinking into saner, more self-satisfying philosophies. Second, we may gain the client's confidence. The simple act of interviewing a spouse may encourage the client to realize that we want to help. Third, the spouse probably could benefit from some saner thinking in his or her life also. Most people do. And perhaps the client is right—the spouse may be more disturbed than the client is. But let us add a word of caution here. RET does not subscribe to the view that every significant figure in the client's life has to change his or her behavior, communicate more accurately, or treat the client more humanely, as desirable as these notions may be. The client's disturbance is not merely a response to other people's disordered behavior. Our task as RET practitioners is to help clients change their evaluations of people's behavior and other antecedents in their lives. When we help spouses change, it is for their benefit and only secondarily to relieve some of the frustration in clients' lives. (Young children are an exception to this rule, as we advocate saner child-rearing practices.)

There are other good reasons to interview the spouse, including the obvious one that the spouse may actually want therapy for himself or herself or may want marriage or relationship counseling. If the spouse has such a desire, it will become apparent. However, the therapist will want to emphasize that the spouse is there not for therapy but to provide information about the client and the client's problems. For if the spouse does not want therapy, and construes the interview to be therapy—meaning he or she should change for the client's benefit—the spouse falls into the category of the "unwilling client." So we recommend careful and explicit structure at the outset of the interview. Even then, some individuals may remain defensive because they simply do not believe us.

What we do after seeing the spouse is critical. If we agree with the client that the spouse must change, we simply encourage irrational thinking in our client by our agreement. However, we may have discovered some new possibilities for the client to try to negotiate a better relationship or to influence the spouse to give up annoying habits, attitudes, and so forth. We discuss these with the client *after* he has made progress on changing self-disturbing perceptions and evaluations. A tack we often take is to agree with the client's version of the spouse, provided it is not too different from our own version of reality. (If it is markedly discrepant, we can work with the client to improve reality testing.) We can point out to the client that the spouse seems unlikely to change very much or very rapidly, and for that reason the client had better work extra hard in changing his irrational beliefs about the spouse, for that is the one way the client can bring himself some modicum of happiness. Thus, the focus is brought back to *B,* the client's beliefs, rather than *A,* the spouse's behavior.

A number of persons have developed expectations of therapy based on the psychoanalytic model. One of the messages such individuals have received—from previous experience in analysis or from articles, novel, or movies they have read or seen—is that insight into past events is crucial for present change. Many clients, whether they expect "analysis" from us or not, do want to explore their recollections of the past. Consequently, we first explain to clients that their interpretations and evaluations of past events (as well as present events) create their disturbance. RET theory rejects the proposition that past messages from parents and other socializing agents constitute the main source of irrational thinking; it is postulated that individuals create perfectionistic and other self-demands without much, if any, aid from parents, who might even try to dissuade them from such unrealistic thinking. Even so, the details of the past can be profitably explored in therapy. There is no reason to rule out such discussions completely, just because we are practicing RET. For instance, Dryden (1979) reports the case of a woman who improved after she discussed her past, *then* disputed the irrational messages she assumed she received from her parents. As long as such explorations do not encourage clients to avoid their present beliefs or to condemn past significant figures or to engage in other activities antithetical to their progress, why not indulge them? We can keep such explorations in perspective and remind our clients that change comes from work, not from insights into the past or recovered lost memories.

Another expectation some clients bring to therapy is that the therapist's warmth, support, and approval is necessary for them to change. Most of these clients probably already have a strong need for approval. They feel adequate only when someone else reassures them, and they refrain from self-denigration only when someone else approves of them. Unfortunately, there is plenty of newsstand psychology to encourage this neurotic need for love. Much of the so-called humanistic psychology is devoted to people's demand for love and attention (to fulfill "needs") and to the obtaining of positive "strokes." Further, many undertrained "counselors" and volunteer workers have little to offer clients other than warmth, support, and encouragement. Although we are not against providing warmth and support or conveying any other humanely motivated attitudes toward clients, there can be danger in actively expressing warmth or liking for a client. We have heard tapes of therapists who say to clients such things as "I really like you." The danger is that the client knows that the therapist does not know everything about him or her, and therefore what is conveyed is, to use Rogers' term, conditional positive reward. Clients, particularly those needing approval, may then continue to behave in ways that have brought this approval, and those ways may not lead to beneficial changes, certainly not to changing the belief "I need another's approval to be a worthwhile person."

Even if the therapist does not actively provide the client with approval, clients who have this expectation, actually the belief that they need approval, may show little progress in therapy. Most clients soon realize that we are pleased with expressions like "RET sure makes a lot of sense to me" or "You're really helping me." What we may be getting is not an expression of progress toward the goal of attitude change but, rather, lip service to a philosophy the client really does not understand but is afraid to tell us for fear that we will disapprove. And although such a client may engage in all sorts of homework assignments, the ultimate goal of attitude change may not take place if the behavior was carried out *in order to* retain the therapist's approval. (This result would be predicted by cognitive dissonance theory, discussed in Chapter Six.)

Since the need for approval is one of the more common problems presented by clients, the message here is simple. If the client believes that he or she needs other people's approval to be worthy or adequate, we can assume that the client also needs the therapist's approval. That approval or potential disapproval (as an activating event) then becomes as much a part of therapy as that of other persons in the client's life. This is the RET version of working with transference. Just as we do not advocate giving approval to the client, we also do not advocate giving disapproval, such as "I don't like you." Instead, we advocate an open discussion of the *possibility* that the therapist may not like the client for one reason or another. For instance, "What if I think you're a louse for not doing your homework?" is worth pursuing or "Even though I like you (perhaps an honest statement), what if I change my mind (an honest possibility)?" Another approach is simply the open discussion of the need for approval, using oneself as the *A*: "You believe that if I don't like you, you're no good. How does that follow?" These are just some examples of efforts to focus on the need for the therapist's (and thus others') approval. For some clients, unless this idea is overtly and actively disputed in therapy, little progress will take place.

Another expectation, perhaps the one that can be most detrimental to progress in therapy, is that change should occur with little effort on one's part. For some clients this may be an expectation developed from experiences with certain medical practitioners, who actively treat the passive patient. For others the expectation derives primarily from a philosophy of low frustration tolerance: "Life should be easy"; "I shouldn't have to do anything that is hard or uncomfortable"; and so forth. Sometimes the first indication we have of this problem is the client's reluctance to engage in homework, particularly behavioral homework. Clients, understandably enough, are often reluctant to attempt behaviors that are different from those they are used to and therefore prefer. There are two main reasons clients give for not carrying out homework tasks. One is the desire to avoid the hassle, inconvenience, or bother of doing so; in other words, to avoid the extra effort they presume it takes to do the homework. Some clients imagine that the homework will consume vast amounts of time, energy, and/or effort or might involve sacrifices too great to bear. The general strategy in working with this problem is to show the client that he or she is exaggerating the amount of difficulty to be encountered. A method of doing this is illustrated below. The second reason clients frequently give for not doing homework is to avoid fear, especially fear of feeling uncomfortable or anxious. Both this fear and the one just described are forms of discomfort anxiety or low frustration tolerance, and both can be treated by the following methods.

First, we may use the *ABC* model to help the client understand the source of her discomfort anxiety or low frustration tolerance. If nothing else, this approach helps clients see that their reluctance is not mere laziness or due to unknown causes. Their inaction, like their other actions, is due to beliefs, perceptions, and desires. Second, the use of cognitive rehearsal, imagery, and step-by-step examination of the anticipated activity can substantially increase the likelihood that clients will do what they have been reluctant to do. We find it particularly helpful to get clients' expectations about the homework activity and to analyze these for their reality content (are the *A*s correctly conceived?) and the evaluative beliefs. Here is a dissuasive dialogue intended to help an accountant reduce his anxieties about mistake making:

T: What homework assignment could you give yourself to work against your perfectionistic philosophy?

C: I guess I'd better not demand perfection of myself.

T: That's a good idea, but not concrete enough. What can you do?

C: Act imperfectly?

T: Sounds good. How about making some mistakes?
C: I couldn't do that. I might get fired.
T: I don't want you to do anything that might threaten your job. What could you do that is relatively harmless?
C: Maybe I could call people by the wrong name—like I forgot their name.
T: How would you feel about doing that?
C: Pretty uneasy.
T: What are you telling yourself to get "uneasy"?
C: That they will think I'm incompetent.
T: And?
C: That they've got to see me as competent.
T: And if they don't?
C: They'll lose respect for me.
T: Let's rehearse. Let's say you're at coffee and you plan to call someone by the wrong name. Can you imagine that? [Client nods.] What would you be feeling?
C: I'd feel very anxious, because I feel that way around them most of the time anyway. I know they'll think I'm an asshole if I make mistakes.
T: How long will you feel anxious?
C: Until I do it. Once I do it, I'll be fine.
T: Sounds like you'd rather not wait. What do you think they will do after you've made your mistake?
C: I don't know. I've never thought about it.
T: Think about it.
C: But I don't think it would be a good idea to try it this week.
T: Why not?
C: I've got a lot to do. Reports to get out. I'll be too busy.
T: How much time do you think it will take? Don't you take coffee breaks every day?
C: Well, yes. But I know I'll worry about it all week.
T: There's an easy remedy for that. Do you know what it is?
C: Do it Monday?

A simple phrase to use to explore and confront irrational ideas and misconceptions is "And then . . . ?" Or we may use the "So what if . . . ?" approach (Lazarus, 1973). The important goal is to get clients to de-awfulize the consequences, experiences, and inconveniences of their homework assignments.

Other factors that lead to reluctance to do homework include negativism, often deriving from the client's belief that no one is going to tell him what to do or has the power to make him change. Most people are more committed to doing things when they have participated in the decision to do them. Thus, it is more effective to ask clients to assign homework to themselves (as in the above dialogue) than to make the assignment like an authoritarian schoolmaster. And, as discussed in Chapter Four, it is also more effective when we can confront clients by saying, "I thought you decided to do . . . ," rather than "I told you to do. . . ." In short, homework is a collaborative effort. Even if we make the assignments in an authoritarian manner, we cannot do the task for the client.

What we can do is to model the activity for the client. Some clients avoid trying new behaviors from ignorance or from a self-defined state of ignorance. The therapist can be supportive and encouraging by modeling the behavior (and the rational thinking that we want to accompany the behavior) for the client. For example, a client who "doesn't know" how to call for an appointment for a job interview can observe the therapist doing this, or the therapist and the client can role-play the telephone call.

Lack of Progress—Therapist Variables

It is often tempting to attribute responsibility for lack of progress to the client. To do so we invoke terms such as "resistance," "transference," "secondary gains," or even "low frustration tolerance," which place fault directly on and within the client. Although the client can impede progress, as we have just discussed, the therapist also can contribute to lack of progress. Since the therapist, as the expert provider of therapeutic services, has the major responsibility for the therapeutic relationship and interaction, lack of progress may be due to the therapist's problems in developing this relationship and in the specific interaction that takes place.

Intrapersonal Problems of the Therapist. Therapists, being as human as their clients, may hold one or more irrational beliefs that can interfere with their clients' progress. One such idea is "I must be approved in order to be worthwhile." Thus, since the goal of the therapist is to be liked, he may not use confrontation when it would be advisable; he may avoid eliciting or discussing painful emotions, for the client might not like that; he may indulge in excessive reassurance and support; he may feel threatened by any expression of annoyance or displeasure toward him by the client. The list can go on.

A second irrational idea that can interfere with clients' progress is "I must be successful in order to be worthwhile." Now the client's progress becomes a measure of the therapist's worth, and any indication of lack of progress becomes a threat. For this idea to lead to feelings of worthlessness, the therapist would also have to believe, "I am responsible for my client's lack of progress." To combat the ensuing guilt if the client does not progress, the therapist may instead believe, "I am not responsible; he is. If he would only cooperate, I could succeed." It is often the need to be successful that leads to conceiving of the client as resistant and makes the therapist particularly susceptible to the power "games" that we will describe later. It is also likely to lead to the related idea "He must improve" and anger when he does not. The anger can be countertherapeutic and sometimes leads to the vicious circle of anger, resistance, more anger, and so on. A different result of the need to succeed is the development of blind spots: assuming progress where none exists. We may go blithely on our way, not checking out the client's progress, for to do so might result in evidence of no change on the client's part, evidence of our failure and thus worthlessness.

The solution for these two irrational ideas that can create problems in the therapeutic process, as well as others we shall discuss, is the same solution we want for our clients—that is, to be aware of them if they exist and to continue to work at changing them. Here is one of the areas in which supervision or consultation can be helpful. Although self-analysis is certainly possible, it is often helpful for a relatively objective observer to point out our problem areas. Some time in personal therapy for those doing therapy is practically always advisable.

Therapists also can interfere with clients' progress by agreeing with clients' irrational ideas. For instance, if a client believes it is awful that a loved one died and we also believe that it is awful, we certainly are not going to try to help the client change that belief. Or the therapist may avoid content areas in which clients have difficulties because she also has fears related to those areas. For instance, if a therapist has doubts about her sexual adequacy and furthermore has the anxiety-creating belief "It would be awful and I'd be no good if I were less than adequate sexually," this therapist may well avoid discussion of sexuality, certainly a disservice to the client if the client also has problems in this area.

Aside from the solution mentioned above, of becoming aware of and working at changing our irrational ideas, a good solution in any particular case is referral. If we recognize that working with a particular client is triggering our own fears and defenses, we can refer that client to another therapist while we continue to work at changing our own thinking. It is not in the client's best interest to keep him or her in therapy with us, using the opportunity to work through our own problems, except perhaps when we have close supervision.

This leads us into the issue of the therapist's self-disclosure in therapy. One rule that seems inviolate is that the therapist is there to give therapy, not to get it. Therapists who share problems in hopes of getting them solved cheat the clients. At the same time, although self-disclosure is probably not therapeutic in itself, it can be useful in establishing rapport and showing clients that the therapist has had the kinds of experiences that promote his understanding of their problems. We can give hope to clients by describing how we overcame a similar problem in the past. Even if we have not completely overcome a problem (which is likely to be the case), say, fear of disapproval, we can mention it, for instance, in the following way: "I used to have severe anxiety attacks, too, so I know what you mean. In fact, I still get anxious from time to time, but now I know how I create my anxiety, and I have ways to talk myself out of it. And, let me tell you, ten minutes of anxiety is a lot different from twenty-four hours' worth." We intend that the client get several messages from such a statement. One is "Here is a person not so different from me. If she can do it, so can I." Another is "Maybe I, too, won't be anxiety free, but that's not so bad." In short, if personal information seems likely to be of benefit to the client, the therapist may decide to use it. If not, there is no valid reason for using it.

Therapists' expectations that may not derive from irrational ideas can also interfere with client progress. One such expectation is that the client can markedly improve in a few sessions. That may be the case for some clients; however, for many other clients change takes much longer. As a result of this expectation, the therapist impedes therapeutic progress by behaviors such as covering a wide variety of client problems in a single session or overloading the client with homework—behaviors we will discuss in more detail later. A solution to the problems created by this expectation is to keep in mind that the term *short-term psychotherapy* does not mean just a few sessions. The phrase came into use primarily as a contrast to classical psychoanalysis, which can last for years.

A related set of expectations is that bright, verbally sophisticated clients will readily understand the difficult concepts we are attempting to teach and that one explanation of these concepts is sufficient. Because of these expectations, we may leap from topic to topic during a session, assuming that the first topic was sufficiently explored and understood; we may do little exploration of rational and irrational ideas, assuming that the distinction is understood; and we may do little actual checking of the client's progress.

The solution to the problems created by these or any other set of expectations is to keep in mind that expectations are based on samples—samples of people, "Most bright, verbally sophisticated clients . . . ," or of events, "Most of the time in the past . . ."—and that there are always exceptions to the rule. If my rule is (we will assume its validity) "Ninety percent of bright, verbally sophisticated clients readily understand the concepts of RET," the question still is "Is my client sitting here one of the 90 percent or one of the 10 percent?" I had better check it out, for in the individual case, given that or any other rule, I am either 100 percent right or 100 percent wrong.

The expectations just discussed are examples of possible assumptions or hypotheses held by the therapist. It is not assumptions per se that can lead to difficulty in the therapeutic process (if we believed that, we would have omitted discussion of RET theory in this book) but *unvalidated* assumptions held by the therapist that may impede progress of the client. Carl Jung is quoted as saying, "Learn your theories as well as you can, but put them aside when you touch the miracle of a living soul" (Kaufmann, 1979, p. 110). There is much wisdom in that statement. We would change it slightly and less poetically: "Learn your RET theory as well as you can, use it as a guide, but check out all theoretical and personal assumptions when you touch the miracle of a living soul."

One assumption that, if not true, can lead to problems in working with a client is "My client and I are working toward the same goal." Clients who believe that the therapist does not understand them or is trying to make them change in ways unacceptable to them may resist actively or passively. A sign of active resistance is arguing. When the therapist finds herself being drawn into an argument with the client, that often indicates a lack of therapeutic alliance. Arguing is seldom therapeutic. The solution is to break off the argument and continue to explore the therapeutic goals with the client. Two people who agree on the same goal and on the means to achieve that goal will not argue. A related assumption, then, is that the client understands the means to achieve his goal—in other words, that he understands the RET approach. Arguing or other forms of resistance signal that this assumption also is to be checked.

Interpersonal Style. Some clients may not progress in therapy because of the therapist's failure to be sensitive to the interpersonal style of the client and her subsequent failure to respond therapeutically to the client's typical style of interaction. The client's inflexibility of interpersonal behavior makes him difficult to work with unless the therapist is flexible. To portray the interactions between therapists and clients, we have used a simple categorization with good results. Two major dimensions emerge in the study of interpersonal behavior: an affective dimension, anchored by words like *unfriendly* or *hostile* at one end of the continuum and *friendly* or *warm* at the other end; and a power dimension, anchored by *dominance* and *submission* at either extreme (Carson, 1969). These two dimensions or factors were identified in Leary's (1957) pre-LSD research and bear a striking resemblance to two of the three main factors—namely, the factors labeled "evaluative" and "potency" —identified by Osgood, Suci, and Tannenbaum (1957) in their analysis of connotative meanings of words. The intersecting of these two dimensions yields a fourfold classification scheme. In Carson's (1969) terminology, the four types are friendly-dominant, friendly-submissive, hostile-submissive, and hostile-dominant. Two propositions have received support: (1) In stable, continuing interactions, there is consistency within the affective dimension; that is, hostile behavior tends to evoke hostile responses and friendly behavior tends to evoke friendly responses. (2) Power relationships are complementary; that is, dominant behavior evokes submissive behavior and vice versa.

Clients who are frozen into the friendly-submissive category typical of anxiety neurotics tend to pull friendly but dominant responses from other people. They tend to seek out and stay with persons who support their weak, passive, inadequate self-image and the resultant acquiescent behavior. If the therapist responds with the socially expected response (friendly-dominant) to the client's weak, anxious manner and statements, the client may like it but probably will not improve. Since the therapist has fulfilled the client's expectations, the client may feel quite satisfied with therapy but become dependent on the therapist. The therapeutic response is to avoid the conventional response and try to move the client out of the category into which he is frozen.

An example: Consider a client who fears committing social errors to the extent that he rarely initiates activities, speaks only when spoken to, and avoids situations in which his behavior could be judged by other people, because "to make a social gaffe would prove me a fool." Interpersonally, he sees almost everyone as his better, and to get along in life he has decided to act friendly toward everyone, to let others choose for him, and to defer to their wisdom. In therapy he, without deliberation or premeditation, assumes the same posture with respect to the therapist. If the therapist is not alert to the client's style, the therapist may unwittingly assume more and more of the responsibility for the therapy and end up doing most of the thinking and problem solving. In other words, the therapist may reciprocate the client's interpersonal style. The therapist may forcefully dispute the irrational beliefs of the client, but the very force with which they are disputed may counteract the therapist's intentions. The tactic we suggest is to assess the client's style and refuse the reciprocal style. Lazarus (1973) uses the phrase *authentic chameleon* to describe the therapist's flexibility and willingness to show many facets of his personality with clients and to choose the ones most helpful to any particular client. Perhaps Carl Rogers' success with neurotics can be explained by his nondirective, warm approach. By refusing the dominant posture, Rogers may have "forced" the client into a less dependent stance.

RET therapists, who have been taught to conduct very directive sessions, may easily fall prey to the temptation to speak too authoritatively, to provide direction about the content of the session as well as the structure, and to tell the client what to think rather than to promote independent thinking. Thus, the suggested tactic with the friendly-submissive client, after the client understands the basics of RET, is to guide him through a self-help session, as in this illustration:

C: I can't go bowling because I'd feel so nervous that I wouldn't be able to roll the ball toward the pins.

T: How do you suppose you'd be getting yourself so nervous?

C: I know that everybody would be watching me, and I'd worry that my ball would go in the gutter or only hit one or two pins.

T: If you were by yourself, would you worry about your performance?

C: No. As long as there wasn't anyone on any of the lanes near me.

T: Does it sound like you're worried about people or bowling pins?

C: People. I know that. I worry about what they are thinking. I know they'd think me an idiot if I bowled badly.

T: Some might; some might not. We don't know. What would *you* be thinking about you?

C: I'd think I was an idiot.

T: And then how would you feel?

C: Pretty nervous.

T: Do you see any connection between what you're thinking about yourself and what you feel?

C: Yeah.

T: Can you describe it?

C: Thinking that I'd be a bloody idiot gets me nervous.

T: Sounds right to me. Can you talk yourself out of that?

C: Poor bowling can't make me an idiot.

T: Right. What can?

C: [Pause.] Well, nothing—when you stop to think about it.

T: I agree. What can you do to stop and think about it?

C: I could tie a string around my finger.

T: As long as that helps you remember. What else can you do to thoroughly impress your insight on your memory?

C: I guess I'd better practice. Is that what you mean?

T: Sure. When are you going to start?

C: I guess I'll go bowling tonight.

Notice that in this dialogue the therapist resisted temptations to state the client's irrational thinking. But the therapist was very active in the dialogue and directed the client's thinking to the *ABC* model of his "nervousness." The frequent use of questions helped to keep the therapist from becoming too dominant. Questions that seek information or opinions from other people place the questioner in a subordinate position. At times therapists use too many questions. Their evocative style may become wearing on the client, who may ask, "What do you want me to say?" This query is a good sign that the questions are keeping the client in the submissive position and not helping him out of it. Nonverbal cues, such as the manner in which the question is asked, may convey to the client that the therapist is asking leading questions and not merely gently guiding the client to insight. (For further discussion of this point, see Beier, 1966.)

This approach resembles transactional analysis (TA). Very dominant responses, whether hostile or friendly, are parental in character. Very submissive responses are childlike in character. Responses that represent neither of the extremes are adult in character. In the following example, a hostile and submissive client is guided into acting responsibly instead of losing her temper with her children:

C: It's no use. Every time I see that messy room, I get furious. I know that you're going to tell me that I get myself furious, but I can't help it.

T: [noting the hostile and submissive tone of voice] How about telling yourself?

C: What?

T: What would the responsible, mature—we might even say rational—part of you say?

C: When I'm thinking rationally, I know that I get myself furious.

T: Let's hear the two parts of you discuss it. What would the mature, responsible part say?

C: Take it easy. Kids will be kids. There is no evidence that they *must* keep their room tidy even though you'd like it. Stop demanding that they do.

T: How do you feel when you say that?

C: Quite a bit less angry. And I realize that I could stop and think straighter instead of getting so upset.

This is an example of the therapist's "talking to the Adult," to borrow a phrase from TA. It nicely disengages the therapist from haranguing the client about *ABC*s and places responsibility gently on the client. By refusing to aid the client's dependence, the therapist (1) breaks up the conventional social pattern, (2) acknowledges the client's responsibility and ability to help herself, and (3) coaches the client in her own internal dialogue, converting it from largely irrational to largely rational.

We borrow another phrase from TA to discuss one of the "games" that clients and therapists can get into. These are dialogues between client and therapist that could become power struggles. They are "games" in the TA sense, because there is a psychological payoff for both parties (Berne, 1964). One hopes that it is the client who initiates them. The solution, once again, is to recognize them and disengage from them. In RET terms, the client's "games" are attempts to compensate for self-downing. By defeating the therapist, the client can temporarily feel superior and raised from a self-defined, self-imposed inferiority. In a typical game, the client repeatedly does not do homework assignments or claims to "not get" the idea that he is not utterly worthless. The client is saying, in effect, "I've talked and talked with you, and I haven't improved. I still think I'm no good." The implication "You haven't helped me" evokes defensiveness in some therapists, who irrationally believe that they should or must help everyone and that "help" means quick change. The conventional social response is to cite progress or to blame the client. The therapeutic response is to recognize the if-I-put-you-down-I-can-put-me-up game and respond accordingly: "Maybe you're right. What do you suggest?" When the therapist shows the client that she is not going to anguish over the accusations or blame anyone for lack of progress, the game is defused. Further, the request for a suggestion underscores the collaborative nature of RET therapy and counseling.

Problems with Technique. Most of the problems discussed here relate to problems with the therapist's assumptions. One problem that has more to do with the therapist's misunderstanding of the RET approach is an almost complete focus on the *A* of the *ABC*s. The therapist spends much of the session challenging and disputing the client's interpretations of events (for example, "Where is the evidence that you are homosexual?") rather than the client's evaluations of the interpretations. Focusing on *A* is not a problem per se, and often we may *choose* to do so for one reason or another. Ellis (1979b, p. 98) states, "I do not devote the bulk of my therapeutic efforts to combating irrational beliefs. Rational-emotive therapy (RET) is an exceptionally multifaceted or multimodal form of therapy that almost invariably includes a number of cognitive methods besides combating irrational beliefs." Focusing on *A*, then, becomes a problem only if the therapist never or hardly ever focuses on *B*, because he does not fully understand the difference between *A* and *B*. The solution, of course, is to acquire a clear understanding of the difference, so that when we choose to examine *B* we are in fact doing so.

Most problems with techniques are related to not checking out assumptions. A major assumption that may go unchecked is "My client understands me." From time to time, all RET therapists engage in explanation—explanation of the therapy itself, the rationale for certain homework, how a particular idea is irrational, and so on. After a brief explanation or at points during a complex explanation, it is important to ask the client, "Do you understand?" or "Does that make sense to you?" However, even if the client says "yes," we would want to check further into his understanding by such inquiries or statements as "Tell me how it makes sense to you" or "Can you tell me how this applies to you?" If the client does not understand, we will find out. A more formal method of checking the client's understanding is to ask for this information after the session. Our colleague Bill Knaus uses a simple printed form containing questions such as "What did you learn or relearn during today's session?" Just as the question "What are your goals for today's session?" indicates that clients have responsibility for setting personal objectives, so the questions about learning during the session suggest that some learning is to take place. But, in addition, the written form gives the therapist some concrete information about the client's understanding of what is important and in what way she understands it.

We call this problem of explaining without checking out the client's understanding "lecturing too much." Related is a problem of "moving too fast," covering too much material in a session. How much is too much? Too much is more than the client can comprehend. Here is an example:

C: If Sally didn't like me, I'd feel pretty inferior.

T: Meaning an inferior person?

C: I guess I do.
T: Do you see that is irrational?
C: Yes, it is.
T: OK, let's get back to your anger problem.

There is no lecturing here, but there is also no real evidence that the client comprehends how the belief that he is an inferior person is irrational. We only know that he agreed with the label "irrational." Again, the solution for "moving too fast" is the same as for "lecturing too much": check the client's comprehension. In the above example, for instance, after the client says, "Yes, it is," we could say, "OK, tell me how thinking you are inferior is irrational."

A final problem related to understanding is the unchecked assumption that our clients understand what we mean and that we understand what our clients mean. We are referring here to vocabulary and semantics. Since all words are abstractions and subject to varying denotations and connotations, it is important that we use a shared vocabulary with the client—specifically, that we define our terms and check out the meaning of the client's terms—and try to keep the dialogue as concrete as possible. Here is an example of a problem where vocabulary was not shared. The client was a bright woman, but with no academic experience beyond high school. In the initial session, she described her "nervousness," for which she was taking tranquilizers. Her goal was to give up the tranquilizers. For the first few sessions, the therapist referred to her "nervousness" as "anxiety." Fortunately for our communication, after several sessions she was brave enough (some clients may not risk appearing ignorant in the eyes of the therapist) to ask, "What is anxiety?" Taken aback, the therapist answered, "Oh, I just mean your nervousness" and apologized for not making that clear. The woman, unfortunately, thought she had some dire new problem. After that time the therapist tried to use the client's term, which would have been better from the start. However, when the therapist slipped and said "anxiety," both knew what was meant. This example points up the importance for therapeutic communication of using a shared vocabulary and shared meanings. If we can get into difficulty with terms like *anxiety,* how much more confusion can result if we or our clients speak of "identity crises," "perfectionism," or "fear of failure," without knowing whether we agree on the meaning.

Related to the rule of using a shared vocabulary is the rule to keep the dialogue as concrete as possible. Doing so serves a dual purpose. Asking for concrete examples is a means of checking out meanings and also of keeping the discussion of clients' problems focused on the real world where they exist and where much behavioral homework can take place. Little progress takes place in the realm of abstractions. If a client says, for instance, "When people yell at me, I get upset," as a description of his problem, it is better to ask him, "Can you tell me about an instance of somebody yelling at you?" or "Has that happened this week?" rather than continuing to discuss the problem at the level of "people yelling at me." A specific example can serve to clarify the *A.* For instance, the client may say, "Well, just this morning my boss told me I wasn't getting enough work out. That upset me." So "people yelling" becomes "boss criticizing," a much more specific *A* and also one that is more salient, since it had recently occurred. Even if the client had said, "When people criticize me, I get upset," we would still want to have him relate a specific example. An example is particularly helpful when we want the client to examine his beliefs about *A.* The client is much more likely to remember and be aware of what he told himself when his boss criticized him this morning than what he believes in general about "people criticizing" him. So the rule of thumb here is to ask for specific examples of problems presented, keeping in mind that the *B* we are looking for can be triggered by any number of specific *A*s.

Probably one of the most important errors that therapists can make relating to lack of client progress—an error that can contribute to any or all of the other errors mentioned in this chapter—is not checking on what progress the client is in fact making. If we find that the client is making little or no progress and if we accept major responsibility for that lack of progress, we will automatically examine our attitudes and behavior in relation to the client and will be likely to discover one or more errors on our part. If we neglect to check on progress throughout therapy, termination may never come.

Termination

The client has made progress toward his goals. Both therapist and client agree that this progress was achieved through attitude change and that the client has acquired cognitive coping skills to combat future irrational thinking. Therapy ends. In RET it is as simple as that. The last session is not essentially different from the one before and the ones near the middle of therapy, except for a somewhat greater emphasis on anticipation of future problems and less emphasis on grappling with present problems. However, as termination nears, we may want to work with our client along two new but interrelated lines.

First, we might consider whether the client would be happier with some new rational beliefs. If his expectations are unrealistic or unlikely to be attained, he can be encouraged to change them. For example, a young undergraduate consulted one of us about his ambition to go to graduate school in psychology. He was irrationally demanding that he succeed in his ambitions and was predictably feeling highly fearful about the future and depressed because his low grades seemed to have assured his getting barred from his goal. The therapist worked with him to help him give up the demands that were bringing him unhappiness. However, he was left with preferences that were certainly rational but that probably would not be fulfilled. So the dialogue shifted to an examination of his values and whether it made sense for him to continue a dream that had such a slim chance of coming true. The therapist shared a personal story about his own ambitions long ago to become a musician—ambitions that he gave up after receiving consistently low evaluations of his talent. Another client wanted to stop getting enraged when his wife objected to his chauvinistic remarks. He quickly learned to give up his self-enhancing demand that she conform to his expectations, but he was still left with a preference (that women cater to his whims) objectionable to his wife. Here the therapist pointed out that if he wanted to get along better with his wife, it would be in his best interest to change his philosophy about women or at least become more circumspect about expressing it.

A second emphasis can be on positive enjoyments. The course of counseling or therapy may end without a probing of what positive enjoyments the client experiences in his or her life. Much of RET literature suggests that the positives will emerge if we rid ourselves of the negatives in life. Nonetheless, some people still will have few positive pleasures. As homework, the therapist can ask these clients to try out new activities and live adventuresomely (having the client come up with specific activities or ways of doing so) or, as our colleague Ray DiGiuseppe suggests, to experience pleasure from daydreaming. Daydreaming can come in handy while one is standing in a checkout line, for instance, and it also builds frustration tolerance, since one now spends unavoidable dead time in a more enjoyable way.

Unlike some therapies, RET spends little time and energy on severing the therapeutic relationship. If, in fact, breaking the relationship does become a major issue, then the client is *not* ready to terminate, for this is an indication that the client relies on the therapist to fulfill some perceived need—perhaps approval, reassurance, or freedom from responsibility. If the client has indeed reduced irrational thinking—thinking that involves demandingness, awfulizing, and evaluation of self and others—and has acquired means of coping with such thoughts, dependency is not an issue. Particularly if the therapist and client like each other, each may approach termination with mixed emotions. The therapist may feel sad about no longer seeing this person but also, and more important, a sense of satisfaction that the client has progressed so far. The client is also likely to feel sad and perhaps a bit apprehensive about the future but, more important, a sense of confidence that life's problems can be dealt with in an autonomous way. RET terminations are primarily pleasant events.

8

A Therapy Session

The session presented here is an actual therapy session that, except for a minute or two of initial chatting and the final minute or so not captured on the forty-five-minute tape, is reproduced in its entirety. The therapist is Lyle Rossiter, a psychiatrist residing in Glen Ellyn, Illinois, who was nearing the completion of the Associate Fellowship program of the Institute for Rational-Emotive Therapy when this session was recorded. Dr. Rossiter submitted the tape to us for supervision, and we both agreed that overall it is a very good representation of rational-emotive therapy with a client who was difficult to work with because he had a strong tendency to seek *A* solutions. Although each client is unique, this tendency is common in many clients in RET. We are grateful to Dr. Rossiter and the client for their permission to reproduce the session in this book.

The client is a 39-year-old businessman with a three-month history of cramping in his left hand, which he interprets as a sign of amyotrophic lateral sclerosis (ALS), an extremely rare muscle-wasting disease sometimes known as "Lou Gehrig's disease." The client is frightened by the possibility that he in fact has ALS and continues to look for reassurance that he does not have the disease. Since doctors could be wrong, reassurance gives him only temporary respite from the anxiety. This is the third session with the client. We intersperse our comments at various points throughout the session.

1 *C:* [Begins by talking about a business deal.] There are more important things to be concerned with. It's been a very tiring week in that it—ah—seems like holidays are and—uh—yesterday morning I read the book—ah—*Overcoming Worry and Fear.* I didn't read, I didn't read [inaudible] by the way. And I read *Worry and Fear* twice. And yesterday morning I outlined it. I have fourteen pages of outlines.

Here is a client who really takes his homework seriously, usually a good omen for therapy. However, as will become clear further into the session, this client appears to use his reading homework (Hauck, 1975) to support his constant attempt to seek *A* solutions. The fourteen pages of notes are our first evidence of obsessive-compulsive symptoms and a need for certainty. As with any hypothesis, T will listen and look for evidence to confirm or disconfirm this hypothesis.

2 *T:* So you really studied it.

3 *C:* Yes, I did, because I felt it to be of value, and it related greatly to what you had discussed with me in the first session. (*T:* Good.) Then I was up until 2:30 this morning working on a job which is due this afternoon.

4 *T:* Burning the midnight oil.

5 *C:* Yeah, but you know what happens? This arm and hand thing I'm finding relates really to a lack of rest (*T:* Um huh.) for some reason. (*T:* OK.) Maybe it's psychological; I don't know. But about midnight I started to feel

> this tightness and so forth (*T:* Yeah.), so I did the worst thing in the world. I started to have a few drinks. So I drank from midnight till 2:30, when I went to bed when I finished this project. Then I feel miserable this morning because one drink gives me a terrible hangover. (*T:* Um huh.) So—uh—you know, not a real healthy state of mind at the present time, but, ah, you had mentioned the last session to think about the thing that is bothering me the most at this time. (*T:* Yeah.) There's probably two things, and it's a difficult decision. I've changed my mind as of this morning when I was having breakfast. I wanted to discuss the problem of speaking before a group (*T:* OK.) because it's very relevant to my job. And yet I've decided I'd rather attack this thing from the standpoint of health (*T:* All right.) Because I still can't get the arm thing off my mind. (*T:* OK.) Like last night as I worked, and as I drank, I continually kept beating the issue. I had to always prove to myself I had strength in my arm (*T:* Um huh.) because I don't know if I'm getting spasms in my arms or not, but as I sit here, or any time, I kinda feel weakness, you know (*T:* Um huh.), and then I have to take my hand and exercise it and clench it to prove to myself I'm OK. And as long as I'm in this state of mind about my health, maybe we should attack that problem (*T:* All right.) and try to equate it, than to other things such as speaking before a group or something, and if it takes more sessions, great, I'm all for it because I'm starting to derive and enjoy something out of this situation.

C (5) is rather rambling. If such rambling was typical of the first two sessions, T probably asked C to pick one problem so that the session could be more focused. As will be seen, T does keep the session focused on C's physical problem. Although the client rambles, T can get many potentially useful insights into C's belief system as well as his means of handling anxiety, in this case procrastination, drinking, and lack of insight, as well as probable perfectionism as C struggles to make the perfect decision. A further suggestion of low frustration tolerance or a need for comfort is C's statement about enjoyment of therapy, highly unusual in our experience.

6 *T:* Is the, the stiffness that you feel in your hands, is that usually the thing that offsets or sets off the anxiety or the worry?

7 *C:* Yes, it definitely is. If I get enough rest, like the day before Christmas I took the day off and I went to bed early on the 23rd. I slept late the 24th. I got up and did some shopping. I really felt good. My arms didn't hurt at all. Uh, they incidentally don't hurt. There's no pain. (*T:* Yeah.) I just sometimes wonder to myself, Geez, I grasp something and I feel a tendency not to release in a normal manner (*T:* Yes.) and that sets me off.

8 *T:* OK, and what is it you feel at the time in reaction to that stiffness or that lack of release that, ah . . .

9 *C:* The initial reaction is "Maybe these doctors are wrong."

Here the client reveals one of his cognitions: that the doctors may be wrong. This is a Step 4 cognition (in the emotional episode), since it is his interpretation of the doctors' statements. Hypochondriacal clients typically misinterpret their bodily sensations, construing them as dreaded diseases and doubting physicians' reassurances. C knows that if he did not have ALS he would be happy, not anxious. This case is a good one to illustrate that if we define as awful even the most improbable event, thinking of the mere chance that it will happen will be sufficient to arouse great anxiety and lead to preoccupation with that event. T (8) asked C what he felt, not what he thought, so T continues:

10 *T:* That's a thought, though; what do you feel emotionally?

11 *C:* Emotionally? Not the emotion or anxiety I did six weeks ago when the whole thing started (*T:* Um huh.), because I immediately, after reading this book, I say to myself, "Now, wait a minute. Think about this." (*T:* OK.) [I've] been to several doctors, including yourself

with a medical background in addition to being a psychiatrist, and even a chiropractor, who isn't of your level of medical knowledge but still knows what he's talking about in terms of muscles. (*T:* Right.) There isn't one person of professional experience who has said to me, "You've got a disease." (*T:* Um huh.) So I said to myself, "Don't be a fool, why worry about this." (*T:* OK.) In fact, one of the things about my new year—ah, in fact, it might be of some value if I stated to you—I'm not going to read this (notes from book), but there are certain points at breakfast this morning I Xed off as being particularly important—uh, one of which, the first step in overcoming fear is to stop making mountains out of molehills. It's a common old saying I've heard a million times, but if you really do stop and think about it, there's a lot of value in it.

A rambling answer typical of this client in this session. Throughout, he tries again and again to reassure himself that he has no need to worry. Note that T, who in a previous session explained the remoteness of C's having ALS, makes no attempt during this session to reassure C that he does not have ALS. T continues to ask for *C,* emotions. Particularly after such a rambling answer as 11, we might tend to forget our original question. T does not.

12 *T:* That's true, but before you begin to tell yourself and remind yourself about what the doctors have said and "Don't be a fool" and "Don't make mountains out of molehills," just after you've experienced the difficulty of release and the stiffness, what is your mood or emotional state at that moment?

13 *C:* I would say it's a little depressed or sad. (*T:* OK.) In other words, I would say immediately, "Gee, I'm going to die." I know I fear death. I don't think about that any more. I really can't answer your question.

14 *T:* So it's more of a depressive or sad feeling than it was a fearful or painful or anxious feeling?

15 *C:* Yeah, like here it is again and I thought I was through with this thing. (*T:* I see.) It's like a person who has an operation for cancer, and in five years later you suddenly feel pain again and think, "God, I thought I was over this." (*T:* OK.) And that's the kind of reaction—and I just say to myself, "To hell with it, I'll just keep on working here," and yet I don't get it out of my mind.

16 *T:* OK, now, what keeps going through your mind? You're telling yourself, "Don't make mountains out of molehills." What are you saying in back of your mind to take you there?

17 *C:* I don't know for sure except to tell you I'm not doing anything constructive to overcome it. In other words, as I read this book and learn what [inaudible] thoughts you *should* institute, I'm not doing that at this point.

18 *T:* OK, I think I can help you with that, but let's first get to what is going on in your head, the imagery or thoughts you continue to feel uncomfortable with.

19 *C:* Well, right now for example I'm feeling in my right forearm a tiredness. (*T:* OK.) I want to go like this [clenches fist?] and say, "Hey, you're not weak, you don't have ALS, OK?"

20 *T:* OK, now suppose you didn't do that, what thoughts and feelings would you continue to have? [Short silence.] What would you be thinking to yourself about that right forearm?

21 *C:* I would try to ignore it. I would try to say to myself, "Hey, forget it."

22 *T:* All right, if you didn't ignore it and didn't—you see, these are both ways of reassuring yourself or distracting yourself. (*C:* I see.) So, let's see if we can get to what's, what the nagging thought is, because what you're doing is avoiding (*C:* Um huh.), understandably enough, because it is a painful thing, but for purposes of our work, let's see if you can neither distract yourself nor reassure yourself with the flexing of your hand (*C:* Yeah.) but instead sink yourself into that feeling. Your arm feels

tired, and the release is kind of stiff. (*C:* Um huh.) What is it you feel and think at that moment?

23 *C:* The only thing I can think of is frustration. (*T:* All right.) Relating back to "Geez, why is this happening?" I'm so disgusted with this situation—why can't my hands just get well again?

T patiently continues to try to evoke C's irrational thinking; C continues to seek other solutions. T (22) explains that C's solutions of reassurance (Step 4 of the emotional episode) and distraction (Step 2) will not work. C's comments (23) are another indication of low frustration tolerance thinking.

24 *T:* OK, what's so disgusting about . . .

25 *C:* Mostly, I'm disgusted with myself for even recognizing it and feeling it and letting it get to me.

26 *T:* Well, OK. You're disgusted with yourself. So that's a second-level problem for reacting to the (*C:* the initial) the initial reaction then. But you're feeling frustrated about having this problem. Now, what are you telling yourself about your hand that generates the frustration?

27 *C:* I've been trying to approach it—I have to really think here because it varies—but I've been trying to approach it positively. Again, as I say, if I have a momentary inability to release; I say to myself, "Hey, Lyle Rossiter, a chiropractor, and two neurologists have said 'Forget it.' " Still, it doesn't solve my problem. I'm still wondering "Why is it here? Maybe they're all wrong."

28 *T:* All right, and maybe they're all wrong and what . . . ? What would that mean if they're all wrong?

It might be tempting to pursue the second-level problem, C's disgust with himself for having the problem in the first place (25), but the first problem, C's fears of having ALS, is still undefined and T wisely continues. Once again, T (28) does not argue about the existence of ALS (avoids a Step 4 intervention) but again probes for the client's beliefs (a Step 5 intervention).

29 *C:* If they're all wrong, it means I might be right (*T:* OK.), and my original thought on the whole matter was I had ALS (*T:* OK.) and therefore I might die.

30 *T:* OK, let's go with that. (*C:* Um huh.) Can you elaborate on that?

31 *C:* Well, I wish—Well, I said to myself in the last week that if I did have a choice between ALS and cancer, I'd rather have cancer, because there is some cancer which is curable (*T:* All right.), and there seems to be hope. And regardless of the type—I'm not a medical man and I know there are some that are just hopeless, but in layman's terms, there's always some hope now, to some degree with some chemicals (*T:* OK, OK.) in some form or another. To my knowledge, anyone with ALS dies. I don't know of anyone who has been cured or has lived twenty or thirty years with ALS. I may be wrong.

32 *T:* OK, let's suppose that's true. (*C:* Yes.) You're telling yourself, "OK, I'm worried that I have ALS and I'm going to die." (*C:* Um huh.) Now, what's the difference between that thought and the thought occurring to you, "I might drive my car off the road this morning and have an accident and die?" Why is it you don't feel depressed, sad, fearful, worried, or otherwise about that?

33 *C:* At this point, the difference is I drive my car everyday. For 39 years I have not died driving my car and therefore I'm used to it; I have confidence in myself. In other words, I'm not going to run a stop sign or a red light, and in fact, when I go through a green light, I look both ways to be sure some other fool doesn't run it.

34 *T:* So you're careful about it.

35 *C:* I control that.

T (32) asked a good contrast question. C (35) gives the answer: With ALS he is not in control. But T does not pursue this response. We recommend pursuing the meaning of the *A*s that the client presents, because it may be more salient to this client to become aware of the beliefs he has about being out of control than about having ALS, which, for him, is one manifestation of not being in control. Dying, except in suicide, is another event over which we have no control.

36 *T:* Well, you have control of your own driving. (*C:* Yeah.) What about the guy that's . . .

37 *C:* I know, that's a hazard I look out for, but it doesn't dwell on my mind.

38 *T:* That's right. But you could. Now I have patients who do. (*C:* Yeah.) OK, they don't think about ALS; they don't think about dying from ALS. They think about dying from an auto accident, so they don't drive, they don't get in the car, something like that. OK, now let's go with the "I might have ALS and die." Suppose . . . you were talking to someone about illness, and the two of you were batting the subject back and forth, and he was saying, "Well, I just had a physical checkup" and you were saying you just had one, and he remarked, "But you know, the physical checkup might have missed something, or I might have been all right at the time of the checkup and I might have developed something since then. The physical checkup was a month ago (*C:* Um huh.) or two weeks ago." Something like that. And another guy was talking, "Yeah, you never know. At any time you could go, could develop a fatal illness that would take you rapidly, a coronary, stroke," something of that sort, OK? And suppose you were to remark, "Yeah, I could even have something like—something esoteric or unusual like amyotrophic lateral sclerosis—and die from that." And at that moment, you'd be just saying it off the cuff. And in this philosophic atmosphere with these guys, let's assume you'd say that "Yeah, I might get a stroke, I might get ALS, I might get a heart attack, I might drop dead tomorrow; you never know." (*C:* Um.) OK, now how is it different? You wouldn't be feeling panicky, fearful, or particularly sad probably (*C:* Right.), if you were keep-

ing the discussion on a philosophical level, "It's true I . . . ," an intellectual level, "It's true I might have ALS and die." Now, how is it different from the way you're thinking about it? Because you're saying something in addition to yourself. (*C:* Um huh.) You're saying something in addition to yourself [other than] "Yeah, I have ALS and will die" when you react to your fingers and your hands. What do think that is? You're adding something. (*C:* Yeah.) You're not just saying philosophically, like this table is wood (*C:* Um huh.) or I might have ALS.

39 *C:* Uh—you're asking my reaction to that casual conversation?

T continues to attempt to evoke C's irrational beliefs. Here (38) he constructs an elaborate scene for C to respond to. T could have taken even more time to do so, obtaining C's reactions and understanding, because "Um huh" and "Right" indicate only that C is listening, not necessarily understanding. The result is a question from T that confuses C (39). T has been working quite patiently with C to evoke C's irrational thinking without putting words in C's mouth. We encourage that approach. However, after making many attempts to evoke irrational thinking to no avail, we usually switch to a more directive approach, such as "I'm wondering if you might not be thinking that it would be awful to die and that must not happen to you?"

40 *T:* No, at the time you're feeling upset.

41 *C:* OK, well that gets into the catastrophizing. (*T:* All right.) This is what I do, as I look upon it—Let me look at some things here [picks up notes] as I talk, uh, because it's important. I try to analyze in my own mind what I'm going through in my thought processes.

42 *T:* I think you're absolutely right (*C:* I know.) [about] the catastrophizing.

C's use of the word *catastrophizing* shows that he has learned from the previous session and/or his readings. However, his use of jargon may simply be a new way to describe his troubles and is no guarantee that he will follow up his awareness of catastrophizing with disputing it. T would have done well to check the client's meaning. But after all the work T did to elicit a probable irrational idea, we can understand why he did not.

43 *C:* If this book is right and your theory is right, then this is what I'm going through, and they cite the five different types of worry, fear, nervousness, phobia—and, incidentally, I conclude in my own mind I have a phobia. [Continues paging through notes.] Now this may not be true, but a phobia by their definition is "a combination of fear and anxiety that occurs when you do not know what it is you are afraid of." (*T:* Um huh.) You think you know. Now, I think I have ALS—incidentally, I don't think this, you know? (*T:* Right.) There are times when I do (*T:* That's right.) because, as I'm talking to you, and maybe because you're a medical doctor and I feel comfort around you. You know, if you saw me sitting here and you saw me picking this up and dropping it and had a weird look on your face, I'd be worried. (*T:* Um huh, um huh.) But when I explain to you I can do this and you shake your head, "Yeah," you're not the type of individual who is just going to let me sit here and crumble away with ALS (*T:* Right.) if I really have it (*T:* OK.) and you're going to say, "Hey, let me get you to a hospital and get this EMA test or EMG (*T:* Right.) or whatever it might be. So I have some—as I talk with you I have some comfort.

T's comments such as "Um huh" and "Right" may unintentionally reinforce and encourage C's rambling statements. T may still be listening for information about C at this early stage of therapy, but he would do better to interrupt C, as he does several times later in this session. When C gives rambling responses, he tends to go back to reassuring himself—a very strong tendency in this client, as we have seen. In C's use of words like *right* and *true,* we again have evidence of a need for certainty.

He also expresses great confidence in T, which is favorable for therapy but has the potential for C's becoming dependent on T for reassurance, comfort, and "truth."

44 *T:* Because you're thinking what?

45 *C:* You're a knowledgeable man in your profession, and if you had any thought that any of the symptoms I've explained to you (*T:* Right.) would be an indication of ALS, you would logically explain to me why I should have a test.

46 *T:* And why would that—what are you saying about that that reassures you, that makes you feel better?

47 *C:* What I'm saying is "Since you haven't said that, I'm reassured." If you were to say it to me (*T:* OK.), I'd go out in left field probably.

48 *T:* All right, now what would you be telling yourself at that moment?

49 *C:* I'd be saying to myself, "He's right." (*T:* About what?) "He's right that I might have ALS."

50 *T:* All right, so what?

51 *C:* Yeah, I know. So what can I do about it. Not much, is there?

52 *T:* OK, but if you were just stuck with that, "OK, maybe I do have ALS. If I have it, I have it. So what? There's nothing I can do. It may take me, or I may get progressively weaker or be in a wheelchair," blah, blah, blah. If you just stuck with that and in a philosophical sense, a resigned sense, said, "Well, I got to go sooner or later; I may have ALS and I may die," then you wouldn't be particularly fearful or go out the window or whatever you said a few minutes ago. (*C:* That's right.) You'd be sad, be disappointed (*C:* Um huh.), which would be appropriate. Now, what's the catastrophizing part? What are you telling yourself that constitutes the catastrophizing about?—it goes beyond "I have ALS and I might die.

53 *C:* Well, I guess I catastrophize in the sense that I think about my family and leaving them alone. I think of all

the future plans we have and how I'm going to miss them. This is sadness (*T:* Right.), but then I turn it into a catastrophe by (*T:* By adding what?) by feeling sorry for myself, I guess. By saying, "Why me?" (*T:* OK.) I probably beat my hands against the wall and everything. You know, I've often thought I would probably commit suicide if I had ALS (*T:* OK.)—at the appropriate time.

54 *T:* What would you be telling yourself about? The "Why me?" is sort of a rhetorical question. What is it really saying?

55 *C:* Well, I think it's self-pity, which is wrong.

56 *T:* How would you put it in a declarative sentence? What do you think you're telling yourself?

57 *C:* Why must I die? What have I done wrong to deserve this? Why not give me life to take care of my children and my wife and happiness? (*T:* OK.) And who am I speaking to when I say that? It could be God. (*T:* All right.) I don't know.

58 *T:* And again, if you take those questions out of the question form and put them into a sentence, how would you be putting it?

59 *C:* Hum?

60 *T:* Where would the catastrophizing come in? Because really you're putting these things in the form of questions, which sounds like a request for information. (*C:* Yeah.) "Why, God?"—you address yourself to God—"Why me? Why can't I stay around and enjoy my children?"

61 *C:* Well, I guess you'd have to phrase it as a—"I'm dying. This is the end. I must face it. And I must do it as a man without fear and make it as easy on my family as I can."

T's doggedness pays off when C (53) reveals his self-pity. In asking for declarative sentences, T (56 and 58) wants C to become aware of his irrational beliefs, which C disguises as rhetorical questions. C (61): "I must do it as a man without fear" is a further indication of LFT, discomfort anxiety. A second clue is "and make it as easy on my family as I can." Many persons with discomfort anxiety also require that everyone else's life be comfortable too.

62 *T:* Those would be pressures you'd be putting on yourself, but what . . . ?

63 *C:* But I'd still be totally destroyed inside. (*T:* How?) By the constant thought of dying and leaving.

64 *T:* All right, what would that constant thought consist of? What would the constant thought be?

65 *C:* Oh, I'd worry. Weirdly enough, I worry about being placed in the ground. I've told my wife several times, I'd rather be in a mausoleum. I can't stand the thought of being buried in the ground and still thinking of myself as still being alive inside of a coffin, trying to get out.

66 *T:* OK, well, let's go with that one. Let's think about—suppose you're thinking of yourself alive in a coffin, can't get out. What is it, what are you telling yourself about that? What are you feeling in response to that idea?

C's response (65) is a very unusual one. But T wisely does not attempt to educate C about the finality of embalming in modern times (Step 3 intervention). Instead, T persistently continues to look for *B*. An alternative that would keep us from getting sidetracked but would also correct C's misconception would be to say, "You'd die in the embalming process if you weren't dead already, but let's just suppose that you are alive in the coffin and can't get out." T (66), while keeping on track, asks two questions, in effect putting C into a bind as to which one to answer.

67 *C:* Uh—What am I feeling? Fear.

68 *T:* Fear, OK. Fear of what?

69 *C:* Being trapped.

70 *T:* Being trapped, OK. What are you telling yourself that's so fearful about being trapped?

71 *C:* The frustration of trying to get out.

72 *T:* What are you telling yourself about [inaudible] be frustrating? If it were only frustrating, it would not have you here.

73 *C:* Well, I mean if you're just smothering (*T:* All right.), if you're still alive and under six feet of earth and in a coffin, you're gonna smother; so it gets back to dying again.

74 *T:* And what would be so catastrophic about that?

75 *C:* The meaning of dying. In other words, maybe you're driving at this point. I haven't thought too much about —I don't fear death as much as I fear the meaning of death.

76 *T:* That's right. You fear dying, the process of dying. Now, let's go with that one. See if you can get yourself into whatever fantasy or imagery or thoughts that are scary about dying.

77 *C:* Well, with the ALS, of course, it's just sitting there and wasting away, with the thought—every morning and every night—that this is going to terminate soon. (*T:* Right.) Uhh, if I had a wish in life, it would be instantaneous death when it has to happen. (*T:* All right.) I can't control when it will happen, unless I kill myself, which I have no intention of doing.

78 *T:* OK, what about sitting there having ALS and wasting away—now, what does that evoke in you?

79 *C:* Uh—sadness. To see my children and realize that maybe next week I won't see my children. See their happy smiles . . .

80 *T:* But again, the sadness isn't the same as catastrophizing. Where is the catastrophizing? See, if you just thought to yourself, "Gee, it would be sad to have ALS because I would be sitting there wasting away and I would know that pretty soon I would be dying, I would be missing my kids, I wouldn't be able to fulfill some of the goals I have," wouldn't that be unfortunate and sad? And it would. You would feel sad and sorrowful, and so on. Now, that's not the same as the catastrophizing and the preoccupation, the fear, the trapped.

81 *C:* I suppose the catastrophizing would be that, uh, I'm not willing to accept the fact that this is going to happen to all of us someday (*T:* I think that's it.) in one form or another.

82 *T:* I think that's right. (*C:* Yeah.) Now, why aren't you willing to accept that?

83 *C:* Maybe because I'm so young. In other words, I don't know if this is right—my mother was visiting . . .

84 *T:* A lot of people die young.

85 *C:* I know, but a lot of people die in their seventies or eighties, and I say to myself, "Gee, maybe I could accept it when I'm seventy or eighty, because my kids would be on their own two feet then, and I would have cared for them properly. I will have lived my full life, and I can go with more peace of mind." Now, I'm not sure I would accept it as readily then (*T:* OK.), any more than I would now.

86 *T:* All right, you might not. But let's go through it now. At your present age and your kids in the present stage of growth and so on, why would it be awful to die, catastrophic to die now, rather than just unfortunate and sad?

87 *C:* Mostly because of the future I dream about, how much happiness I hope for.

88 *T:* And you wouldn't have that. It would be unfortunate too, but why a catastrophe?

89 *C:* It's hard for me to answer. I mean, I shouldn't catastrophize, first of all, as a logical . . . (*T:* Well . . .) But I do, or in what form I do it . . .

90 *T:* Well, you just suggested in a sense that maybe the key, the key element here [is] "I will not accept me dying young." (*C:* Hm.) "Maybe other people, but not me." (*C:* Um huh.) "I will—I refuse to accept that possibility." And it happens that your fantasy about the worst way to go is with ALS. For some people it might be burning in a fire, who knows? (*C:* Yes.) Cancer or congestive heart failure or whatever it might be. But for you it seems to me what you're saying to yourself that

is most central to this point so far, the most central to your problem, is "I refuse to accept that. I won't accept that. I won't, won't, won't" (*C:* Um huh.), though it is in fact a real possibility in this real world.

91 *C:* Um huh, that's true. I won't accept that.

92 *T:* Well, why not?

93 *C:* Because I don't deserve to die at a young age in that manner. Now, (*T:* Who does?) if I was a murderer—Well, let's take [names presumed criminal]. (*T:* OK.) Now, I always wondered about—I'm not a religious person—I'm trying to be, incidentally. In fact, I carry a Bible with me, which I look at once in a while for certain passages. And I say to myself, why in God's name does [presumed criminal] walk this earth—I think he's still alive—free and healthy (*T:* OK.) when a man like you and me may have to die tomorrow of a heart attack?

94 *T:* All right. Now, what does that tell you about your—your actually philosophical statement of just a moment ago, "Because I don't deserve to die"? What does that tell you about reality and deserving? What is your experience?

95 *C:* Well, I must be fantasizing that, since I try to live a decent, beneficial life to everybody else (*T:* That's right.), then I don't deserve this type of punishment.

96 *T:* That's right. Now, what do you think of the reality of the, the appropriateness of that belief, because that's a philosophical belief?

97 *C:* Yeah, and it's an inaccurate belief.

98 *T:* That's correct. And why is it inaccurate?

99 *C:* Because God or whoever decides when you're going to die doesn't judge you on that basis.

100 *T:* That's right. The universe is not set up on the basis of fairness. (*C:* Yeah.) It's set up on the basis of gravitational forces and electromagnetic forces and a few others that we know about, but not fairness. (*C:* Um huh.) Where's the fairness? Where's the fairness of little kids burning to death in a house? (*C:* Um huh.)

Where's the fairness of a 12-year-old kid dying of leukemia?

101 *C:* So how do you—how do you fight that? Well, fight isn't the proper word. You have to accept that, don't you?

102 *T:* Well, you fight your irrational belief in what?

103 *C:* I'd fight my irrational belief?

104 *T:* Yes, I'd say—what would be appropriate would be to fight your irrational belief that the world is set up on what basis?

105 *C:* Uh—well, put a different way, it's not set up on the basis of fairness.

106 *T:* That's correct; that's exactly right.

107 *C:* You can't fight that, can you? You have to accept that.

108 *T:* No, you'd better accept, you don't have to, but you'd better. Because if you don't accept the reality that the universe is frequently unfair and that people get lots of things they don't deserve and don't get lots of things they do deserve—in other words, that deserving is a concept, a philosophical idea, a religious idea, a belief that men have made up from time immemorial; that if you go to school, go to church, pay your dues, clean your room, whatever it is (*C:* Yeah.), keep your nose clean, cover your mouth when you cough, whatever the local bullshit is—if you do that, then you will have a happy life and live a long time. (*C:* Um.) That's just all what?

109 *C:* Just a lot of garbage.

110 *T:* A lot of garbage, right. But this is what you're believing. You're believing, "Since I live a good, clean, decent life, I must and should live a long, carefree, or disease-free life. And die at 70 or 80 instead of 39."

111 *C:* That brings up a point [paging through notes] that I remember in the book. "Life is full of danger, heartache, and injustice, and if you focus on them unduly, you create more danger and heartache . . . uh, emotional peace is talking yourself out of overconcern.

Life's problems will not vanish, but changing your thinking about these situations is what will finally bring peace of mind."

112 *T:* Right. And what we're trying to get here is changing your thinking in a specific way about your own specific beliefs about the world, which are getting you into trouble. (*C:* Um huh.) You're saying, let's go through it again, "I refuse to accept the possibility of my early death by a severe muscle-wasting disease" because what—"I refuse to accept it" because what?

T has been working well through here to confront C and help him achieve insights into his thinking. To do so, T interrupts C three times (80, 84, and 90). We mention this because some beginning therapists and counselors are hesitant to interrupt their clients, thereby allowing digressions to occur that waste therapeutic time. At 94, T moves into disputing C's belief that life should be fair. Note that T (98) does not stop with C's conclusion that his belief is "inaccurate" but asks him to explain the reasons why it is. Again, C (109) concludes that his belief is "a lot of garbage." T (112) continues to dispute C's belief. Since C has already concluded that it is irrational, at this point it would be better for T to change tactics and work to get the client to act on his insights rather than to "go through it again." For instance, T could ask here, "Now, what can you do this week to remind yourself that life is not fair?" or "How about going through the newspaper each day and keeping a tally of reports of unfairness?"

113 *C:* Are you asking me now from a rational . . .

114 *T:* Not from a rational, no, no. I want to be sure we're clear on the irrational. (*C:* The irrational?) Yeah. In other words, what would you be saying?

115 *C:* Well, basically because I don't think I deserve it.

116 *T:* I don't deserve it. (*C:* All right.) It wouldn't be fair. And the world must and should be fair. (*C:* Yeah.) So this is where you're getting yourself in trouble with this death thing.

117 *C:* I'm not willing to just accept life as it is.

118 *T:* That's right. You're not willing to accept the reality of the possibility, the very real possibility, you may get ALS and die. Now, it's a remote possibility, because ALS is not a common disease.

119 *C:* I know. That's something I've thought about. Ah, I've focused on it at the moment because of this experience with my hands. (*T:* Yeah.) But in my subconscious I must have been thinking about it because the minute that thumb went I said, "God, I've got ALS" (*T:* That's right, that's right.), because I fear the type of disease that it is.

120 *T:* Yeah, and you might also ask, then, why that type of disease is so troublesome to you, because you again may be saying something comparable to, about that type of disease. What do you think that might be?

121 *C:* Well, you know, what I fear about ALS is death.

122 *T:* But you could get that from any disease (*C:* I know.) —fatal disease. (*C:* I know.) Now, why ALS? Why do you single ALS? You just said something about the type of disease; it has a particular significance.

123 *C:* Well, the debilitating nature of the death that results.

124 *T:* Now, what are you telling yourself about having a debilitating disease?

125 *C:* I'll tell you, I could accept a debilitating disease if it weren't going to be a terminal disease. My main focus in life is to remain here in one form or another. (*T:* All right.) I really do think if I was totally paralyzed from the waist down (*T:* Yeah.), I could be a relatively happy person. (*T:* So you could somehow accommodate to that.) I do think I could because as long as my wife and children are here and I could see them and talk to them and have my senses to some degree (*T:* All right.), I just don't want to leave them. (*T:* All right.) So ALS—incidentally, I, ah—Well let me ask you. Has anybody lived twenty or twenty-five years with ALS?

126 *T:* Well, I'll have to look that up again.

By going over the same ground, T has given C the opportunity to get back to his preoccupation with ALS.

127 *C:* Well, the neurologist told me there are forms of ALS, and some can go for six months and others are relatively benign. (*T:* Yeah.) So, you know, here again I'm making a mountain out of a molehill. Let's assume I did have ALS. My first reaction would be, "My God, I'm going to die," because Lou Gehrig dies and everyone else dies. Uh, and then the neurologist says, "You're in the wrong age group even." I think Gehrig got it when he was like 35 and died when he was 39 or 40. (*T:* Um huh.) And, you know, everybody that I know of, I don't know anybody personally with ALS, but those I've read about have been in my age group, so I don't know what this guy was talking about. I don't know if he means my chances come later in life or if I've passed the stage of ALS. (*T:* Um huh, um huh.) I have no idea. I grasp with these things and try to rationalize myself out of the thought that I even have it, you know.

128 *T:* Yeah, but you see, the part that is making that hard for you is that you're immediately trying to reassure yourself, without getting at the, the anxiety and fear and depression-generating thoughts. You're immediately trying to use the Norman Vincent Peale method, think positively (*C:* Um huh.), rather than first finding out exactly, precisely what the negative thinking is—to what degree is it irrational or overreactive—and then you can fight it, then you can start countering it. For example, once you get to the "I cannot, and will not, and refuse to accept the idea that I will, might get ALS and die, I refuse to accept that," then you can counter that by saying what?

To get back on the track, T is reminding C once again about the *ABC*s and reminding C that it is *B* that creates his fear.

129 *C:* The chances of getting that are relatively minor.

130 *T:* Relatively minor. You could dispute the certainty of your statement because you've been saying "I will get it" (*C:* Um huh.), and you could dispute, "I probably won't because it's a rare, rare disease and the chances are remote; it's much more likely that I'll die in an auto accident (*C:* Um huh.) or fall off a ladder or something like that. And then you'd have something logically to dispute it with. So far, you're only saying, "Well, I hope I don't have ALS; I hope I don't have ALS; I hope I don't have ALS." Well, if you keep that up, you're almost putting yourself into more . . . (*C:* Yeah.) So really the, so far this morning what we've established is, tentatively—we want to confirm it as we go along, but tentatively we've established, "I've refused (a) to accept the idea that the universe is not organized according to fairness and deservingness and justice, and (b) I refuse to accept the idea I might die young and leave my children behind and not ever see my wife again. I know I accept the fact that other people do, it happens to people even younger than 39, but I refuse to accept it in my own case."

131 *C:* I can objectively agree with you. I could tell you that or—and my next-door neighbor (*T:* Right.), but I have a hard time accepting that rationalization for my own . . .

C is using the term *rationalizing* for rational thinking. It is clear that he does not mean "rationalizing" in its precise meaning, and T properly does not correct him. Although this would be proper procedure with some clients, with C a correction might lead to a long discussion of the "right" use of these terms.

132 *T:* Right. And what you'd better do to get to these parts of, ah, of—There's probably a little more to it, a couple of thoughts which you're plaguing yourself or catastrophizing with. What you'd better do is fight

these irrational beliefs that the world is set up on the basis of fairness and justice and, secondly, I refuse to accept my early death—the possibility of it—and maybe a third thought that, uh, since the world is set up on the basis of fairness, and since I've been fair and a good guy and a decent citizen, I should not and must not get an early disease.

133 *C:* Um huh, it's a stupid thought (*T:* That's right.) because it isn't going to be that way. (*T:* That's right.) I know that.

134 *T:* And you may live till you're 90, but it won't be because you're a decent guy or because of anything that has to do with fairness, OK? (*C:* That's right.) And you don't—you're not yet convinced of that, see, you probably—if you do that today, if you continue to think like you do now, you'll be saying [mimicking an old man's voice], "Well, I've lived till 90 because I've been a goddamn good man. I've supported my children. I've been honest with my dealings with other people," blah, blah, blah—which is horseshit!

T concisely summarizes C's main demand and dramatizes it by affecting an old man's voice. It would have also been desirable for T to dramatize at other times during the session to avoid the overintellectual discussion this client seems to want.

135 *C:* Yeah, I know it is, I know it is. Yeah—you think in this book, they talk about conscious and unconscious (*T:* Um huh.), ah, fears. I think they use the word *neurotic behavior.* (*T:* Um huh.) Do you think my thought process is conscious at this point, or is it back there when I was 5 years old? I hope it's not back there when I was 5 years old.

136 *T:* No, no, it's not back there when you were 5 years old. It's what we would more accurately call preconscious. In other words, it takes, ah, it's not that it's deeply repressed so much as it's going on in the back of your mind, but you don't easily, and most of us don't, vir-

tually nobody puts his finger right away on those thoughts that are in the back of your mind. They tend to go unnoticed because you immediately tend to defend yourself from them by occupying yourself with squeezing your fist, or occupying yourself with positive thinking or distracting yourself (*C:* Um huh.) or drinking yourself into distraction, or something like that. You see . . .

137 *C:* I don't attack the problem properly.

It would be appropriate here for T to ask C something like "And what is the problem?" Here as well as in other parts of the session, it appears that T and C have two different definitions of the problem and therefore different goals. T has been working with C's problem of anxiety and the beliefs that create the anxiety, while C continues to be concerned with the problem of having ALS and the solution of ridding himself of that problem. It would be helpful for the therapeutic alliance if T, from time to time, asked C whether he wants to feel less anxious or, if C had agreed, to remind him of that goal.

138 *T:* That's right. But you haven't been trained to yet, but you're learning to. That's what we're doing this morning with my urging you to keep thinking about the—imagining you having ALS, imagining you're gonna die, and so on, what do you tell yourself about that? And you've come up with a couple of things that you didn't know heretofore. (*C:* Um huh.) You have a couple of bullshit beliefs about the universe being organized on the basis of fairness, and you, in particular, will not, must not, cannot have that kind of thing happen to [you].

139 *C:* Well, there's a statement in the book [paging through notes]. I can't find it at the moment, I was looking for it, where they make the statement that neurotic people are sensitive people, ah, sensitive to the feelings of a child or someone who is suffering. The book makes a statement, "Look, you've just got to be cold-hearted

about life," and that isn't the word they use, and I even wrote it in and I can't find it. [Continues to page through notes.]

For the next few minutes, C is only half listening to T as he continues to search for the exact quote, which he eventually finds (151). This again can be seen as another symptom of this client's need for exactness and certainty.

140 *T:* Let me suggest a different way of putting that. That when we act neurotic—there's no such thing as a generally neurotic person because there's always some areas where he's rational—but when you're acting neurotically, you're almost invariably holding a belief, "I am special with regard to this particular issue that I'm having a neurosis about. I am, in this case, I am special about not dying at an early age. Others do, but it must not be me, because I have a special relationship with the universe, or I have a—I should have and must have a special exemption from the possibility of a death at a relatively young age." Now, that's an irrational belief. (*C:* Yeah.) You don't have such a special exemption, and what you're doing is demanding that "I must have that special exemption. I must not . . ."

141 *C:* I'm just not accepting it.

142 *T:* You're not accepting it. Because if you accepted it . . . ?

143 *C:* I wouldn't be here, would I?

144 *T:* You wouldn't be here. If the thought of having ALS occurred to you and you really accepted that, how long would it last in your mind?

145 *C:* If I accepted it?

146 *T:* Yeah, how long would you think about it?

147 *C:* I wouldn't think about it.

148 *T:* That's right. It'd be just like the thought of dying in an auto accident or dying of a stroke or dying of falling off a ladder or something. Some guy—if you were shooting the shit with your neighbor and he said,

"Well, you know you could go at any time, you might fall off a ladder and break your neck and die from it," and the thought would occur to you, "Yeah, I might fall off a ladder, break my neck and die. Yeah, so I might. That'd be too bad. Now, let's see, what am I going to do for the rest of the day? Maybe I'll play some golf (*C:* Yeah.) or do something in the house."

149 *C:* Right. You see, it's strange to me that there are people who would worry about that type of thing. (*T:* That's right.) And yet that same guy would look at me and say, "What in the hell is ALS?" He's never heard of it. (*T:* Right.) You know, if I hadn't heard of the disease, then this cramp in my thumb would have been nothing more than a cramp to me. [Continues paging through notes.]

150 *T:* And what he might ask you then, and what he might ask himself is, if he had heard about it, "Why is this guy worrying about ALS, which is a remote possibility (*C:* Um huh.), or why isn't he accepting the fact that he, like me, could die early? What's so special about him that he is entitled to a guarantee that he will live till he's 90 or 70 or 80 or whatever he'd think was an acceptable age?"

151 *C:* On page 109 of the book they make a statement, this is what I'm looking for, quote: "It is necessary to develop a cold-hearted outlook toward people and reality, and it is healthy to look at things objectively and with little sentimentality." (*T:* OK.) Maybe that's the essence of it. (*T:* Well . . .) Kind of a cold, cruel way to put it, ah . . .

152 *T:* I don't know if I would quite agree with cold-heartedness or, or what that implies. But more the willingness to accept that life sometimes is sad and tragic, and if you want to think for a few minutes about the sadness or the tragedy of life, with the possibility of unfairness and cruelty and all the rest of the ills of the world, go ahead. But why preoccupy yourself with it? That's what you're doing. You're preoccupied with it; you're dwelling on it.

153 *C:* [Sighs.] Let me explain an event in my life that may have some relevance in here. If we're over time that's OK with me, but if you have other things just let me know.

154 *T:* Go ahead, we can go for another five or ten minutes.

T doesn't mind changing the subject, also believing that it would be relevant. In the notation we used briefly in Chapter Five, having ALS is a_1. For this client, a_2, a_3, a_4, and so on—events triggering the same irrational thinking—probably will be variations on a need for control or certainty.

155 *C:* OK, when I was younger, shortly before I got married, I lived at [names apartment]. I lived there for eight years; I really had a great time. I was a single guy. They had a bar there, and over a period of time it started to get populated by Hell's Angels type characters, real sons of bitches, you know. (*T:* Um huh.) And I had a run-in with one of them one time, and it just about came to a fight, and, you know, the guy was drunk. He didn't know who I was the next time he saw me. But there was this guy in the complex who got in a fight with one of them. For some reason they mistook me for him [same first names], and the word was out that they were going to knock off me. Ah, I called one of these characters on the phone, I knew where they worked, and I said, "You guys want a piece of me, fine, I'll be at the bar tonight. Let's just settle this thing," because it was getting to me. I was up awake at night; I was looking through my window; I was looking for these bastards to come in and try to wipe me out.

156 *T:* Um huh, you were preoccupied . . .

157 *C:* Yeah, totally. (*T:* Yeah.) So I challenged them. So I showed up at the bar—and don't get the idea that I'm some sort of fighter or anything, but I wanted to get this thing resolved. (*T:* That's right.) But they didn't show up. But you know what I did for about a month? I carried a .38 revolver with me. Because I decided if

these sons of bitches were going to jump me out of the bushes and drag me off in a car and kidnap me and butcher me (*T:* Um huh.), I'm going to kill them before they do it. Now—that's irrational.

158 *T:* Well, you see, the irrational part of it is, would be this: "I can't stand the uncertainty of it" (*C:* Um huh.), because that sounds like what you were dealing with. "I got to settle it tonight, because I can't stand this day-after-day (*C:* That's . . .) feeling of [not] knowing whether they're going to get me or not."

159 *C:* That's a very important part of my life. I can't stand the unknown. I just can't tolerate it. (*T:* All right.) for any length of time.

160 *T:* Well, why can't you?

161 *C:* I don't know. (*T:* OK.) I worry about it. (*T:* That's right.) That's why I can't tolerate it, because it preoccupies all my moments and I can't enjoy life.

162 *T:* I must have certainty. I must have predictability in my life.

163 *C:* And yet, to—only to some degree. If God came down and said, "You're going to die when you're 45 (*T:* Um huh.), I'd start worrying right now about my death in six years, saying, "Oh God, you mean I got to go so soon?" (*T:* Yeah.) If God came down and said, "You're going to live to at least 90," I'd probably sit back and be the happiest guy in the world. (*T:* OK.) ALS wouldn't disturb me because . . . [Tape ends.]

C is a difficult client to work with and is not likely to be dramatically helped in one session. Continued patience and persistence are T's best strategy. Particularly with an obsessive client like this one, we want to avoid a purely intellectual approach and use creative, imaginative tactics to reach mutual goals. T alludes to imagery and fantasy at several points, but he does not use them in this session. An example of another intervention, which avoids C's intellectualizing and which T used in a later session, is to reverse roles and ask C to talk T out of the need for certainty about death or ALS. Behavioral homework assignments, of course, are a prime means of encouraging C to achieve more than a purely intellectual solution. These would be developed in the therapy with C, but here are two possibilities: C could drive to an unfamiliar place and not take a map with him, or C could give a speech without using notes. The intent of each of these is to encourage C to face uncertainty and the associated anxiety rather than avoid it through drinking, distraction, or reassurance, so that he can have the experience, not just the idea, that uncertainty and discomfort can be tolerated.

9

Working with Groups

There are many formats in which RET can be and has been applied to groups. A major application by Ellis and his associates is the offering of time-limited problem-oriented workshops; for example, focusing on procrastination, assertiveness, women's sexuality, or shyness. RET has also been applied to one-day or weekend marathon groups, including marathons for couples. Ongoing therapy groups include the treatment of couples or families. This chapter will be devoted primarily to applying RET in an ongoing therapy group composed of individuals, usually unrelated, seeking help for personal emotional or behavioral problems. Some of the material, particularly that on initiating a group and teaching the basics of RET, is certainly applicable to other formats. (Readers interested in applying RET to couples and to families may want to consult Ard, 1977; Hauck, 1977; and Ellis, 1978a, 1979c.)

Unless a therapist or counselor is already experienced in working with groups, we advise learning to use RET with individual clients first. The communication patterns and dynamics of interaction are more complicated in groups than in individual therapy. For example, in individual therapy, there is one two-way communication channel; in therapy with couples, there are three channels; and in a group of seven clients and one therapist, there are twenty-eight potential channels. Not all channels may get used in a group, but the possibility for confusion exists. Stated simply, using RET with groups requires skills in group management and discussion leading as well as in the theory and tactics of RET. This chapter, then, is addressed to therapists and counselors who have basic knowledge of RET. It does not describe general principles of working with groups. (For information about group dynamics in general, see Olmsted and Hare, 1979.)

The advantages of group therapy far outweigh the disadvantages for many clients, although such clients sometimes may not be convinced of the advantages of group over individual therapy, especially when their problems involve a good deal of interpersonal anxiety. One method we have used to encourage such clients to enter a group is to remind them that their problems for the most part do involve other people, "not trees or rocks," and therefore that the group is an ideal situation in which to work on their problems. However, a disadvantage is the lessened amount of time for personal attention from the therapist. For clients with significant emotional problems or who are facing a life crisis, individual treatment may be the format of choice, at least initially.

The advantages of group therapy are many. First, groups are cost efficient; the therapist can see several clients and teach rational principles to many people at one time. Second, members of a group can learn that they are not unique in having a problem or in having specific kinds of problems. Third, the group can provide a forum for preventive psychotherapy, since members can hear others discussing problems which they may not have faced or may not be currently facing in their lives, but which may help them learn rational techniques for handling these problems should they arise. Fourth, group members can help themselves by learning to help others. One of the best ways to learn a skill is to teach it to someone else. By teaching rational thinking to others in a group, clients are, in effect, teaching themselves. Fifth, some activities and exercises (see examples given later) can be done only in groups. The group may also provide a forum for practicing shame-attacking or risk-taking exercises. Sixth, some group exercises may be advantageous in bringing out specific emotions, which can then be dealt with *in vivo* in the group setting. Seventh, certain problems—for example, interpersonal or social skill deficits—can be most effectively dealt with in a group. The therapy group can function as a living laboratory, in which, under the guidance of an experienced therapist, the client can try out new ways of relating to other people and practice new social behaviors. Eighth, a group setting allows clients to receive feedback from a number of persons about their behavior, and such feedback may be more persuasive in motivating them to change than that of a single therapist in an individual session. Ninth, when therapeutic efforts are focused on deriving practical solutions to life problems, group members probably can give many more suggestions than is possible for any one therapist. Tenth, the group members can provide a source of peer pressure, which may be more effective in promoting compliance with homework assignments than that of the individual therapist. Finally, the group can provide a phasing-out experience for clients who have been in individual therapy. Such clients may have learned their irrational ideas and how to dispute them but require additional practice to complete the process.

Characteristics of RET Groups

One of the first decisions the group leader makes is what role to take. Shall the leader be active, talk more than any group member, and take responsibility for uncovering irrational ideas and disputing them or remain passive and let the group do most of the work? We recommend that the leader of an RET group take a very active role. It is the leader who has the basic knowledge of human emotional disturbance, and, although not having all the answers, the leader probably has a good many more of them than the group members have. To highlight the central role of the leader of an RET therapy group, we shall refer to him or her as the *therapist.* This choice of terms may seem obvious, but we hope that it will serve as a reminder that the therapist is not a "facilitator."

The RET group therapist's role is to see that the main focus of changing self-disturbing cognitions and resultant feelings and behavior is not lost. Groups easily get sidetracked, fall into the giving of personal advice, and wander from the problem they started to solve. The therapist, therefore, had better be especially active and directive. However, the therapist can also be *too* active. If he or she dominates the discussion to the point that the members seldom get a chance to talk, group members will probably lose interest and become, at best, mere spectators. Being too active also detracts from most of the advantages previously mentioned of group therapy over individual therapy.

High degrees of cohesiveness and intimacy are not necessarily sought in RET groups, although, given enough time and a stable group membership, they usually develop anyway. Many therapists think that something special must be done in order for a group to develop cohesiveness and intimacy. However, almost any group of people, if left to interact freely, will develop special feelings of liking for each other. Many work groups show this. Members may feel more positively toward each other (exchange confidences and the like) than they do toward their own families, probably because being a member of a family usually involves less freedom of choice than being a member of a work group (Brown, 1965).

Cohesiveness within a therapy group can present problems. A highly cohesive group may resist the introduction of new members or develop a norm or unwritten rule that says, in effect, "We don't confront each other here; we support each other rather than challenge." The introduction of new members is especially critical if the group is ongoing. Ellis's groups have been ongoing for over twenty years, with several hundred percent turnover in clientele. New members typically get quickly absorbed into the group because there seems to be an absence of the specialness or elitism that characterizes some other forms of therapy groups.

Initiating an RET Group

As we have mentioned, it is best not to start applying RET in groups until the principles and procedures of RET have been mastered. The management of group discussion and interaction requires skills and experience which, if the therapist does not already have them, may distract from doing effective RET. Once the therapist can probe for irrational beliefs, dispute them, and construct helpful homework assignments, he or she is probably ready to lead an RET group.

What kinds of clients and how many should be in an RET group? The answer to how many is pretty much the same as considered optimal for most other ongoing therapy groups—between six and twelve. Below six, it is difficult to sustain discussion, and above twelve the group becomes unwieldy. For time-limited workshops, however, where the purpose is primarily to provide a beginning understanding of RET principles applied to specific problem areas, group size can go well beyond this arbitrary number.

The answer to what kinds of characteristics to look for in a potential client for an ongoing RET group is best given in the negative. Ellis has two criteria for screening out potential group members. First, is the client a compulsive talker who will dominate the group session? Second, can the client participate in an appropriate manner? Note that these criteria are both based on the client's potential to disrupt the group, not on diagnosis. Obviously, these criteria will rule out certain individuals who are highly disturbed, perhaps psychotic. But they do not rule out for group membership a person *because* he or she is seen as psychotic. In fact, many individuals labeled psychotic will not, for the most part, be disruptive to the group. The criteria are aimed at eliminating those persons who cannot contribute to the group's task, even though they themselves might benefit. Should someone develop into a compulsive talker or become highly disruptive, the therapist may remove that person from the group and refer him or her to individual therapy.

Experience has shown that it is not necessary to select clients with particular problems or diagnoses for an RET group. Nor does the group have to be homogeneous by age, background, or other demographic variables. It is desirable, however, to have about equal numbers of men and women, for many problems brought up in the group concern relating to members of the opposite sex.

Let us assume that the group has had no introduction to RET or even to group therapy. Here are some suggestions for orienting a group to RET: Begin by letting the group members know why they are there, what they can get from being there, and what their task will be. They are there for therapy or counseling. They can benefit by gaining some solutions to their personal problems. Their task is to talk about their own problems and to help solve other people's problems. Discuss these and related points as much as seems necessary to satisfy the questions raised by the clients. Be sure to describe the therapist's role. You are there to teach them how to solve personal problems more effectively and to begin to do some things they have wanted to do or to stop doing some things that they want to stop. Also discuss these and related points as much as seems necessary to provide an orientation.

At this point it is helpful to have a get-acquainted activity if the group members are strangers to each other. Many such activities abound in the literature of groups and are not unique to RET. Simple introductions will do, with members giving their names and saying something about themselves. An example of a more elaborate exercise involves pairing off group members for a ten- to fifteen-minute discussion. Their discussion is structured by the following incomplete sentences which can be delivered aloud or printed on cards:

- My name is . . .
- Some things I'd like you to know about me . . .
- What I hope to get from coming to this group . . .
- Some areas I wouldn't like to talk about . . .

The group is told not to worry about completeness; the purpose of this exercise is to acquaint each client with one other person, not to exhaustively discuss each point. When time is up, the group is reassembled and the partners are asked to introduce each other to the rest of the group, saying what they now know about the other person. Finally, the therapist checks to see that everyone knows everyone else's first name, including the therapist's.

If the group members already seem eager to talk, a less time-consuming exercise is simply to have them say their names, but with this variation: Seated in a circle (therapist included), the person to the left of the first person repeats the first person's name, then adds his or her own name. The next person repeats the first two names, adding his or her own, and so on. The second and last time around, each person is to repeat every other person's name. This simple exercise quickly and effectively allows everyone a chance to remember all the names.

Thus far, the group members have been oriented and introduced to each other. Assuming that they know little or nothing of RET, it is time to teach them. We recommend a short presentation about human disturbance, emphasizing the following points:

1. Everyone has problems, and each problem usually has two parts—a practical part and a psychological or an emotional part.
2. Most often we can solve the practical part better, or learn to live with it better if it cannot be solved, if we solve the psychological part first.
3. The psychological part can be understood by means of a simple formula: activating events (*A*), combined with our beliefs (*B*) about them, result in emotional and behavioral consequences (*C*).
4. Most of our disruptive emotions and behavior come from beliefs that have absolutistic commands and demands in them, usually signaled by the word *must*.
5. From these commands and demands, we derive several illogical conclusions: It is awful if it is not the way I say it *must*

be. I can't stand it if it is not the way I say it *must* be. I am worthless if it is not the way I say it *must* be. ("I," "you," or "the world" can be substituted for "it" in each of the above.)

6. These illogical conclusions result in disruptive feelings and behaviors: anxiety, depression, guilt, shame, anger, avoidance, inertia, self-punishment, and direct or passive verbal or physical aggression.
7. If you want to solve the psychological part of the problems and feel and act differently, discover your beliefs and change those that are unrealistic.

It is best to hold the presentation of the basics of RET to about fifteen minutes, for even though we have defined the therapist as the "expert," one of our tasks as therapists is to encourage the group to participate. If the therapist does too much of the talking during the first session, he or she may induce a set or expectation that will be hard to change. Because the group is ongoing, the therapist will have plenty of time to reiterate the above points in the context of the problems that clients present.

Major Group Strategies

Although all RET groups are oriented to problem solving, there is a choice of models at this point. The therapist can structure the session so that the format consists of each client, in turn, presenting a specific problem; about a half hour is then spent on each problem. Or the therapist can adopt a more experiential format to reinforce the presentation of basic RET principles. We recommend that the therapist incorporate both individual problem solving and experiential exercises. We turn our attention first to problem solving.

Following the presentation and discussion of RET basics, the therapist asks who would like to present a problem. As in an individual session, he puts the problem into *ABC* terms and shows the client precisely what he or she is doing to create emotional disturbance. But, because this is group therapy, the therapist also tries to involve the other group members by calling on them by first names and asking them for comments on the formulation of the problem. For instance, the therapist can ask, "Has anyone else had a similar problem?" or "Have you ever felt that way, Sue?" The therapist attempts to get everyone focused on the *A*, the *B*, and the *C*, and to underscore the idea that disturbance comes from the *musts* in our heads.

Once the clients have been shown how they are disturbing themselves, the therapist attempts to get members of the group to question the validity of the irrational beliefs. The therapist can model for them a few good questions; for example, "Where's the evidence?" or "Why must it be the way you demand?" Although group members are usually not very effective in disputing irrational ideas at this early stage, the therapist keeps them involved, models for them, and coaches and corrects their errors. If time permits, the therapist can explore the practical part of the client's problem. Many group members want easy, practical solutions to their difficulties and want to offer such solutions to others. Practical solutions have their place, for indeed many clients do lack social and other practical skills. But—as in individual therapy—RET first, practical problem solving second. In any case, the therapist ends the discussion with the first client by assigning homework that the client can report on during the next session. Homework assignments given in the group can be the same as those used in individual therapy (see Chapter Six).

The therapist then asks for another problem and repeats the procedure outlined above. This, in general, is the format of a problem-oriented focus. Group members will soon learn to bring in problems each time they meet and to report on homework assignments. In fact, a good way to begin subsequent sessions is with reports on homework accomplishments. The first session is ended with an assignment to all group members to read some RET literature, so that they can become better acquainted with the approach.

As the group gets better trained in RET group procedures, the therapist can move more and more into a coaching role. In the initial sessions, the interaction occurs primarily between the therapist and the focal client and secondarily between the focal client and the other group members. In later sessions, most of the interaction can take place between the group members themselves as they try to help the focal client. The therapist can move to the sidelines, observe and correct when necessary, and guide the discussion rather than conduct the discussion.

The ideal outcome for the RET group is to have it function well without the therapist. When each group member understands the basic principles of RET and is able to use them to help the others, the group can become a self-help group. It is not easy to reach this point, however, because some problems are difficult to pin down. Even though the basic *ABC* model is simple, people's problems may be more complex and require an experienced and skilled therapist to unravel them enough to put them into *ABC* format. A common example of a problem that may require the therapist's assistance is anger. Most group members can learn to look for the *must* ideas that lead to anger (for example, "You must do things to please me") and their conclusions (for example, "and I blame you, you no-good bastard, for displeasing me!"). But anger can mask unassertiveness, which can derive from low self-esteem and resultant anxiety. The most important problem, the client's self-judgments, may therefore not receive attention even though the anger is correctly dealt with.

Even a stimulating problem-focused group will tire eventually of hearing the same people present similar problems. To relieve the tedium, experiential exercises can be introduced occasionally. Some groups can be conducted almost entirely by means of experiential exercises. An exercise becomes a vehicle to evoke feelings and behavior *in vivo,* not as an end in itself but to provide a common experience around which to center group discussion of the underlying beliefs and attitudes. The experiential approach alone is difficult with an ongoing group. Like too much of any good thing, exercises can also become tiresome. However, with a time-limited group, especially one designed to increase personal awareness rather than for therapeutic purposes, and as a relief from the sameness of problem solving in an ongoing therapy group, we highly recommend use of experiential exercises.

The therapist who chooses to emphasize the experiential focus will introduce exercises immediately after the presentation of basic RET principles. An exercise such as the one we shall describe can be used to show the effects of thoughts on feelings. Like many RET exercises, it probably has its origins in one of the games described in the encounter group literature. RET practitioners have not invented many new exercises; but, simply by processing the experience according to the *ABC* model, they can easily adapt most exercises designed to uncover feelings or expose typical interpersonal behaviors.

T: I'm going to ask you to think of some secret, something about yourself that you normally would not tell anyone else. It might be something you have done in the past or something you're doing now in the present; some secret habit or physical characteristic. [Pause.] Are you thinking about it? [Pause.] Good. Now I'm going to ask someone to tell the group what he or she has thought of . . . to describe it in some detail. [Short pause.] But since I know everyone would want to do this, and we don't have enough time to get to everyone, I'll select someone. [Pause—looking around the group.] Yes, I have someone in mind. [Pause.] But before I call on that person, let me ask what you are experiencing right now?

Words like *anxious, tense,* and *nervous* are commonly mentioned. Ideas such as "I hope you don't call on me!" are expressed. At this point, the group can be shown that the thought of doing something, not the thing itself, led to their feelings. The therapist then asks questions about what kinds of thoughts led to these feelings, particularly to anxiety. Typical responses are "If I said something foolish or embarrassing, people would laugh at me, and that would be awful." "If they would find out something about me I wouldn't want them to know, that would be awful." Once the discussion is begun, it often picks up momentum as people realize that their strongly evaluative thinking about what might happen led to their anxious reactions. This is the point that the therapist wishes the group to learn from the experience.

As the discussion progresses, the therapist can show the group members that they may be demanding that they follow implicit norms in the situation. A thought that may coexist with those mentioned above is "I must do what the leader says." The anxiety-producing conclusions are obvious: "And if I don't do what he says, he and the others will think that I've copped out or can't take it or have some other weakness. That would be awful, and it would prove what a worthless person I truly am!"

Further discussion can show people their defensiveness and self-protectiveness. For example, some people will admit that they would not have revealed anything too embarrassing, just something that sounds risky but really is "safe." Others will admit that they thought of leaving the room. Such responses can often be generalized to other situations as well. The therapist can ask questions like "Is your reaction today typical of the way you usually act when put on the spot?"

Following discussion of how this self-disturbance was created, the therapist moves to disputing irrational beliefs and tries to involve the group in this process as much as possible. Homework is then assigned to the group, to individuals, or both. The individual assignment can arise from the discussion of a particular problem, and the group assignment can be preplanned. For example, the group members might be assigned the task of taking a risk in some other setting, perhaps the risk of saying something personal without knowing what the reaction will be.

An exercise such as the one just described is a good way to start a new group. Once clients have been introduced to RET principles and have worked together for a number of weeks, other exercises can be used to identify irrational beliefs and to help dispute them. For example, exercises such as the gestalt hot seat or body exploration are appropriate. The exercise is conducted in a typical gestalt therapy manner, but afterward the clients are assembled in a group and asked to identify their feelings during the exercise and to explore and challenge their belief systems behind the feelings. These exercises can help get at the *ABC*s and bring these elements to the clients' awareness. The rational-emotive therapist typically goes on to active disputation to maximize the helpfulness of the exercise. Although we are describing the use of exercises in a rational framework, at times the therapist may want to use them for the purposes originally intended: building group rapport, developing trust, building intimacy, establishing self-disclosure skills, and so forth.

Problems with Group Therapy

A common problem in group therapy is the giving of advice by group members. Practical advice, even if it is sound, may be poorly timed and can prevent a member from facing his disturbing irrationalities. While we are certainly not opposed to practical advice, a client's ability to utilize suggestions will be maximal only after he has disputed his irrational beliefs and reduced his emotional distress. The therapist's job, therefore, is not one of inhibiting practical advice but of assuring its proper timing. Poor advice is another matter. For example, after group therapy one night, some members strongly advised a habitually unassertive woman to speak up to her boss when he did something she disliked. She did—and got fired. Had the therapist been there, she could have clearly alerted the client to the risks of speaking up as well as the advantages.

Another problem often encountered is clients' delving into too much detail. For example, after a client has stated that she is upset because her mother-in-law is critical of her, other group members may pursue this problem with:

- What does she say to you?
- Does she really say you're incompetent?
- Does your husband go along with her?
- How often do you see her?

While some exploration of the details of the situation is desirable, groups can waste time by endlessly going after details about activating experiences or the facts about the problem, just as some clients like to engage in seemingly endless narrations about their activities and problems. In such instances, the therapist will want to remind the clients that people are not disturbed by events but by the view they take of events.

Unbalanced participation by clients is another problem. The therapist's role includes preventing some dominant members from taking over the discussion and encouraging the members who seldom say anything to join in. Therapists who have been in leaderless groups and nondirective "growth groups" may be surprised at how directively an RET group therapist acts in controlling the discussion. The RET therapist does not believe that asking a client to talk less will do psychological damage or that silent members should be left alone to speak up when they are "ready." Therefore, the therapist may say to the silent client, "What do you think about this problem, George?" or "Has anything that John is describing ever happened to you, Grace?" or "You've been quietly thinking, Mary; I wonder what's on your mind right now?" This last question is particularly good, since there is undoubtedly something on her mind, and if she does not want to talk about it, her reluctance can be investigated in *ABC* terms. Silent members, if they are not otherwise highly disturbed and thus inappropriate for the group, usually fear criticism for speaking in public, even in a therapy group where people are largely accepting. This fear is appropriate for group discussion.

Many problems can develop from the dynamics of a group. In any group of interacting individuals, certain patterns of interaction emerge over time. Members sort themselves out into a hierarchy on the basis of how much they speak or how good their ideas are perceived to be. It is not necessary for the therapist to construct a sociogram in order to discover who is seen by the others as most helpful. If the most helpful knows RET, the high ranking can work well. If the most helpful does not, it is important for the therapist to counteract his or her suggestions.

Informal norms emerge in an ongoing group. These unwritten rules cover what can be said and what cannot be said. For example, some groups may agree to the unwritten rule "I won't confront you if you won't confront me" or "We all need to protect Bob; he's too fragile for discussion" or "It's all right to keep secrets even though the therapist says it's against the rules." While there is less chance that informal norms will develop in an RET group, because the therapist provides the structure for each session, it nonetheless can occur. When a group norm emerges that thwarts therapy, the therapist would do well to take measures to expose it. For example, the therapist can discuss the norm and point out to the group members how their behavior has conformed to this unwritten rule, or she can create an experiential exercise in which norm breaking is a featured part of the activity. For example, if a norm forbids members from confronting each other, group members can be instructed to act confrontively toward a specific member, toward the therapist, or toward an empty chair; or each member can be assigned to say something critical about every other member of the group.

The therapist has the responsibility for initiating the challenging and exposing of norms, because the group members will react against any member who frequently or seriously breaks the norm. Therapy groups react predictably, just as every other group does under such circumstances. First, they attempt to control the behavior of the deviating member—perhaps by criticism or by giving information or by a warning. If this fails, then very likely they will reject the offender and perhaps even say that the member should be expelled from the group. That this reaction is typical of groups highlights the importance of the therapist's setting the climate of undamning acceptance of everyone in the group, even those who break norms.

The group process can be used to therapeutic advantage if the group members react against a person who breaks a norm and the norm-breaking behavior is mediated by irrational thinking. For example, a norm of every therapy group had better be that members bring up personal problems and work on them. If a member never brings up a personal problem, especially if he actively and persistently offers advice to others, the other members will focus on him. They may ask questions such as "Why don't you ever bring up anything?" or "Are you just here to help with *our* problems?" or "Do you think you're the therapist?" If some group members are angry, the therapist can use the *ABC*s to show them that they are needlessly upsetting themselves with the deviant's behavior. Then, if the therapist also believes that the "deviant" is avoiding his own problems, she can try to find out why by looking for anxiety and/or low frustration tolerance.

Finally, boring leaders can be hazardous to group effectiveness. Groups are probably more successful, and certainly more interesting, if the therapist has a lively, stimulating manner. A sense of fun is highly desirable in an RET therapist, and the judicious use of wit and humor can have therapeutic impact. A wisely used sense of humor is likely to be even more important in group therapy than it is in conducting individual therapy.

Conduct of Group Members

It may be clear by now that the RET therapist is not an equal member of the group. He or she is a specialist, and special rules of conduct apply to the therapist. The therapist's conduct is governed by the codes of ethics of his or her professional organization. Besides behaving unethically, the therapist can behave in a number of other ways that can impede the progress of clients in a group. Since the problems discussed in Chapter Seven apply equally to individual or to group therapy, we will mention only one special rule for the group therapist here: Do not socialize with clients. Although this rule applies equally to individual therapy, the temptation to do so may be greater with a group. Socializing can detract from the professional relationship. In addition to creating undue problems of transference and countertransference, socializing can feed into clients' need for approval or their need to manipulate an authority figure.

Members of a therapy group, whether RET is used or not, are also subject to ethical rules. Cardinal among these is the rule that everything that is said is confidential if it concerns another group member. If a member wishes to quote to a friend the therapist's wisdom about the "nature of human nature," that is permitted. But to say that John is thinking of leaving his wife is strictly forbidden. There are difficulties in enforcing rules of confidentiality, since each member's behavior cannot be kept under surveillance for the entire week. Each is bound to abide by the rules himself, and should any infractions come to the group's attention, they can be dealt with accordingly.

While it is unwise for client and therapist to socialize, clients are permitted to socialize with others in the group. Such socializing, however, has certain disadvantages. For example, a cohesiveness may develop that is disadvantageous to therapeutic progress. If the cohesiveness is coupled with a dedication to irrational thinking, therapeutic change will prove difficult. Clients who socialize outside the group with other group members also may gossip about what has been revealed in the session. If the socializing includes people who do not belong to the group, such gossiping can result in a serious breach of confidentiality. Another serious disadvantage to socializing with other group members is the possibility that an individual will become dependent on the group for outside social contact and not take the risk of socializing with people he knows less well. An obvious result is that social skills will fail to develop, and fear of social rejection may be strengthened.

On the advantage side, group members may come to know each other better and support each other in their attempts to change. They may develop close ties, perhaps for the first time, and this is beneficial—provided these are not the only ties developed. Furthermore, members may support each other's attempts to think more rationally. One rule we recommend about socializing outside the group is that everything that is said among group members can be brought up for discussion during a later group therapy session. Thus, if John has begun an affair with Mary, the rules say that they are to report this to the group. Failure to do so provides an opportunity for therapeutic inquiry: What did they fear about openly revealing their secret?

Rather than burden both therapist and clients with a long list of rules, we simply urge all therapists to use good judgment, keep ethical considerations (particularly confidentiality) in mind, and remember that the purpose of the group is therapy. Anything that interferes with therapy belongs on the taboo list.

Illustration of a Group Session

Unlike the individual session in Chapter Eight, the session illustrated here is not part of an actual session but one we have created to illustrate some of the principles described in this chapter. We provide annotations to describe critical events in this session.

1 *Therapist (T):* Who wants to bring up a problem?

2 *John:* I do. I've got a job interview coming up later this week, and I feel very anxious about it.

3 *Mary:* You're finally getting an interview? How nice!

T starts in typical fashion: T structures the session by asking for specific problems. In the unlikely event that no one volunteered, T could (1) wait silently; (2) encourage volunteering; (3) check on previous homework assignments; (4) introduce an exercise; or (5) ask a group member, especially one who has not presented a recent problem, how he or she is faring. John did speak up, but it was probably not a sudden decision on his part. Group members learn to expect opportunities to work on personal problems and plan what they will say. They may write notes to give to T as they enter the room. Mary's response shows that members are often mutually supportive and, unless quite disturbed, take genuine interest in each other's fate. It is not unusual for some members to know more personal information about each other than T does, since T's focus is on philosophies of living rather than on details of the client's past or current life circumstances.

4 *John:* Yeah. It's been a long time since I had a chance to get a really good job. But I'm scared I'll blow the interview.

5 *Tom:* What makes you think you'll blow it?

6 *John:* Because I'm so nervous about it.

7 *T:* Sounds like you've got two problems: One, you'll get nervous; and, two, you'll blow the interview if you get nervous. Let's look at the second one. How would you feel if you blew the interview?

8 *John:* Terrible. I've waited so long. I'd get down on myself.

9 *Tom:* Depressed?

10 *John:* Yeah. And angry too.

11 *Pete:* That happened to me one time. I figured I'd never get another chance.

12 *T:* John, I wonder if you can figure out what you'd be saying to yourself if you blew the interview. How would you get yourself angry and depressed?

T (7) structures the discussion by focusing on the problem of failure and probes for emotional consequences. After eliciting depression and anger, T (12) probes for mediating beliefs.

13 *John:* I guess—like Pete, I think this is my last chance. . . .

14 *Pete:* [interrupting] But it's not.

15 *John:* I know. But it feels like it is.

16 *T:* It feels like it is because you're defining it that way. But let's assume that it is your last chance to get a job this good—it's probably not, but let's assume that it is—why would that be awful?

T does not offer support as Pete does (11 and 14); rather, T underscores the contingency between thoughts and feelings and assumes the worst outcome, just as the client does. Note, however, that T subtly sides with Pete ("it's probably not") while tentatively agreeing with John's construction of the situation. T does not yet want to focus on the truth or falsity of John's report of *A*; T wants to work with John's belief system.

17 *John:* I'd never be able to work at what I want to do.

18 *Mary:* How do you know you won't?

19 *T:* Mary's right. You probably would get another chance. But let's assume the worst. Now, why would it be awful if you didn't get to work at the job of your choice?

T redirects John's attention to his belief system while supporting Mary's comment. T does this because Mary's comment pertains to the probability of the occurrence of what John anticipates (*A*), and T wants John to work on his philosophical beliefs rather than on his accuracy of forecasting outcomes. However, by speaking in this manner, T works at two levels (*A* and *B*) at once.

20 *John:* I don't think I could be happy doing anything else.
21 *Pete:* But you're not that unhappy now, are you?
22 *John:* No.
23 *Tom:* Yeah, since you've been coming to group, you don't seem nearly so unhappy.
24 *T:* Right! Happiness is relative. Can you imagine yourself being unable to work at what you want *and still* being relatively happy?

Again T supports a group member's comment and tries to take John's thinking another step forward. The idea of relative happiness is important, especially for clients who think in absolute or dichotomous ways. T could expand on this point by distinguishing between satisfaction compared with an ideal (absolute satisfaction) and satisfaction relative to available alternatives (relative satisfaction). The latter is obtainable while the former usually is not.

25 *John:* Yeah. I guess I can.
26 *T:* What could you do to make yourself happy?
27 *John:* Try something else. Hey, I think I see what you mean. Have I been demanding that I get the job I want and no other?
28 *T:* Let's ask the group. What do you think, Janet?
29 *Janet:* I think so. John, I think you've been like a baby,

demanding to have this job. I gotta get what I want.

30 *Tom:* I think so too. [Others nod agreement.]

31 *T:* It would be better for you to give up that demand if you want to feel better. Now let's look at your nervousness.

T involves Janet (28), who has been silent, and then the rest of the group. T then turns to John's more immediate problem (31). T does this because John already knows that he is making unrealistic demands (27), and T hypothesizes that the same cognitive statements or rules of living underlie the "nervousness" problem.

32 *John:* I think part of it is due to wanting to do so well because I have to get the job. But if I don't demand to get the job, I won't feel so nervous. The two are connected.

33 *T:* Good insight. But isn't there more to it than that?

34 *Janet:* John is still worried about what they'll think of him.

35 *John:* Of course. If they don't think I'm any good . . .

36 *Janet:* But wait a minute. Don't you remember the difference between judging your ability and judging you? Which one are you worried about?

37 *John:* I guess that they'll judge me. That they'll think I'm an asshole for even applying to them.

38 *Tom:* That's a put-down!

39 *Pete:* How could their rejecting you for the job make you an asshole?

40 *Mary:* It couldn't, John. Do you see that?

41 *John:* But it's so hard not to think that way—and they might really think I'm an asshole.

42 *Tom:* Do you need their approval?

43 *John:* No.

44 *Tom:* You sound like you do. [Others nod.]

45 *T:* If they really think you're an asshole, you, of course, are an asshole. I'll prove it to you with the help of the group. Let's all think to ourselves,

"John is an asshole." [Silence, followed by a few laughs.]

The group (34-44) is doing well in talking with John, so T stays out of the discussion. Here T switches to a paradoxical approach. Since it involves humorous exaggeration, it is somewhat risky—John may wrongly conclude that T and the group are having a joke at his expense. But John seems insightful and the group positive in its attitude toward John, so the risk is slight. Demonstrations are often more memorable than logic, even if they seem stagy and contrived.

46 *T:* John, are you turning into an asshole?
47 *John:* [Laughs.] No.
48 *T:* We're not trying hard enough. Let's say it out loud: "John, you're an asshole!"
49 *All:* [except John] "John, you're an asshole!"
50 *T:* Again, louder! It's still not working.
51 *Group:* "John, you're an asshole!"
52 *John:* OK! OK! I get the point. I *don't* need their approval of me.
53 *T:* I'm sorry our magic didn't work, but it did seem to help you think more clearly. Now, you'll probably feel a little tense during the interview, and that's good because you won't be complacent or dull. Remember, John, we'd like to see you get the job, even though your world won't end if you don't. Let's try some rehearsal; would you like that?

T actually encourages a bit of anxiety, subtly contradicting the common tendency to want to feel perfectly untense. T uses role playing to reduce anxiety through overpreparation. New erroneous thinking might emerge as a result of the role playing; even if it does not, practical benefits can be derived from the rehearsal.

54 *John:* Yeah. If it will help me get ready.
55 *T:* Who'd like to role-play the interviewer?

56 *Pete:* I would. I've had plenty of experience on the other side of the desk. Now's my chance.

57 *T:* OK. The rest of us will observe and make suggestions.

58 *John:* [begins to role play] My name's John and I'm here to interview for the job. I'm feeling very nervous.

59 *Mary:* I've got to interrupt!

60 *Tom:* You don't *have* to; you mean you want to.

61 *T:* Tom's right, but let's not pick nits.

Some overzealous clients spot every *should, must, have to, got to,* and so on, whether they are meant absolutistically or not. T supports the ideal of vigilance without dwelling on it or allowing it to sidetrack the discussion.

62 *Mary:* Don't tell him you're nervous, John. That makes a poor impression. [Others nod and murmur agreement.]

63 *John:* OK. I'll skip that part.

64 *Pete:* [role playing] Now, just what are your qualifications, John?

65 *John:* Uh—I don't think he'll ask that.

66 *Pete:* I got asked that a couple of times. It's better to be ready.

67 *John:* [role playing] Thank you for asking. I know a bit about your company and here's what I think I can do for you.

68 *Tom:* Hey, that's good! Where did you learn that?

69 *John:* From a book on how to interview for jobs. Mary recommended it one night when you weren't here.

70 *T:* We'll fill you in later, Tom. Can we get back to the role playing? Let's raise the ante. Pete, put some more pressure on him.

71 *Pete:* [role playing] Now, young man, just what makes you so sure you can do anything for us?

72 *John:* [Laughs.] Here's what I've done lately and my relevant experience. [Laughs.] Pete, nobody would be as tough as that. But if they are, I'm ready.

73 *T:* We can rehearse some more.

T has remained out of the dialogue since the group's effort is relevant to John's practical problem solving. Collectively, they may have some more information than T has.

74 *John:* No, I feel confident about what I'm going to say, and as long as I remember not to put myself down I'll be OK.

75 *T:* How about giving yourself a reminder?

76 *John:* You mean write myself a note?

77 *T:* Sure. Pilots use a checklist when they take off and land a plane, so that they don't have to rely on fallible human memory. You can do the same.

Clients frequently overlook practical aids or feel ashamed to use them because they think they are a sign of weakness or dependence. T quickly legitimizes mnemonic devices without confirming whether or not John would feel ashamed to use them. Another member of the group might have the problem or might simply benefit from a rational reminder. Even if the reminder is totally gratuitous, it takes very little time to mention it.

78 *Janet:* What homework assignment do you want to give yourself, John?

79 *John:* I don't know. I guess to keep reminding myself that I'm not an asshole if I don't get the job and that it's not the end of my world. I can still be happy.

80 *T:* That's fine. But how about something with more action in it? Where you do something?

81 *John:* Anybody got a suggestion?

82 *Tom:* You're already doing something by going for the interview.

83 *John:* I could deliberately screw up the interview.

84 *T:* No! Don't sabotage yourself. That's what other people are for. Homework is intended to make life easier, not cut you off from going after what you want. How about trying to make some more appointments to interview? That way you could

work on the self-acceptance solution to nervousness and help yourself by having a few more interviews lined up.

85 *John:* Sounds practical. And I'm to accept myself while I risk getting turned down for interviews?

86 *T:* Right.

87 *John:* I'll let you know what happens.

Janet (78) seems to have become the "assistant therapist." Since her remarks are helpful, T allows it. However, recalling that Janet was silent at first, T makes a mental note to monitor her participation to see whether Janet is avoiding her own problems by helping others. T (84) advocates behavioral-experiential homework, not thinking homework alone. T emphasizes practical aspects of risk taking rather than the foolish testing of one's mettle. John probably knows he will be asked what happened. His statement (87) reflects this. We hypothesize that clients who make a public commitment to a homework activity are more likely to follow through, especially when they believe they will be asked to report on it.

10

RET and Other Forms of Psychotherapy

Despite the difficulties in combining theoretical and procedural approaches, many practitioners want to use RET occasionally rather than exclusively. Still other practitioners prefer an eclectic approach, in which they take the most appealing features of several systems and combine them into a personal system of therapy and counseling. We are obviously biased in favor of comprehensive RET. However, we also wish to bridge gaps between it and other forms of therapy and counseling. We wish to help practitioners who want to integrate RET into their usual approach to treatment, for we are convinced that RET has much to offer. We wish to work toward a goal of recognizing convergences among all successful approaches to counseling and therapy, for we hope that eventually there will emerge a unified theory and practice of psychological helping. Therefore, we offer this attempt at an integration of RET and other approaches and add it to those of Raimy (1975) and Dolliver (1979). We fully realize that we have not represented the views of other systems as accurately as we can RET, and we welcome corrections. We also hope that our effort will prompt others who know more about other therapies to make similar attempts.

RET as Cognitive-Behavior Therapy

The central assumption of RET and the other cognitive-behavior approaches to treatment (Raimy, 1975, pp. 195-196) is that "cognitions control emotions and feelings; disruptive affect is the result of faulty perceptions, beliefs, and convictions. . . . The alternative point of view, that emotion or affect is somehow an independent entity which can be modified or eliminated by 'expressing it,' is an outmoded doctrine." Cognitions include thoughts, meanings, images, and beliefs. They serve as mediators between stimulus events and psychological and behavioral responses. In broad terms, they are simply elaborations of Woodworth's S-O-R paradigm. However, various cognitive-behavior theorists have given greater importance to some types of cognitive mediators than to others. Ellis (1977d) identifies beliefs or *evaluative thinking* as the controlling cognitive mediator. In Beck's (1976) view, *meanings* are the crucial mediating cognitive variables. Lazarus (1978) emphasizes the importance of *images.* Watzlawick (1978), who does not claim to be a cognitive-behavior theorist, stresses the importance of "world view" and, like most of the others mentioned in this paragraph, quotes the philosopher Epictetus: "It is not things themselves that worry us, but the opinions that we have about those things."

Comprehensive RET acknowledges the importance of all these cognitive mediators, of the multiplicity of tactics for producing change, and of the desirability of flexibility in using tactics in working with clients. We are not aware of any tactic reported in published reports of cognitive-behavior approaches that is alien to RET. Cognitive-behavior approaches to therapy include all approaches that attempt to utilize thoughts in the control or modification of behavior, both verbal and nonverbal. Comprehensive RET overlaps the entire field of cognitive-behavior therapy and has points in common with some nonbehavioral approaches as well. We do not imply that cognitive-behavior approaches are subdivisions of RET or that comprehensive RET is a subdivision of cognitive-behavior approaches. Rather, we are talking about bridging gaps. A brief description of the main cognitive-behavior approaches will show some similarities to and differences from RET. References cited may be consulted for more extensive descriptions of each approach.

Except for some relatively minor points, in practice comprehensive RET is virtually identical with Lazarus's (1976) multimodal behavior therapy. Like RET, the multimodal approach employs behavioral and experiential methods in addition to cognitive tactics. Lazarus advocates a more systematic approach to the various modalities, to which he has given the acronym BASIC ID: behavior, affect, sensation, imagery, cognition, interpersonal behavior, and drugs. Since he has written relatively little about a theory of disturbance, we cannot say that multimodal therapy makes the same theoretical assumptions that RET makes. Further, he does not emphasize philosophical change to the same extent that RET does, although he probably gives it more emphasis than other forms of therapy do.

The cognitive therapy of Beck (1976) is strikingly similar to RET. Beck's emphasis is on the client's perceptions, descriptions of reality, logical inferences, and, to a lesser extent, evaluative thinking. In comprehensive RET, the emphasis is reversed in principle but not necessarily in practice. We hypothesize that, when jargon is omitted from a session with a depressed or an anxious client, comprehensive RET and Beck's cognitive therapy will be virtually identical.

Maultsby's (1975) rational behavior training (RBT) began as a restatement and an elaboration of RET. In some of his earlier writings, Maultsby equated RET with RBT. RBT gives very little emphasis to philosophical change and a great deal of attention to accurate perceptions and descriptions of activating events. In this way, RBT resembles Beck's cognitive therapy more than it does RET. RBT also relies mainly on two techniques: rational self-analysis (a form of written homework) and rational-emotive imagery (a form of cognitive rehearsal that differs slightly from Ellis's version of rational-emotive imagery).

Meichenbaum's (1977) cognitive-behavior modification uses cognitive self-statements to modify behavior. Little attention is given to changing emotional responses, but, rather to controlling behavioral reactions to emotional responses. In Meichenbaum's view, there is little that can be done to prevent anxiety, but one can learn to act in spite of it. Therefore, by focusing on the behavior response portion of the emotional episode, he attempts to control behavior after the behavior-producing thoughts and feelings have occurred. In RET, rational coping statements, which clients learn to make in place of the dysfunctional statements that create disturbance, are the counterparts of the Meichenbaum "talking to yourself" approach. Meichenbaum's procedure is similar to Maultsby's in this respect. A seasoned RET practitioner may use self-statements–such as "Don't worry; worry won't help anything" or "I can control how I feel"–in working with some kinds of clients, particularly those who are too young or unintelligent to rethink their evaluative attitudes.

Although Spivak, Platt, and Shure (1976) have recently developed a social problem-solving approach, problem solving has been used in RET, especially in groups, for many years. Often clients are trained in how to solve problems, anticipate consequences, and acquire specific skills. Although this approach is "inelegant," since it does not stress unconditional self-acceptance and a philosophy of tolerance, in any given session RET practitioners may emphasize problem solving and increasing the accuracy of perceptions, descriptions, and inferences about reality. One would also find a good portion of behavioral rehearsal, practical advice-giving, and many more activities in addition to classical disputing.

Strategic psychotherapy, as presented by Rabkin (1977),

has a great deal in common with RET. Rabkin's approach to treatment seems almost atheoretical in its eclecticism. He offers a variety of devices to induce clients to think and act differently. All these devices have been used by RET practitioners and no doubt by therapists of other orientations. Finally, among several other cognitive approaches, Greenwald's (1973) direct decision therapy and Farrelly and Brandsma's (1974) provocative therapy overlap significantly with RET.

There are very many cognitive-behavioral techniques (see Foreyt and Rathjen, 1978). All form an important part of the RET practitioner's skills. The RET practitioner does not rely solely on cognitive interventions but uses any means within ethical limits to produce attitudinal and behavioral changes. It is unfortunate that most RET literature is devoted to cognitive tactics of intervention, leaving the impression that they alone are used (see Wilson, 1978)—whereas, in fact, cognitive disputing rarely is used alone.

Relations to Other Therapies

Comprehensive RET not only is coextensive with cognitive-behavior therapy but overlaps with nonbehavioral approaches as well. There are striking similarities between RET and the now almost forgotten therapy of Paul DuBois (see Raimy, 1975, for a discussion). Kelly's (1955) fixed-role approach also bears many similarities to RET. Although Lewin (1935) did not create a system of psychotherapy, his influence is felt in the group dynamics movement, and for many years his was the only cognitive statement of personality theory. Lewin's formula, $B = f(p, e)$ (Behavior is a function of the person's characteristics and his perception of the environment), easily translates into $C = f(B, A)$ (Emotional and behavioral consequences are a function of a person's belief system and his perception of activating events). The conclusion is clear that RET has a decided phenomenological component. Subjective appraisals of reality and of values are the substance of RET and are what make it distinctive as a cognitive-behavior therapy.

Freudian Psychoanalysis. Psychoanalysis as a theory has

some points of correspondence to RET; for example, the demandingness of the id and the moral imperatives of the superego. Freud was a cognitive theorist of sorts, although he maintained that the key cognitions are unconscious. Freud was also a biological theorist in that human sexual motives derive from physiological processes; however, their representation in the mind has to be cognitive—that is, they are mental processes. The treatment goal of Freudian psychoanalysis is to replace unconscious motives with rational decisions: Where the id was, the ego shall be. In addition, Freud and Ellis both employ the principle of hedonism in their conceptions of personality. Freud spoke of offsetting hedonistic strivings by sublimating them, whereas Ellis flaunts hedonism by frankly declaring that pleasure is good—particularly when both long-term and short-term pleasures are calculated and an optimal balance struck. While Freud wanted to tame id impulses, Ellis wants to enjoy them.

The differences between RET and psychoanalysis are great. Freudian orthodoxy has been a favorite target for many of Ellis's most vigorous attacks. RET postulates no structural unconscious. Some thoughts are unconscious in the sense that they are not in awareness, but people can fairly easily become aware of them. The American habit of looking left when starting to cross a street may remain out of one's awareness until a trip to England, where traffic moves in the opposite direction. But this, of course, is not Freud's construct of the unconscious. The assumption of unconscious motivation of all significant behavior suggests that humans are not quite responsible for their actions. This assumption clashes harshly with the ethical values of humanism and with those of the Judeo-Christian religions. RET is decidedly existential in its emphasis on human responsibility. As Ellis (1977b) put it to music in one of his rational songs, "I could, of course, refuse to be crazy, but I, alas, am just too goddamned lazy." By adopting (often with difficulty) rational outlooks on one's life, one can control emotions as well as actions.

Another major difference between RET and Freudian psychoanalysis concerns the basic causes of disturbance. Freud changed his position on this issue, settling on the threat of expression of id impulses as the cause of anxiety. The need to defend against anxiety then leads to the ego defense mechanisms and neurotic patterns of behavior. Ellis has consistently maintained that it is primarily strongly evaluative thinking—one's system of beliefs—that creates emotional experiences. Childhood events, relationships with parents, and other prominent features of Freud's theory play little or no part in RET. While they may influence the shaping of one's beliefs, they are not the sole determining factor. Ellis, like George Kelly, rejects childhood experiences, pathogenic mothering, and passive conditionings by the environment as significant factors in determining one's cognitions.

Traditional psychoanalytic treatment differs greatly from RET. Instead of passive listening, RET features active participation by the therapist. In place of encouraging transference, the RET practitioner encourages independence and the client's own ability to reason. Rather than "working through" unconscious conflicts, the client does behavioral-experiential homework.

"Analytic" Psychotherapy. We use this term to cover a range of approaches, from neo-Freudian to Sullivanian. When "analytic" approaches emphasize ego processes, they converge with RET. When they dwell on presumed unconscious processes, they diverge. The more active the analyst, the more similarity with RET as it is usually practiced.

Alfred Adler is sometimes classed as a neo-Freudian, although his developed theory of personality widely diverged from that of Freud. Adler's theory shares with RET (and George Kelly's personal construct theory) a focus on philosophy, values, and personal goals. A major theoretical difference is Adler's emphasis on social interest, as opposed to Ellis's emphasis on self-interest. (For an extensive comparison, see Ellis, 1973.) There are, however, many similarities in methodology (Lemire and McCullough, 1978; Rule, 1977).

Another neo-Freudian, Karen Horney, developed a theory that was a source of ideas for RET. Her term *tyranny of the should* summarizes beliefs that people neurotically impose on themselves, beliefs that sound very much like an Ellis list of basic irrational beliefs. Horney's (1942) list of ten "neurotic needs" easily fits current RET:

1. For attention and approval.
2. For a partner to take over one's life.
3. To restrict one's life to narrow borders.
4. To control self and others.
5. To exploit others.
6. For social recognition or prestige.
7. For personal admiration.
8. For personal achievement.
9. For self-sufficiency and independence.
10. For perfection and unassailability.

Beneath these similarities lie some wide differences. There is an obvious difference in therapeutic procedure, since Horney remained fundamentally a psychoanalyst despite her disagreement with Freud's views about biological motivation. But there are also theoretical differences. Horney postulated the neurotic need as a defense against basic anxiety stemming from infantile helplessness. Ellis's position is that irrational beliefs are acquired first and that their failure to be fulfilled, or the risk that they will not be fulfilled, creates anxiety. The relation between anxiety and neurotic need is reversed. In practice, RET therapists could join Karen Horney in her fight against the Ideal Self, but for different theoretical reasons. Horney said that anxiety causes alienation from the Real Self. Ellis says that alienation from the Real Self causes anxiety. In this respect, Ellis is much closer to Carl Rogers' position than to Horney's.

Client-Centered Counseling. In their conduct of therapy and counseling, Carl Rogers and Albert Ellis have little in common. However, if one looks at their theories of disturbance and their goals of counseling and therapy, several striking similarities emerge. In short, although their methods diverge sharply, their objectives converge.

Both approaches have roots in psychological phenomenology. Both make self-image or self-concept a central construct in the theory of disturbance. Ellis emphasizes elegant self-acceptance—that is, not damning or praising self for any reason; Rogers emphasizes the lifting of conditions of worth placed on self. Both say that lack of self-acceptance or conditional self-acceptance is an important source of anxiety. While Rogers has focused on the client's gaining self-acceptance as a result of the unconditional regard the therapist conveys to the client, Ellis has taken more direct approaches, such as advocating a philosophy of self-acceptance, teaching its central role in anxiety, and challenging people to prove that they are unworthy or can be evaluated at all. Rogers and his followers suggest that change is made possible by an understanding, empathetic, congruent therapist or other facilitator of growth. Ellis clearly states that understanding is not enough. Dissuasive attempts to counteract self-defeating philosophies of living are required for change to occur. Ellis gives homework assignments to allow people opportunities to practice self-acceptance while courting the disfavor of other people. Ellis shows nondamning acceptance rather than positive regard, because positive regard is another form of evaluation or rating the person. Any attempt to assign a global rating to a human is illegitimate in RET.

In addition to differences in conducting therapy or counseling, there are some important differences in assumptions about human nature that separate Ellis from Rogers. Where Rogers emphasizes each human's positive potential for growth, Ellis emphasizes *both* the potential for growth (rational thinking) *and* the negative potential for defeating oneself (irrational thinking). Self-defeating behavior, according to Ellis, then, is largely due to one's innate tendency to think irrationally, while for Rogers it is due to environmental and social conditions that block one's tendency to actualize. Whereas Rogers sees conditions of worth as largely learned—that is, we learn to judge ourselves because others fail to give us unconditional positive regard—Ellis claims that people are born with the tendency to self-evaluate and might learn to denigrate themselves even if others expressed only unconditional positive regard.

Can client-centered counselors use RET? We believe that they can, provided they overcome inhibitions to speak up and gently counter the client's irrationalities. Persons with nondirective orientations are generally reluctant to disagree with clients, because, we believe, they confuse the rejecting of a client's statement with the rejecting of the client. As we have shown in this text, a counselor need not sound like Albert Ellis in order to practice RET. Ellis agrees (1977c, p. 17-18): "Even the most direct and persuasive form of RET can be done with a Rogerian-oriented manner. . . . On the other hand, therapeutic warmth that leads to dependency . . . has its distinct limitations." If the no-nonsense, very active approach seems foreign, then a more low-keyed style of RET is appropriate. Confrontations can be supportive and oblique, as well as brusque and frontal.

Transactional Analysis (TA). Eric Berne (1961) developed a theory of human behavior and disturbance that is highly complex, though couched in simple language. In particular, his conceptions of human interaction can be highly instructive to RET practitioners. TA practitioners can also learn much from RET's emphasis upon actively changing beliefs rather than simply becoming aware of them. It is one thing to become aware of adopting a life script at an early age. It is quite another to work consciously and conscientiously at changing it.

The irrational beliefs that specify what a person should or must do can be thought of as TA's Parent Ego State, especially the Critical Parent Ego State. The impulsive low-frustration-tolerance philosophy statements like "I must have what I want when I want it" echo the Child Ego State. Rational beliefs, by definition, correspond to the Adult Ego State. But whereas TA can allow people to avoid responsibility by claiming that their ego state messages ("tapes") were given to them by parents and other socializing agents, RET holds that early socializing agents may have had little to do with the initial acquiring of irrational beliefs and that some are so widespread that we all seem to have had the same parents!

Both Ellis and Berne have focused on social interaction. Ellis shows clients that the neurotic need for approval is a way of rescuing the self from its own degradation (or, as Ellis puts it, "Other people's approval rescues you from your own shithood"). Berne theorized that people work to get "strokes," or recognition from other people, because they have an innate need to do so. When pathological "games" are involved, people are moved to get temporary respite from a life script that describes them as inadequate or worse—I'm not OK. The notion of

"I'm OK" is compatible with RET if it is interpreted to signal self-acceptance—that is, the absence of self-judgment—rather than self-esteem or high self-rating.

The notion of life script does not have a precise corresponding concept in RET. Related to Adler's concept of life style, it seems very much like self-image, an idea or theory of who we are. The self is an abstraction, albeit one that is easily reified. According to RET, the evaluation or rating of that abstraction is at the very heart of much disturbance. The giving up of self-rating is the key to change from neurotic to nonneurotic. By viewing the client holistically rather than working with isolated irrational beliefs, the RET practitioner in effect works with the life script.

Gestalt Therapy. This approach resembles RET less than any other popular approach to therapy or counseling. Gestalt therapists who follow Fritz Perls take an antiintellectual stance, while RET therapists, following Albert Ellis, take a prorational position. Perls (1969) holds that if people can increase their awareness and thus become integrated, they will no longer experience disturbing emotions, while RET assumes that philosophical change and realistic thinking will accomplish the same results.

There are clearly some real differences, and the two positions may not be reconcilable. However, certain similarities suggest possible areas of convergence. Both Perls and Ellis, in the spirit of Karen Horney, stress the "tyranny of the should." (Carl Rogers does too, in different words, as does Eric Berne.) Hence, the so-called gestalt prayer, "You do your thing and I do mine," could be part of an RET session, except that an RET practitioner would add, "Sometimes my doing your thing is in my best interest." Certainly the message of responsible independence is common to both RET and gestalt therapy, as well as to most psychotherapy and counseling systems. Like RET, Perls' version of gestalt therapy is intentionally persuasive. Raimy (1975) has identified twenty-six different attempts to persuade made by Perls during a short segment of work with a client. As we noted in Chapter One, persuasion need not be direct or obtrusive.

In practice, RET counselors and therapists make use of some gestalt exercises but process them in a manner consistent with the *ABC* model of disturbance and treatment (see Chapter Nine). We might also point out that some gestalt exercises were originated by Jacob Mareno and the psychodrama movement; so both RET and gestalt therapy are borrowers (Nardi, 1979; O'Connell, 1967).

General Semantics. Developed by Korzybski (1933), general semantics has become an influential approach to the study of language and meaning (Fabun, 1968; Hayakawa, 1952; Johnson, 1946). Bandler and Grinder's (1975) analysis of psychotherapy using concepts from general semantics is intriguing to those interested in a cognitive approach to therapy. Bandler and Grinder call their approach neurolinguistic reprogramming, many aspects of which can easily be combined with RET, due to their common emphasis upon dissuasion and semantics. Ellis has explicitly used many concepts from general semantics. But the fullest integration of RET and general semantics has been accomplished by the Dutch psychologist René Diekstra (Diekstra and Dassen, 1979). Since Diekstra's work is not available in English, we will go into some detail about his integration.

The first assumption is that reality is a process—things are never quite the same from moment to moment. The room in which you are reading these words is not identical to the same room an hour ago. Slight changes have occurred: there are different air molecules, new dust, the light may be changed. Reality is dynamic, ever changing, however slight and imperceptibly. There are many potential stimuli in the reality of one's environment at any given time. Individuals do not perceive all stimuli available to them at any given moment, and hence their perceptions are reductions of reality.

The perceiver can describe stimuli, either to himself or to other people, as he perceives them. Descriptive statements are most accurate when they include the perceiver-describer in the account and when they specify time, place, and circumstances. Description is a symbolic behavior and corresponds to the *A* of Ellis's *ABC* theory, although Diekstra prefers to categorize all symbolic behavior under *B* (similar to the practice of Maultsby, 1975). The resolution to the disagreement is to use the *ABC*s as a didactic and mnemonic device for clients and to base theoretical discussions on the emotional episode.

The next level of abstraction consists of inferences about descriptive statements. To illustrate: "I saw a person driving into a service station at ten o'clock this morning" (descriptive statement). "The person was going to buy gasoline at that service station" (inferential statement). A descriptive statement is a fact that can be verified; an inferential statement is an opinion stated as though it were a fact.

The most significant inferential statements occur when some form of the verb *to be* is used to describe a thing or event or oneself. Known in general semantics as "the is of identity," it is the process of equating a thing with its label. Hence, it is not correct to describe oneself in terms of "I am . . ."; it is preferable to say, "I act this way under these specific circumstances." At one time Albert Ellis made "the is of identity" a central feature of RET (Moore, 1977). He wrote four books in "*e*-prime"; that is, in English without any form of the verb *to be.* While this practice underscored his position against global evaluations of anything, especially of the self, it proved to be an awkward mode of writing, and he later abandoned the practice. Although *e*-prime is a cumbersome mode of writing, and nearly impossible to speak, the basic notion remains an important feature of RET.

At the highest level of abstraction, and the one most removed from reality, are evaluative statements—statements about the goodness or badness of some thing or event, as though the thing or event were good or bad in itself. It is not the thing that is good, bad, beautiful, or ugly, for these are people's views or opinions or judgments of the thing. This is not a good typewriter. It is a typewriter that I evaluate as good at this time, in this place, for this purpose. We can turn an evaluative statement into a descriptive one by including the evaluator, the time, the place, and other circumstances of the evaluation. Evaluative statements are equivalent to irrational beliefs. Descriptive statements in which one expresses an opinion are rational beliefs. Thus, the task of RET, according to Diekstra, is to reduce evaluative statements to descriptive statements that emphasize *personal* preferences, likes, and dislikes.

General semantics promotes clear thinking and helps one

to avoid overgeneralizations that can be disturbing. Overgeneralizations about oneself or another person fail to take into account human complexity. Whether the label is self-denigrating or self-aggrandizing, it can hardly do justice to one's complexity. A familiar phrase in general semantics is "The map is not the territory." Clear descriptions of other people's actions or other events can counter tendencies to make catastrophes of life. Clear talking and clear thinking can help us see that the catastrophe is what we add to the perception by our inferential and evaluative statements. The catastrophe is not reality.

Other Approaches. Currently, a much-publicized approach to therapy outside the cognitive-behavioral array is Bandler and Grinder's (1975) neurolinguistic reprogramming (NRP). In many ways this approach is a variation on the theme in gestalt therapy that "awareness is curative." However, in actual practice it seems to be more attuned to dissuasion of the client. Many aspects of NRP can easily be combined with RET, probably because of their common emphasis on dissuasion and semantics.

RET as RET

RET cannot be easily grafted onto any other system of therapy or counseling, because its account of human nature and disturbance is not fully compatible with other approaches. This same statement is true of any two systems: there are areas of convergence and areas of divergence. For example, where RET overlaps with one system, it may diverge from another. Where it diverges from gestalt therapy, psychoanalysis, and radical behavior therapy on the role of cognitive mediators, it converges with Kelly, Beck, Lazarus, and many others.

There are several distinctive features of RET. First, the very fact that it overlaps with many other approaches to therapy and counseling shows that it is not narrowly doctrinaire. While the important emphasis of RET is on evaluative thinking, other important aspects of human functioning are not ignored. The eight-step model of the emotional episode highlights this characteristic of RET.

Second, RET is grounded in psychology in general. RET takes both a learning approach to treatment *and* an attitude change approach. It includes the usual behavioral concerns for stimuli and responses and reinforcing consequences, as well as for perceptual and cognitive processes.

Third, because of its comprehensiveness, RET can be applied to a wide variety of human problems. It is action oriented, stressing behavioral change, experimentation, and experience, whereas the so-called insight therapies work toward self-enlightenment and understanding as goals in themselves. Unlike strict behavioral approaches, RET willingly includes examination of values that people live by and at times suffer by—issues of guilt, shame, moral right and wrong, and ethical and existential anguish that cannot be touched by behavioral technology. Thus, RET combines the strengths of rigorous behavioral methods with the humanistic qualities of insight approaches.

Fourth, RET is parsimonious in that it postulates no mysterious psychic energies or bodily quirks and yet allows for the influence of somatic events on psychological processes.

Fifth, RET is a multimethod approach to treatment, unified by a theoretical model of disturbance. RET does not rely solely on argumentation, direct confrontation, or exceptionally strong language. RET attends to clients' misperceptions, demoralizing expectations, illogical mental operations, and maladaptive social behavior, and to their own structuring of their interpersonal environments.

Sixth, RET is a multifunctional approach to treatment. It aims for emotional change and behavioral change and cognitive change. RET can, therefore, easily incorporate newly devised tactics from other approaches to counseling and therapy and from other fields, such as philosophy, into its diverse multimethod intervention techniques.

Self-Supervision Inventory

The Self-Supervision Inventory presented here is modeled after the Competency Checklist for Cognitive Therapists developed by Jeffrey Young, Karen El Shammaa, and Aaron T. Beck (see Beck and others, 1979). Some items were taken from the Competency Checklist without modification; others have been slightly altered. Most of the items pertaining to RET are original. Russell M. Grieger collaborated in earlier versions of the Self-Supervision Inventory. The inventory can be used for self-supervision or as a guide for RET supervisors. It represents personal characteristics we deem important for therapists and counselors and minimal skills to practice RET effectively. The inventory also summarizes the most important principles presented in this book.

I. Therapist Variables: General

Genuineness

The therapist

- seemed to be saying what he or she sincerely felt or meant;
- seemed honest and "real."
- seemed open rather than defensive.
- did not seem to be holding back impressions or information or evading client's questions.
- did not seem patronizing or condescending.
- did not seem to be playing the role of a therapist; did not sound contrived or rehearsed.

Concern

The therapist

- seemed supportive of client's goals.
- did not judge or rate the client.
- seemed client oriented rather than theory oriented.
- conveyed interest by tone of voice and nonverbal behavior.
- did not ridicule the client but seemed free to criticize or disapprove of the client's behavior.
- did not seem cold, distant, or indifferent.
- seemed optimistic about client's potential for change.
- responded to and displayed humor when appropriate.

Empathy

The therapist

- accurately reflected what the client explicitly said.
- accurately reflected the client's most obvious emotions.
- accurately reflected the most subtle nuances of feeling or implicit beliefs.
- communicated through verbal and nonverbal behavior that he or she understood the client's feelings and was responding to them.

Aptitude

The therapist

- seemed intelligent and able to express his or her thoughts.
- showed reasoning ability.
- seemed able to synthesize what the client said.

seemed persuasive and convincing without sounding manipulative.
persisted even when client showed little change.

Adjustment
The therapist
showed evidence of good reality testing.
seemed to have a self-accepting (nonjudgmental) attitude.
showed high frustration tolerance (patience) with the client.
did not "awfulize" or express other exaggerated evaluations.
did not directly or indirectly express irrational premises or evaluative conclusions.

Professional Manner
The therapist
conveyed confidence through tone of voice and nonverbal behavior.
made clear statements without frequent hesitations or rephrasings.
seemed relaxed and did not seem to be anxious or "trying too hard."
did not seem effusive, possessive, or overinvolved with the client.

II. Therapist Variables: Specific

Interviewing Skills
The therapist
used open-ended questions appropriately.
used few questions requiring yes-or-no responses.
avoided rapid-fire questioning.
interspersed questions with reflective statements, illustrative examples, or capsule summaries.
avoided using too many questions; that is, did not work evocatively when a more declarative style would be better.
seemed aware when his or her questions or statements focused on *A*-, *B*-, *C*-type material or were attempts to dissuade.

Structuring of the Session

The therapist

responded therapeutically rather than socially.

was in control of the session; was able to shift appropriately between listening and leading.

provided structure for the session, following the *ACBD* model or the *CABD* model.

was flexible enough to include important issues that arose during the session.

spent limited time on peripheral or tangential topics.

limited unproductive discussion on relevant topics.

disengaged from the client's attempts to play "games."

periodically recapitulated or reformulated problems being worked on in the session.

summarized progress made on identified problems during the session or asked the client to summarize.

III. The Therapeutic Alliance

The Relationship

Both client and therapist

seemed to have at least minimal rapport; did not seem over-defensive, cautious, or restrained.

displayed a smooth flow of verbal interchange.

displayed good affective interaction.

The client revealed personal information; did not seem to hold back.

The therapist

used vocabulary appropriate for the client and frequently used the client's words.

responded to client's feedback and/or suggestions; did not ignore or negate them.

involved the client even when using an educative model.

asked for the client's understanding of points he or she (the therapist) was making.

checked periodically for his or her own understanding of key points made by the client.

periodically summarized key points or asked client to summarize key points made by the therapist.
explained rationale for specific tactics to be utilized in dealing with problems.
elicited client's feelings and reactions to the present session.
elicited feedback regarding previous session(s).

Goal Setting
Both therapist and client
agreed on appropriate goals of therapy.
agreed on appropriate goals for the present session.
stated goals in positive as well as negative terms, such as "I'd like to feel annoyed rather than angry and act assertively rather than aggressively in this situation."

Conveying the ABCs
The therapist, in the first session and periodically thereafter,
explained to the client the connection between specific beliefs and affect.
obtained the client's acknowledgment that specific beliefs are the determinants of target feelings.
when appropriate used other tactics, including:
imagery.
role playing.
rational emotive problem simulation.
behavioral homework.

IV. Assessment

Problem Assessment
The therapist
skillfully blended questions and other techniques to elicit data regarding problems, life situations, current expectations, thoughts, feelings, and (where applicable) past experiences.
converted vague, general complaints into concrete problems.
showed understanding of basic RET propositions about disturbance and identified and focused on specific problems based on them.
identified issues that are central as well as peripheral to the client's problem.

identified problems appropriate for treatment at this time.
concentrated on one or two problems instead of skipping around.
used the *ABC* model to lead client to identify *iB*s and *rB*s.
used direct questions to help client discover *B*s.
dialogued with client to explore and identify *B*s rather than only pointing them out in a didactic, interpretive fashion.
clearly and accurately advanced hypotheses derived from both client statements and the *ABC* model to help the client become aware of *iB*s.
gave up hypotheses when client data failed to confirm them.
accurately conceptualized problems about problems, such as anxiety about anxiety.
separated ego problems from low frustration tolerance ones.

Assessment of Progress
When the client reported insight or change, the therapist
challenged the client's rational statements.
obtained feedback that *B*, not *A*, is changing—by means of techniques such as:
nonleading questions.
written homework.
role reversal.
rational-emotive imagery.
checked on how client would deal with potential future problems.

V. Change Tactics

Dissuasion, in Session
The therapist
disputed specific *iB*s relevant to the problem rather than vague, general ones.
disputed appropriately within the time allotment (neither too ambitious nor too limited).
did not use exhortations exclusively to "talk the client out of" *iB*s.
helped client evaluate evidence and draw conclusions.

helped client analyze the validity of ideas by systematically collecting evidence.
used questions to show incongruities or inconsistencies in client's ideas or conclusions.
used questions to help client examine arbitrary or absolute conclusions or ideas.
used questions to help client consider alternative explanations.
used questions to help client predict positive and negative consequences of a proposed idea or action.
effectively and appropriately provided information and clarified misconceptions.
effectively used a variety of tactics in helping client dispute his or her irrational ideas—tactics such as:
rational-emotive imagery.
role reversal.
cognitive rehearsal.
role playing.
examination of means-ends relationships.
time projection imagery.
paradox.
exaggeration and humor.
allegories and parables.
appropriate modeling and self-disclosure.
hypnosis.

Dissuasion, out of Session (Homework)
The therapist
negotiated homework assignment with the client rather than unilaterally assigning it.
assigned homework appropriate for identified problems.
explained homework specifically and clearly.
got commitment from client to attempt homework assignment.
assigned homework that is specific ("Ask five women for their telephone numbers") rather than vague and general ("Try to get a date this week").
rehearsed client in homework, including role playing and/or time projective imagery.
used a wide range of assignments to tailor the homework to the client—assignments such as:

written homework.
rational-emotive imagery.
bibliotherapy or audiotherapy.
shame-attacking exercises.
risk-taking exercises.
antiprocrastination exercises.
counterphobic activities.
rational proselytizing.
diary, log, or other record keeping.

Adjunctive Tactics (in Session or Homework)

The therapist used when appropriate

assertiveness training.
practical and social problem solving.
relaxation training.
social skills training.
rational coping statements.
reattribution.

Checking on Homework

After the first session, the therapist

asked for a report on assigned homework.
summarized conclusions or progress derived from homework or asked the client to summarize.
reinforced successful attempts at homework, including partially completed homework.
corrected errors in written homework.
did not judge or rate the client for failing to complete the assignment.
asked for reasons if homework was not completed.
reexplained rationale for homework or verified client's understanding if client cited lack of understanding as a reason for not completing homework.
made low frustration tolerance or discomfort anxiety the focus of early part of session if homework was not completed for one of these reasons.
obtained commitment to do noncompleted homework if appropriate or negotiated a new assignment.

References

Abelson, R. P., and Rosenberg, M. J. "Symbolic Psycho-Logic: A Model of Attitudinal Cognition." *Behavioral Science,* 1958, *3,* 1-13.

Ard, B. N., Jr. "The Rational-Emotive Approach to Marriage Counseling." In J. L. Wolfe and E. Brand (Eds.), *Twenty Years of Rational Therapy.* New York: Institute for Rational Living, 1977.

Arnold, M. *Emotion and Personality.* New York: Columbia University Press, 1960.

Bandler, R., and Grinder, J. *The Structure of Magic.* Palo Alto, Calif.: Science and Behavior Books, 1975.

Bandura, A. *Principles of Behavior Modification.* New York: Holt, Rinehart and Winston, 1969.

Bard, J. A. "Rational Proselytizing." *Rational Living,* 1973, *8* (2), 24-26.

Beaman, A. "Rational-Emotive Therapy and Christian Contrition." *Rational Living,* 1978, *13* (1), 17-18.

Beck, A. T. "Thinking and Depression." *Archives of General Psychiatry,* 1963, *9,* 324-333.

Beck, A. T. *Cognitive Therapy of the Emotional Disorders.* New York: International Universities Press, 1976.

Beck, A. T., and others. *Cognitive Therapy of Depression.* New York: Guilford, 1979.

Beier, E. G. *The Silent Language of Psychotherapy.* Chicago: Aldine, 1966.

Bergner, R. M. "Transforming Presenting Problems." *Rational Living,* 1979, *14* (1), 13-16.

Berne, E. *Transactional Analysis in Psychotherapy.* New York: Grove Press, 1961.

Berne, E. *Games People Play.* New York: Grove Press, 1964.

Brown, R. *Social Psychology.* New York: Free Press, 1965.

Carson, R. C. *Interaction Concepts of Personality.* Chicago: Aldine, 1969.

Combs, A. W., Richards, A. C., and Richards, F. *Perceptual Psychology: A Humanistic Approach to the Study of Persons.* New York: Harper & Row, 1976.

Criddle, W. D. "Guidelines for Challenging Irrational Beliefs." *Rational Living,* 1974, *9* (1), 8-14.

DeSoto, C. B. "The Predilection for Single Orderings." *Journal of Abnormal and Social Psychology,* 1961, *62,* 16-23.

Diekstra, R. F. W., and Dassen, W. F. M. *Inleiding tot de Rationele Therapie* [Introduction to Rational Therapy]. Amsterdam: Swets and Zeitlinger, 1979.

Dollard, J., and others. *Frustration and Aggression.* New Haven, Conn.: Yale University Press, 1939.

Dolliver, R. H. "The Relationship of Rational-Emotive Therapy to Other Psychotherapies and Personality Theories." In A. Ellis and J. M. W. Whiteley (Eds.), *Theoretical and Empirical Foundations of Rational-Emotive Therapy.* Monterey, Calif.: Brooks/Cole, 1979.

Dryden, W. "Past Messages and Disputations: The Client and Significant Others." *Rational Living,* 1979, *14* (2), 26-28.

Ellis, A. "Outcome of Employing Three Techniques of Psychotherapy." *Journal of Clinical Psychology,* 1957, *13,* 344-350.

Ellis, A. *The American Sexual Tragedy.* New York: Lyle Stuart, 1960a.

Ellis, A. *The Art and Science of Love.* New York: Lyle Stuart, 1960b.

Ellis, A. "A Weekend of Rational Encounter." In A. Burton (Ed.), *Encounter: The Theory and Practice of Encounter Groups.* San Francisco: Jossey-Bass, 1969a.

Ellis, A. *Sex Without Guilt.* New York: Lancer Books, 1969b.

Ellis, A. "Rational-Emotive Psychotherapy." In R. J. Corsini (Ed.), *Current Psychotherapies.* Itasca, Ill.: Peacock, 1973.

Ellis, A. *Growth Through Reason.* North Hollywood, Calif.: Wilshire, 1974a.

Ellis, A. *Humanistic Psychotherapy.* New York: McGraw-Hill, 1974b.

Ellis, A. "The Biological Basis of Human Irrationality." *Journal of Individual Psychology,* 1976, *32,* 145-168.

Ellis, A. "Fun as Psychotherapy." *Rational Living,* 1977a, *12* (1), 2-6.

Ellis, A. *A Garland of Rational Songs.* New York: Institute for Rational Living, 1977b.

Ellis, A. "Intimacy in Psychotherapy." *Rational Living,* 1977c, *12* (2), 13-18.

Ellis, A. *Reason and Emotion in Psychotherapy.* Secaucus, N.J.: Citadel Press, 1977d. (Originally published 1962.)

Ellis, A. "RET as a Personality Theory, Therapy Approach, and a Philosophy of Life." In J. L. Wolfe and E. Brand (Eds.), *Twenty Years of Rational Therapy.* New York: Institute for Rational Living, 1977e.

Ellis, A. "A Rational-Emotive Approach to Family Therapy, Part 1." *Rational Living,* 1978a, *13* (2), 15-19.

Ellis, A. "Toward a Theory of Personality." In R. J. Corsini (Ed.), *Readings in Current Personality Theories.* Itasca, Ill.: Peacock, 1978b.

Ellis, A. "Discomfort Anxiety: A New Cognitive Behavioral Construct, Part 1." *Rational Living,* 1979a, *14* (2), 3-7.

Ellis, A. "On Joseph Wolpe's Espousal of Cognitive-Behavior Therapy." *American Psychologist,* 1979b, *34,* 98-99.

Ellis, A. "A Rational-Emotive Approach to Family Therapy, Part 2." *Rational Living,* 1979c, *14* (1), 23-27.

Ellis, A. "Discomfort Anxiety: A New Cognitive Behavioral Construct, Part 2." *Rational Living,* 1980, *15* (1), 25-30.

Ellis, A., and Harper, R. A. *A New Guide to Rational Living.* Englewood Cliffs, N.J.: Prentice-Hall, 1975.

Ellis, A., and Knaus, W. J. *Overcoming Procrastination.* New York: Institute for Rational Living, 1977.

Erikson, M. H., Rossi, E. L., and Rossi, S. I. *Hypnotic Realities.* New York: Irvington, 1976.

Eschenroder, C. "Different Therapeutic Styles in Rational-Emotive Therapy." *Rational Living,* 1979, *14* (1), 3-7.

Fabun, D. *Communication: The Transfer of Meaning.* Beverly Hills, Calif.: Glencoe Press, 1968.

Farrelly, F., and Brandsma, J. *Provocative Therapy.* San Francisco: Shields, 1974.

Festinger, L. *A Theory of Cognitive Dissonance.* Stanford, Calif.: Stanford University Press, 1957.

Foreyt, J. P., and Rathjen, D. P. (Eds.). *Cognitive-Behavior Therapy: Research and Applications.* New York: Plenum, 1978.

Försterling, F. "Attributional Aspects of Cognitive Behavior Modification: A Theoretical Approach and Suggestions for Techniques." *Cognitive Therapy and Research,* 1980, *4,* 27-37.

Frank, J. D. *Persuasion and Healing.* Baltimore: Johns Hopkins University Press, 1961.

Gardner, M. *In the Name of Science.* New York: Putnam's, 1952.

Greenwald, H. *Direct Decision Therapy.* San Diego: Edits, 1973.

Hauck, P. A. *Overcoming Depression.* Philadelphia: Westminster Press, 1973.

Hauck, P. A. *Overcoming Frustration and Anger.* Philadelphia: Westminster Press, 1974.

Hauck, P. A. *Overcoming Worry and Fear.* Philadelphia: Westminster Press, 1975.

Hauck, P. A. "Irrational Parenting Styles." In A. Ellis and R.

Grieger (Eds.), *Handbook of Rational-Emotive Therapy.* New York: Springer, 1977.

Hayakawa, S. *Language in Thought and Action.* London: Allen & Unwin, 1952.

Heider, F. *The Psychology of Interpersonal Relations.* New York: Wiley, 1958.

Horney, K. *Self-Analysis.* New York: Norton, 1942.

Johnson, W. *People in Quandaries.* New York: Harper & Row, 1946.

Kahn, R. L., and Cannell, C. F. *The Dynamics of Interviewing.* New York: Wiley, 1957.

Karlins, M., and Abelson, N. I. *Persuasion.* (2nd ed.) New York: Springer, 1970.

Kaufmann, Y. "Analytical Psychotherapy." In R. J. Corsini (Ed.), *Current Psychotherapies.* (2nd ed.) Itasca, Ill.: Peacock, 1979.

Kelly, G. A. *The Psychology of Personal Constructs.* Vol. 2. New York: Norton, 1955.

Knaus, W. "Cognitive-Behavioral Strategies for the Therapeutic Armamentarium." *Rational Living,* 1975, *10* (1), 41-43.

Korzybski, A. *Science and Sanity.* Lancaster, Pa.: Lancaster Press, 1933.

Lazarus, A. A. "Learning Theory and the Treatment of Depression." *Behavior Research and Therapy,* 1968, *6,* 83-89.

Lazarus, A. A. *Behavior Therapy and Beyond.* New York: McGraw-Hill, 1971.

Lazarus, A. A. "Multimodal Behavior Therapy: Treating the 'BASIC ID.' " *Journal of Nervous and Mental Disease,* 1973, *156,* 404-411.

Lazarus, A. A. *Multimodal Behavior Therapy.* New York: Springer, 1976.

Lazarus, A. A. *In the Mind's Eye.* New York: Rawson Associates, 1978.

Lazarus, R. S. *Psychological Stress and the Coping Process.* New York: McGraw-Hill, 1966.

Leary, T. *The Interpersonal Diagnosis of Personality.* New York: Ronald Press, 1957.

Lemire, D., and McCullough, L. "Irrationality and Mistaken Goals." *Rational Living,* 1978, *13* (2), 23-27.

Levy, L. H., and House, W. C. "Perceived Origins of Belief as Determinants of Expectancy for Their Change." *Journal of Personality and Social Psychology,* 1970, *14,* 329-334.

Lewin, K. *A Dynamic Theory of Personality.* New York: McGraw-Hill, 1935.

McGuire, W. J. "The Nature of Attitudes and Attitude Change." In G. L. Lindzey and E. Aronson (Eds.), *The Handbook of Social Psychology.* Vol. 2. Reading, Mass.: Addison-Wesley, 1969.

Mahoney, M. "Reflections on the Cognitive-Learning Trend in Psychotherapy." *American Psychologist,* 1977, *32,* 5-13.

Maslow, A. H. *Motivation and Personality.* (2nd ed.) New York: Harper & Row, 1970.

Maultsby, M. C., Jr. "Emotive Imagery Increases the Effectiveness of Written Homework in RET." *Rational Living,* 1971, *6* (1), 24-26.

Maultsby, M. C., Jr. *Help Yourself to Happiness.* New York: Institute for Rational Living, 1975.

Meichenbaum, D. *Cognitive-Behavior Modification: An Integrative Approach.* New York: Plenum, 1977.

Moore, R. H. "The 'E-Priming' of Bob Moore." In J. L. Wolfe and E. Brand (Eds.), *Twenty Years of Rational Therapy.* New York: Institute for Rational Living, 1977.

Nardi, T. J. "The Use of Psychodrama in RET." *Rational Living,* 1979, *14* (1), 35-38.

O'Connell, W. E. "Psychodrama: Involving the Audience." *Rational Living,* 1967, *2* (1), 22-25.

Olmsted, M., and Hare, A. P. *The Small Group.* (2nd ed.) New York: Random House, 1979.

Osgood, C. E., Suci, G. J., and Tannenbaum, P. H. *The Measurement of Meaning.* Urbana: University of Illinois Press, 1957.

Perls, F. *Gestalt Therapy Verbatim.* Lafayette, Calif.: Real People Press, 1969.

Posner, M. E. *Cognition: An Introduction.* Glenview, Ill.: Scott, Foresman, 1973.

Premack, D. "Toward Empirical Behavioral Laws. I: Positive Reinforcement." *Psychological Review,* 1959, *66,* 219-233.

Rabkin, R. *Strategic Psychotherapy.* New York: Basic Books, 1977.

Raimy, V. *Misunderstandings of the Self: Cognitive Psychotherapy and the Misconception Hypothesis.* San Francisco: Jossey-Bass, 1975.

Rimm, D. C., and Masters, J. C. *Behavior Therapy: Techniques and Empirical Findings.* (2nd ed.) New York: Academic Press, 1979.

Rogers, C. R. *On Becoming a Person.* Boston: Houghton Mifflin, 1961.

Rule, W. R. "Increasing Self-Modeled Humor." *Rational Living,* 1977, *12* (1), 7-9.

Russell, B. *The Conquest of Happiness.* New York: New American Library, 1930.

Schachter, S. "The Interaction of Cognitive and Physiological Determinants of Emotional State." In L. Berkowitz (Ed.), *Advances in Experimental Social Psychology.* New York: Academic Press, 1964.

Selye, H. *The Stress of Life.* (rev. ed.) New York: McGraw-Hill, 1976.

Simkin, J. S. "Gestalt Therapy." In R. J. Corsini (Ed.), *Current Psychotherapies.* (2nd ed.) Itasca, Ill.: Peacock, 1979.

Spivak, G., Platt, J. J., and Shure, M. B. *The Problem-Solving Approach to Adjustment: A Guide to Research and Intervention.* San Francisco: Jossey-Bass, 1976.

Tosi, D. J., and Reardon, J. "The Treatment of Guilt Through Rational Stage Directed Therapy." *Rational Living,* 1976, *11* (1), 8-11.

Warren, R., and Hymen, S. P. "Getting Back to the Roots of RET." *Rational Living,* 1980, *15* (1).

Watzlawick, P. *The Language of Change.* New York: Basic Books, 1978.

Wegner, D. M., and Vallacher, R. R. *Implicit Psychology: An Introduction to Social Cognition.* New York: Oxford University Press, 1977.

Wessler, R. L. "Evolution of Irrational Thinking." *Rational Living,* 1977, *12* (2), 25-30.

White, R. W. *Ego and Reality in Psychoanalytic Theory: A Proposal Regarding Independent Ego Energies.* New York: International Universities Press, 1963.

Wilson, G. T. "Cognitive-Behavior Therapy: Paradigm Shift or Passing Phase?" In J. P. Foreyt and D. P. Rathjen (Eds.), *Cognitive-Behavior Therapy: Research and Applications.* New York: Plenum, 1978.

Wolpe, J. *Psychotherapy by Reciprocal Inhibition.* Stanford, Calif.: Stanford University Press, 1958.

Young, H. "Counseling Strategies with Working Class Adolescents." In J. L. Wolfe and E. Brand (Eds.), *Twenty Years of Rational Therapy.* New York: Institute for Rational Living, 1977.

Zajonc, R. B. "Feeling and Thinking: Preferences Need No Inferences." *American Psychologist,* 1980, *35,* 151-175.

Zastrow, C. *Talk to Yourself: Using the Power of Self-Talk.* Englewood Cliffs, N.J.: Prentice-Hall, 1979.

Zimbardo, P. G., and others. "Communicator Effectiveness in Producing Public Conformity and Private Attitude Change." *Journal of Personality,* 1965, *33,* 233-255.

Index